KT-558-162

'A bold attempt to rewind political ... political variable ... It moves in and ... great agility, weaving together complex questions of class, culture and identity with a lightness of touch. Jones torches the political class to great effect.'

Jon Cruddas, *Independent*

'It is a timely book. The white working class seems to be the one group in society that it is still acceptable to sneer at, ridicule, even incite hatred against ... Forensically ... Jones seeks to explain how, thanks to politics, the working class has shifted from being regarded as "the salt of the earth to the scum of the earth".'

Carol Midgley, *Times*

'A lively, well-reasoned and informative counterblast to the notion that Britain is now more or less a classless society.'

Sean O'Hagan, *Observer*

'Impassioned and thought-provoking ... I genuinely hope his voice is heard.'

Claire Black, *Scotland on Sunday*

'A trenchant exposure of our new class hatred and what lies behind it.'
John Carey, author of *The Intellectuals and the Masses*

'The stereotyping and hatred of the working class in Britain, documented so clearly by Owen Jones in this important book, should cause all to flinch ... the stigmatization of the working class is a serious barrier to social justice and progressive change.'

Kate Pickett and Richard Wilkinson, authors of *The Spirit Level*

'A fascinating piece of social reportage and insight, there are echoes of George Orwell's brilliant non-fiction in *Chavs*'.

Doug Johnstone, *Big Issue in Scotland*

'*Chavs* is persuasively argued, and packed full of good reporting and useful information ... [Jones] makes an important contribution to a revivified debate about class.'

Lynsey Hanley, author of *Estates: An Intimate History*

'Jones's analysis of the condition of the working class is very astute ... A book like this is very much needed for the American scene, where the illusion is similarly perpetuated by the Democrats that the middle class is all that matters, that everyone can aspire to join the middle class or is already part of it.'

Huffington Post

'A blinding read.'   Suzanne Moore, *Guardian*

'[A] thought-provoking examination of a relatively new yet widespread derogatory characterization of the working class in Britain ... edifying and disquieting in equal measure.'

Publishers Weekly

'A fiery reminder of how the system has failed the poor.'

Peter Hoskin, *Daily Beast*

'Seen in the light of the riots and the worldwide Occupy protests, his lucid analysis of a divided society appears uncannily prescient.'

Matthew Higgs, *Artforum*

'A passionate and well-documented denunciation of the upper-class contempt for the proles that has recently become so visible in the British class system.'

Eric Hobsbawm, *Guardian* Books of the Year

'Mr. Jones's book is a cleareyed examination of the British class system, and it poses this brutal question: "How has hatred of working-class people become so socially acceptable?" His timely answers combine wit, left-wing politics and outrage.'

Dwight Garner, *New York Times*

CHAVS
The Demonization of
the Working Class

OWEN JONES

VERSO
London • New York

This updated edition first published by Verso 2012
First published by Verso 2011
© Owen Jones 2011
www.owenjones.org

11

Verso
UK: 6 Meard Street, London W1F 0EG
US: 20 Jay Street, Suite 1010, Brooklyn, NY 11201
www.versobooks.com

Verso is the imprint of New Left Books

ISBN-13: 978-1-84467-864-8

British Library Cataloguing in Publication Data
A catalogue record for this book is available from the British Library

Library of Congress Cataloging-in-Publication Data
A catalog record for this book is available from the Library of Congress

Typeset in Fournier by MJ Gavan, Truro, Cornwall
Printed and bound by CPI Group (UK) Ltd, Croydon, CR0 4YY

Contents

Preface to the New Edition

Nobody expected *Chavs* to attract half as much attention as it did. And if it had been released even three or four years ago, I doubt that it would have done so well. But the book's impact had less to do with the provocative title and everything to do with the fact that class is back with a vengeance.

During the boom period it was possible to at least pretend class was no more—that 'we're all middle class now', as politicians and media pundits put it. As chancellor of the exchequer, Gordon Brown had pronounced the end of 'boom and bust', and it seemed as though a future of rising living standards beckoned for all. At a time of economic chaos, this period looks like a golden age—even if we now know our sense of prosperity was built on sand. Yes, it was true that real wages stagnated for the bottom half and declined for the bottom third from 2004 onwards—that is, four years before the economic collapse began. But the availability of cheap credit helped paper over Britain's growing class divisions, which, despite the hubris of the political and media elite, were as entrenched as ever.

Chavs was my contribution to ending the conspiracy of silence over class. But, unexpectedly, it pushed at an open door. Economic crisis helped to refocus attention on the unjust distribution of wealth and power in society. Throughout 2011, living standards for the average

Briton were declining at the fastest rate since the 1920s. The Child Poverty Action Group warned that poor families faced a 'triple whammy' of benefit, support and service cuts, stating that the coalition government's 'legacy threatens to be the worst poverty record of any government for a generation'.[1]

But it remained boom time for the people at the top. In 2011, board-room pay for Britain's top one hundred companies soared by 49 per cent; the previous year, it had shot up by 55 per cent.[2] The wealth of the richest 1,000 Britons, meanwhile, increased by a fifth, after leaping by 30 per cent—the biggest increase ever recorded—in 2010. Shortly after arriving in office, the Conservatives' austerity Chancellor George Osborne had claimed 'we're all in this together'. As the statement veered between ludicrous and offensive, few were now making the case that class division no longer mattered in Britain.

Although I wanted to encourage a broad debate about class, the title I chose proved contentious. For some critics, the book failed to acknowl-edge that the object of demonization was an identifiable subgroup of undesirables—a workless Burberry-wearing underclass—rather than the working class as a whole. Sometimes, said these critics, I got bogged down in discussing the origins and definition of the term 'chav'. Given that I had plastered the word across the book's cover, it would have been brash to refuse to engage in such a debate. But the book wasn't simply about the word. It aimed to challenge the myth that 'we're all middle class now': that most of the old working class had been 'aspirational' and joined 'Middle Britain' (whatever that was), leaving behind a feckless, problematic rump. This was often racialized and described as the 'white working class'. 'Chavs' was the term—encompassing a whole range of pejorative connotations—that best summed up this caricature.

Shortly after *Chavs* was published, a study by polling organization BritainThinks revealed just how demonized working-class identity had become. As *Chavs* pointed out, most polls have consistently shown between 50 and 55 per cent stubbornly self-identifying as working class, despite the 'we're all middle class' mantra being drummed into us. But BritainThinks revealed that 71 per cent self-identified as middle class, with just 24 per cent opting for working class. Undoubtedly the contrasting results had much to do with the fact that, while only one 'working-class' category was offered, there were three 'middle-class' options to choose from (lower, middle and upper). But there was a more profound and disturbing explanation. According to Britain-Thinks's Deborah Mattinson, a former pollster for Gordon Brown:

> There was a strong feeling in the focus groups that the noble tra-
> dition of a respectable and diligent working class was over. For
> the first time, I saw the 'working-class' tag used as a slur, equated
> with other class-based insults such as 'chav'. I asked focus group
> members to make collages using newspaper and magazine clip-
> pings to show what the working class was. Many chose deeply
> unattractive images: flashy excess, cosmetic surgery gone wrong,
> tacky designer clothes, booze, drugs and overeating.

Members of one focus group self-identified as middle class; another opted for working class. Their backgrounds, jobs and incomes were almost exactly the same. The difference was that the 'middle-class' self-identifiers were trying to distance themselves from an unappealing identity in favour of one with a strikingly positive image. As Deborah Mattinson put it: 'being middle class is about being, well, a bit classy'. The working-class label was no longer something people felt that they could wear with pride. Far from it: it had effectively become synony-mous with 'chav'.[3]

The minority that did describe themselves as working class strug-gled to come up with positive contemporary images to express their own identity. Focus group participants suggested the 1960s as the heyday of working-class Britain. When asked to define what it meant to be working class, a common theme was it 'tends to just mean being poor'.[4]

The BritainThinks studies identified some of the consequences of the social and political forces that *Chavs* had tried to identify. First, the Thatcherite assault on many of the pillars of working-class Britain, from trade unions to traditional industries. Secondly, a political consensus established by Thatcherism: that we should all aspire to be middle class, and that being working class was no longer something to be proud of. Thirdly, the almost complete absence of accurate representations of working-class people in the media, on TV, and in the political world, in favour of grotesque 'chav' caricatures.

The term 'chav' is used by different groups of people throughout British society. Practically nobody, except in jest, self-identifies as a chav. The term is almost always an insult imposed on individuals against their consent, but its exact meaning changes depending on who is wielding it, and the context in which it is used.

That said, as I have shown in the book, the term is undeniably used in a classist fashion.

Take ChavTowns, a pretty nauseating website which—I'm proud to say—has added my name to its roll call of villains. ChavTowns ridicules entire communities. As it happens, my own hometown of Stockport gets a bit of a battering at the hands of anonymous individuals brimming with undiluted class hatred: 'To be fair, Stockport has some very wealthy areas. Unfortunately, it has more than its fair share of scummy ones too,' says one. Another moans that 'I have to admit I feel ashamed to have to write Stockport on my address, despite being from one of its much, much nicer suburbs (yes they do exist).' Yet another post, written by someone describing themselves as living in the 'charming village of Cheadle Hulme', savages people living on Stockport's council estates.

But that's not to say this demonization is straightforward. In her review of *Chavs*, Lynsey Hanley—author of the brilliant *Estates: An Intimate History*—argued that class hatred wasn't simply 'a one-way street', but a 'collusive, often subtle, process which demeans everyone. In fact a great deal of chav-bashing goes on *within* working-class neighbourhoods, partly because of the age-old divide between those who aim for "respectability" and those who disdain it.'

Chav-bashing can often come from working-class people as an expression of frustration at anti-social elements within their own communities. *Chavs* attempted to put anti-social behaviour in a social and economic context: it was more likely to happen in communities with high levels of poverty and unemployment. But it's also true that the impact of anti-social behaviour and crime are class issues. Both are statistically more likely to affect working-class people than middle-class people. Those on the receiving end often—unsurprisingly—have little sympathy for the perpetrators, particularly if they share a similar set of difficult economic circumstances but do not themselves resort to anti-social behaviour.

It's also not the case that hostility to supposed 'benefit cheats' is the sole preserve of middle-class *Daily Mail* readers—the net-curtain-twitching types who rant about gays and Gypsies. If you are someone scraping by in a low-paid job, the feeling that there are people down the street living it up at your expense may well infuriate you more than anything else. It's an age-old example of the 'poor against the poor', and right-wing politicians and journalists exploit such sentiments ruthlessly. Extreme examples of 'benefit fraudsters' are hunted down with relish by the tabloids, and are passed off, not as isolated examples, but as representative of an endemic and far bigger problem. The 'scrounger' has become the public face of the unemployed in Britain.

That's not to say there isn't a widespread understanding about the causes behind the increase in long-term unemployment. As one working-class self-identifier put it in the BritainThinks study, 'We've now got this benefit generation which started when Thatcher closed all of the industries.' *Chavs* attempted to present a corrective to these exaggerated tales of benefit fraud. Such fraud, indeed, represents less than 1 per cent of total welfare spending, and up to 60 times less than tax avoidance at the other end of the economic spectrum. Meanwhile, the idea that there are plenty of jobs if only people could be bothered to drag themselves down to the Jobcentre is risible. All the evidence shows that most unemployed people desperately want work: they can't find any. At the end of 2011, the *Daily Telegraph* reported that there were twenty-three jobseekers in the UK chasing every job vacancy. For every retail job, there were forty-two applications; in customer services, it was forty-six.[5] In some communities, the picture is even bleaker. In Hull, there are 18,795 jobseekers chasing 318 jobs. There are simply not enough jobs to go round. But with this reality largely banished from our newspapers and TV screens, and with tax-avoiding businesspeople a distant, abstract concept for most, it is a challenging case to make.

The demonization of working-class people also stems from insecurity, or 'social distancing' from those in superficially similar circumstances. BritainThinks revealed that those belonging to groups most likely to be stigmatized as chavs can often be among the most vociferous in their chav-bashing. One long-term incapacity benefit claimant denounced chavs who were supposedly milking the system; so did two unemployed teenage mothers. This isn't classist contempt: it comes from a fear of being lumped in with a demonized grouping. Here is one ugly consequence of persistent attacks on the unemployed and teenage mothers: prejudice can even be voiced by those who are themselves targeted.

In large part, the demonization of the working class is the legacy of a concerted effort to shift public attitudes, which began under Thatcher, continued with New Labour and has gained further momentum under the coalition. Poverty and unemployment were no longer to be seen as social problems, but more to do with individual moral failings. Anyone could make it if they tried hard enough, or so the myth went. If people were poor, it was because they were lazy, spendthrift or lacked aspiration.

The latest Social Attitudes Survey, published at the end of 2011, shows just how successful this project has been. Even as economic crisis swelled the ranks of the unemployed and poor, attitudes towards them hardened. With nearly 2.7 million people out of work, over half of those surveyed believed that unemployment benefits were too high and were deterring people from getting a job. Of course, few would have known from reading newspapers or watching TV that the Jobseekers' Allowance was worth just £67.50—and even less for those under the age of twenty-six. Another 63 per cent believed that a factor driving child poverty was parents 'who don't want to work'. Depressing stuff, but not surprising given the Thatcherite onslaught, New Labour's refusal to challenge Conservative dogma on social problems, and the airbrushing in the media concealing the reality of poverty and unemployment.

And of course, such attitudes have political consequences. If you think poverty and unemployment are personal failings rather than social problems, then why have a welfare state at all? The Social Attitudes Survey revealed that support for the redistribution of wealth had fallen to just a third; towards the end of Margaret Thatcher's reign in 1989, it was over half. Demonization serves a useful purpose in a divided society like our own, because it promotes the idea that inequality is rational: it is simply an expression of differing talent and ability. Those at the bottom are supposedly there because they are stupid, lazy or otherwise morally questionable. Demonization is the ideological backbone of an unequal society.

Another criticism facing *Chavs* was that it glorified a golden age that never existed, presenting a rose-tinted view of an industrial world that was finished off by the Thatcherite experiment. But I do not believe that this was the argument presented in the book. As *Chavs* emphasized, industrial work was often backbreaking and dirty. Women were often excluded from these jobs; and when they were not, they did not have the same status as men. There were countless other problems that a dewy-eyed portrait of the industrial past written by an author in his mid-twenties would fail to address.

My point, however, was a different one: that the vacuum left by the massive disappearance in industrial work was often not filled properly, leaving entire communities bereft of secure, well-regarded work. Service-sector jobs are on the whole cleaner, less physically arduous, and are better at including women (even if they are still disproportionately concentrated in the lowest paid and most insecure work). But such work is often less well paid, lacks the same prestige, and is more likely to be hire-and-fire. Call centres and supermarkets do not form the basis of communities in the same way that the mine, factory, or dock did. I was not, though, calling for young men to be sent down the pits again. Just because I was arguing that what replaced these industries was in some important ways worse doesn't mean that I advocated a return to a vanished world.

It was also suggested that I had a very one-dimensional view of the working class: that what I was actually talking about was a male, white working class. But in fact many of the key examples of demonized figures portrayed as representative of larger groups of people were women—Karen Matthews, Jade Goody and Vicky Pollard, for example. Indeed, class hatred and misogyny often overlap. I also wanted to emphasize the explosion of women in the workforce in the last few decades: indeed, they now account for over half of all workers—though of course it must be pointed out that women have always worked, as well as doing much of the unpaid housework men traditionally refused to do. 'A low-paid, part-time, female shelf-stacker' was one of my suggestions for a symbol of the modern working class. We cannot understand class without gender; but that works the other way, too. Women's liberation must address class: but the retreat from class has often stripped it from the agenda here as everywhere else.

Chavs was sometimes referred to as a book solely about the white working class. One of the purposes of the book was to take on this narrow, exclusive image of the working class. Though chavs are often regarded as 'white working-class' figures, it should be noted the book was intentionally titled 'the demonization of the working class' rather than 'the *white* working class'. After long arguing 'we're all middle class', the media and politicians started talking about the working class again, but in a racialized form. The problems of the 'white working class' were ascribed to their whiteness, rather than their class. But *Chavs* argued against this false portrait. Indeed, working-class communities and workplaces are more likely to be ethnically diverse than their middle-class counterparts. Problems faced by working-class people who are white—like the housing crisis, the lack of good jobs, poor rights at work, declining living standards, safe communities—are to do with class, not race. These are problems shared by working-class people of all ethnic backgrounds.

Where race does come into it is the fact that working-class people from ethnic minority backgrounds suffer from other forms of oppression and exploitation. The majority of British Bangladeshis and Pakistanis, for example, live in poverty, while black people are far more likely to be stopped by the police. Although it is important to address issues common to all working-class people, it would be wrong to ignore the extra oppression suffered by minority groups.

One of the main reasons that politicians and media commentators started talking about the 'white working class' was the emergence of far-right populism, as most prominently expressed by the British National Party. But *Chavs* argued that such movements were, above all, driven by social and economic insecurities. This, of course, does not mean outright racist bigotry isn't part of the story, too. Despite the great strides made by the struggles against racism in post-war Britain, prejudice, bigotry and discrimination remain massive problems at every level of society.

Some felt that, in exploring an interesting premise, I had got distracted by an outdated grudge against Thatcherism. As Philip Hensher put it in the *Spectator*, 'The spread of contempt for the urban working classes is an important subject, but here it got lost under a welter of old-school moans about Mrs Thatcher, as if anyone still cared.' I would hardly wish to hide my deeply held antipathy towards Thatcherism, and *Chavs* can hardly be accused of doing so. But the book is, inescapably, about the legacy of the Thatcherite 1980s. I do not believe it is possible to divorce class contempt from broader social and political trends. One of the book's key arguments was that this new classism had everything to do with an offensive against working-class Britain, including unions, industries, housing, communities and values. We still live in the Britain that Thatcherism built: a critique of it can hardly be dismissed as 'old-school moans'.

It was also suggested by some that the book suffered from a lack of theoretical explanation. I make no apologies for this. Although in recent years the idea of class has not been the subject of much discussion among academics and leftists, literature still exists on the subject. Unfortunately, it remains largely unread outside small circles of specialists. One of the purposes of *Chavs* is to present ideas about class to a wider audience; it also aims to promote left-wing ideas at a time when the left is very weak. That's why it was written in a way that was intended to be readable—I hope it succeeded in this.

All these criticisms, indeed, were part of a wider debate. Getting people to talk about class—whether they disagreed with me or not— was exactly what I had intended. But the debate took an unexpected turn a couple of months after the book was published. For a few days in August 2011, it looked as though England was staring into an abyss of social chaos—and the demonization I had written about flourished like never before.

August is normally the height of Britain's silly season. With Parliament in recess, news channels end up featuring extra helpings of fatuous celebrity gossip, when not speculating about one or other embattled party leader's future or covering stories about talented animals. But 2011 was quite unlike normal years. In a year of upheaval, silly season was cancelled—and communities across England were overwhelmed with rioting, looting and arson.

The unrest began after the police shot dead twenty-nine-year-old Mark Duggan in the London borough of Tottenham on 6 August 2011. Duggan was black, and in Tottenham the relationship between the local black community and the police has a fraught history. In 1985, after Cynthia Jarrett—also black—died during a police raid of her house, Tottenham exploded in the riots that took their name from the estate on which they focused, Broadwater Farm. A policeman, PC Keith Blakelock, was killed during the unrest: it was the first death of a police officer during a riot for over 150 years. Though relations have improved since 1985, many in Tottenham—particularly young black men—harbour resentments against the police, who they feel harass them. Indeed, a black person is thirty times more likely than a white person to be stopped and searched under Section 60 by the police in England and Wales.[6] The police kept Duggan's body from his family for thirty-six hours. Initial reports from the Independent Police Complaints Commission that he had fired on the police were widely disbelieved and later discredited. On the afternoon of Saturday, 6 August, hundreds gathered in a peaceful protest outside Tottenham Police Station, but within hours the mood had turned ugly. People across the UK awoke the following morning to blanket media coverage of mayhem and smoking rubble on Tottenham High Street.

What happened next was for most an entirely unexpected and terrifying disruption to normality. By Monday, the riots had spread to my own London Borough, Hackney. It was my birthday and, with celebratory drinks cut short as nervous friends fled home, I cycled past boarded-up shops on Kingsland Road that were being defended by groups of Turkish men. From Barnet in the north to Croydon in the south, London's shops were looted and burned; crowds of rioters rampaged through the streets. On Monday and Tuesday, unrest spread to other English cities: Birmingham, Manchester, Liverpool, Leeds, Nottingham. There was a sense, even among more rational observers, that the country was descending into chaos. 'Not since the blitz during World War II have so many fires raged in London so intensely at one time,' claimed *Time* magazine.[7]

Amid the chaos, commentators looked at *Chavs* in a new light. Partly, I suppose, because the word 'chav' was being bandied around to describe the rioters, particularly on Twitter and Facebook. Fran Healey, lead singer of Scottish soft-rock band Travis, described the unrest as the 'Chav Spring' in a Tweet, referencing the Arab Spring. Fitness chain GymBox—which appears in *Chavs* as the promoter of a 'Chav Fighting' class—announced that it would be shutting early due to the 'chav infestation'.

But, above all, a link was made with *Chavs* because the riots shone a light on Britain's fractured, divided society. I was one of the few commentators during that turbulent week asked to challenge the dominant narrative that this was mindless criminality, end of story. Challenging this consensus, especially at the time, was not popular. People felt terrorized in their communities and Britain was in the throes of an angry backlash. Two days into the riots, nine-tenths of those polled supported the use of water cannon; two-thirds wanted the army sent in; and a third supported using live ammunition on rioters. Attempts to understand what was happening were seen as attempts to justify it. There was little appetite for social and economic explanations for the disorder sweeping English cities. People just wanted to feel safe and for those responsible to be punished.

Inadvertently, I found myself at the centre of one of the ugliest episodes of the backlash. Along with author Dreda Say Mitchell, I was put up against Tudor historian David Starkey on the BBC's current affairs programme *Newsnight*. In a now infamous intervention, Starkey began by quoting Enoch Powell's 'Rivers of Blood' speech, which warned that immigration into Britain would plunge the country into violent chaos. Powell was—as Starkey accepted—wrong in his prediction that it would bring inter-communal violence. Instead, what Starkey called 'black culture' had turned white people into rioting thugs. 'The whites', he pronounced, 'have become black.'

Attempting to scapegoat black people for the rioting, Starkey used a tortured argument to navigate around the fact that most rioters were not black. His increasingly baffling—but clearly carefully planned—rant took an even more alarming turn when he argued that if someone were to hear prominent black Labour MP David Lammy without seeing him, they would conclude he was white. Almost paralysed by the scene unfolding before me, I responded that he was equating black with criminality and white with respectability.

What unnerved me most about Starkey's rhetoric were the possible consequences. Could David Starkey become a new Enoch Powell, with critics like me dismissed as a liberal elite trying to crack down on a brave historian for telling the truth? Would badges and t-shirts be produced proclaiming 'Starkey Is Right'? Would there be marches in his support, like there was in 1968 when Powell was sacked from the Conservative Shadow Cabinet for his racist bigotry? My fear was that he had introduced race at a time of intense anxiety, when people were angry and scared. But what sympathy there was for him was not particularly strong or deeply felt. Since World War II, struggles against racism had transformed how people looked at race: for example, just over fifty years ago, a Gallup poll found that 71 per cent were opposed to interracial marriage. The number admitting such a prejudice today is virtually non-existent. Although racism was far from being purged from British society, Britain had changed and the public ramblings of a TV historian were not going to reverse that.

As the riots subsided following a surge of police officers onto Britain's streets, the Government pledged a crackdown on those responsible. With a mood of widespread fury, a furious right-wing backlash followed, carefully nurtured by senior Conservatives. One traditional target of right-wing moralizers was singled out for particular opprobrium: the single mother. 'Children without fathers' was one of the factors identified by Tory Prime Minister David Cameron; it was a point echoed by right-wing commentators. The *Daily Express* appeared to find no contradiction in claiming that 'we have bred feckless, lawless males who pass on to their own children the same mistakes' and, in another paragraph, that 'fatherlessness is the single most destructive factor in modern society'.

It smacked of the arguments of US right-wing pseudo-sociologist

Charles Murray, who claimed that rising illegitimacy among the 'lower classes' had produced a 'New Rabble'. This was classic demonization, reducing complex social problems to supposed individual failings and behavioural faults.

Pervading the backlash was the talk of a 'feral underclass'. This was the idea of the Victorian 'undeserving poor' taken to a new level: the rioters and their families weren't just undeserving, they were barely human. Some commentators took this rhetoric to its logical extreme: right-wing journalist Richard Littlejohn used his *Daily Mail* column to describe rioters as a 'wolfpack of feral inner-city waifs and strays', calling for them to be clubbed 'like baby seals'. The idea of a 'normal' middle-class majority versus a problematic underclass was ubiquitous in post-riot commentary. According to Conservative Work and Pensions Secretary Iain Duncan-Smith, 'Too many people have remained unaware of the true nature of life on some of our estates. This was because we had ghettoised many of these problems, keeping them out of sight of the middle-class majority.'

In the febrile atmosphere that followed the riots, the government proposed that rioters living in council homes should be evicted, along with their families: in other words, collective punishment. It 'should be possible to evict them and keep them evicted', Cameron told MPs, and local councils—such as Nottingham, Salford and Westminster—announced their intention to do precisely that. Further plans were unveiled to dock the welfare benefits of those convicted of committing crimes during the riots. In this way, a link was made between the rioters, council tenants and people on benefits as a whole—all of which reinforced the notion of a feral underclass. But a precedent was set in Cameron's Britain: if you were poor and if you committed a crime, you would be punished twice—once through the justice system, and again through the welfare system.

Cases were rushed through the courts, but the sentences handed down were, it seems, as much about retribution as justice. 'Mum-of-two, not involved in disorder, jailed for FIVE months for accepting shorts looted from shop', boasted Greater Manchester Police's Twitter feed. 'There are no excuses!' The police force in question was subsequently forced to apologise. Twenty-three-year-old Nicholas Robinson, a man with no previous convictions to his name, was imprisoned for six months for stealing £3.50-worth of bottled water. Two young men were jailed for four years—more than many manslaughter sentences—for using Facebook to incite riots in their local towns. Riots that never happened.

Steal bottled water and end up in prison for six months. But help push the world into the most catastrophic economic crisis since the 1930s and expect to face no legal sanctions whatsoever. Even as much of the West's bankrupt financial system remains propped up by trillions of taxpayers' pounds, dollars and euros, not a single banker has ended up in the dock. What is more, many of the British politicians baying for justice post-riots had, in the very recent past, helped themselves to millions of pounds of taxpayers' money. Two years before the riots, MPs had been found systematically milking the expenses system. Only three ended up behind bars. Some had embezzled funds to pay for the same sorts of widescreen televisions that were later carted out of shops by rioters, admittedly in a more disorderly fashion. When Labour MP Gerald Kaufman was found to have claimed £8,750 of public money for a Bank & Olufsen television set, he was simply asked to pay it back. Post-riot Britain trashed the myth that Britain's justice system is blind to wealth and power.

Just as an economic crisis caused by the market was transformed into a crisis of public spending, the post-riots backlash demonstrated just how effective the right is at manipulating crises for its own advantage. The riots were once again used to reinforce the view that social problems were the consequences of individual failings, and that there was an out-of-control feral underclass that needed to be brought firmly under control.

I felt that the riots magnified a number of the issues explored in *Chavs*. Weeks after calm had returned to England's streets, facts emerged that challenged the dominant narrative. Iain Duncan-Smith had blamed gang culture, yet only 13 per cent of those arrested were members of gangs. But, according to the government's own figures, 42 per cent of the young people involved were eligible for free school meals, more than two and a half times the national average. The adults arrested were almost three times as likely to be on out-of-work benefits as the population as a whole. Nearly two thirds of the young rioters lived in England's poorest areas. Here, then, was a sliver of Britain's burgeoning young poor.

It would be simplistic to argue a straightforward cause and effect: that unemployment and poverty had provoked the unrest. After all, the vast majority of people who were out of work or poor did not riot. But there are growing numbers of young people in Britain with no secure future to risk. Youth unemployment is running at over 20 per cent. There is a crisis of affordable housing, the biggest cuts since the 1920s, and falling living standards; university tuition fees have trebled and the Educational Maintenance Allowance for students from poor backgrounds has been scrapped. Many young people have been left with very little to hope for. For the first time since the World War II, the next generation will be worse off than the generation before it. Of course, we all have agency: we don't all respond to the same situation in the same way. But it only takes a small proportion of young people who have nothing much to lose to bring chaos to the streets.

It is also impossible to ignore the fact that men featured so prominently among the rioters. Nine out of ten apprehended rioters were men. Britain's rapid de-industrialization and the disappearance of so many skilled middle-income jobs were particularly disruptive—given that such work often excluded women—to the lives of working-class men. Over a generation ago, a young working-class man could leave school at the age of sixteen and have a decent prospect of getting an apprenticeship, training that might open a gateway to a skilled, respected job that could give life some structure. But when the jobs and the apprenticeships that supported them disappeared, there was nothing to take their place.

Although the old industrial heartlands are generally associated with mining and manufacturing areas in the North, industry disappeared in parts of the South too. Hundreds of thousands of mostly light industrial jobs disappeared in London and southern England. In October 2011, the Government's Cabinet Office published a report on the riots, based on interviews in five of the worst-hit areas. In Tottenham, for example, the report found that 'Decline in local industry and subsequently in retail on its high street were factors seen as being responsible for the lack of jobs. Interviewees described the hopelessness of some young people in the face of limited opportunities.'[8] Again, this disappearance of opportunities has affected a large proportion of young working-class men, the overwhelming majority of whom did not riot. But with so many leaving school with nothing much to look forward to, it should not be all that surprising if a small minority should respond to their bleak prospects in this way.

A toxic combination of inequality and consumerism also undoubt-edly played its part. In 1979, Britain was one of the most equal Western societies. After three decades of Thatcherism, it is now one of the least equal. The Gini coefficient—which measures levels of inequality in a society—has shot up from .25 to .40 in three decades. London is one of the most unequal cities on earth: the richest 10 per cent is worth 273 times more than the poorest 10 per cent.[9] London is not—yet—like Paris, where the affluent are concentrated in the centre, and the poorest are more likely to be found in the *banlieues* (the suburbs). In London, the rich and the poor live almost on top of each other. On a daily basis, the least well-off are able to see what they will never have. Take Clapham Junction, one of the scenes of August 2011's riots. A railway separates the affluent south from deprived estates to the north. 'If they [young people] ever wanted reminding of what they don't have, this is a good place to be,' one 'community stake-holder' told the Cabinet Office investigators.[10]

Britain is a hyper-consumerist society. Status has so much to do with what we own or wear. The vast majority of young people want to be part of this consumerism, but many face huge financial obstacles. What surprised me least of all about the looting was the targeting of trainers. When I was growing up, they were a huge status symbol: to have an unfashionable pair could bring ridicule. No wonder, then, that Foot Locker was looted, while more upmarket stores were simply burned to the ground. The goods may have been worth more, but they had no relevance to the lives of young people: they brought no status.

Hostility towards the police was an important factor, too. Since the riots, I have spoken to a number of young black men about their experiences with the police. Like me, they have never been charged with an offence. But there was one major difference: while I have never been stopped and searched by the police, it was an experience they have all endured throughout their lives. One told me that he was first stopped and searched at the age of twelve when he was on his way to buy milk for his mother. Sometimes the police officers were sympathetic, or even almost apologetic; at other times they were aggressive or threatening. Some officers acted as if 'we're the biggest gang around here'—a sentiment that cropped up in interviews with convicted rioters. Indeed, interviews with rioters conducted by the Reading the Riots study—a collaboration between the LSE, the Joseph Rowntree Foundation, and the *Guardian*—found that rioters identified anti-police sentiment as the biggest single cause of the unrest.[11]

Of course, many of the rioters got involved because they saw an opportunity to steal with impunity. For others, it was a vicarious thrill; a chance to show off in front of friends, and to be able to boast that they were a part of the action. Some just got caught up in a crowd, sensing that accepted social norms had temporarily been suspended. Others looked at the shameless greed of the bankers and politicians, feeling that if those at the top could get away with it, why couldn't they? And there were others who felt frustrated, angry, disillusioned, or bored. The specific motives varied from case to case; for some, there was a combination of reasons. But what united the rioters and looters of England's hot August was there was not much for them to put at risk, and a lack of faith in—or outright antipathy towards—the local police.

No one can predict whether there will be a new wave of riots. But it is certain that the most drastic cuts since the 1920s will have a devastating impact on Britain's social fabric. Growing numbers of people (of all ages) will inevitably have a mounting sense that there is a bleak future ahead. In those circumstances, anger and frustration will surely only increase—and unless it is organized and given political direction, it could manifest itself in the ugliest of ways.

2011 was a year of turmoil across the globe: not least because of a deepening economic crisis, and the courage and determination of millions of Arabs in rising up against the brutal, senile tyrannies that ruled over them. This new era of unrest represented another shift taking place, one with profound implications for my arguments. *Chavs* is, in large part, a story about the legacy of defeat: that is, the consequences of the pounding suffered by the British labour movement and many working-class communities in the 1980s. I argued that the demonization identified was 'the flagrant triumphalism of the rich who, no longer challenged by those below them, instead point and laugh at them'. But even as *Chavs* was published, this triumphalism was under attack.

At the end of 2011, *Time* magazine named 'The Protester' as its 'Person of the Year'. Indeed, whether it was uprisings against murderous despots or mass demonstrations against austerity, the protest made one of its biggest comebacks since the 1960s—including in Britain, which experienced waves of demonstrations, occupations, and strikes. Although, as yet, there has been no sustained challenge to the position of the wealthy elites, it has once more become clear that it is possible to resist.

In Britain, the new age of dissent arrived on 10 November 2010, when the National Union of Students called a demonstration against the proposed trebling of tuition fees. Only 20,000 or so were expected to turn up; the actual number on the day was around 52,000. Most of those who had taken to the street were newly politicized, and they found the experience of marching alongside young people both exhilarating and empowering. A section of the demonstration occupied Westminster's Millbank Tower, where the Conservative Party has offices. Although the scenes became the focus of a self-righteous media eager to condemn 'violence'—even though there was hardly any—the Millbank occupation became a symbol of resistance for many radicalized young people. Despite the lack of support from the National Union of Students leadership, the following weeks saw a series of protests, while dozens of occupations were staged at universities across the country.

Amid all the moral outrage and focus on smashed windows, the media missed one of the most interesting elements of the protests. Many of the most vocal, determined protesters were not middle-class students, but working-class teenagers who were furious at the scrapping of the Educational Maintenance Allowance—means-tested government subventions given to those from poorer backgrounds to keep them in education. Many of them felt that a government of millionaires was slamming the door in their faces. Previously they had been dismissed as, at best, an apathetic mass with few interests outside *X-Factor* and iPhones; and, at a worst, a social threat that had to be contained. But here they were: politically astute, indignant, and determined to make their long-ignored voices heard.

The students did not stop the government forcing the trebling of tuition fees through Parliament, but the myth of British passivity was shattered. Trade unions—still drastically weakened and lacking in confidence—looked on at the protesting students with more than a little interest. In the words of Len McCluskey, leader of Unite—the biggest trade union in the country—the students had put trade unions 'on the spot'. In 2011, the unions' turn came.

As austerity began biting into jobs and living standards, the trade union movement called on people to 'March for the Alternative' on 26 March 2011. It was the biggest workers' protest for over a generation. Here was a cross-section of the modern British working class, hundreds of thousands strong, standing up to a government that was forcing them to pay for a crisis they had no role in causing.

The protest marked the beginning of a new wave of trade-union resistance. After assuming office, the Conservative-led government announced so-called reforms to public sector pensions—'reforms' being a term that had long since changed in meaning from 'social progress' to 'rolling it back'. Arguing that public sector pensions were becoming unaffordable, the government unveiled plans to make workers pay more and work longer for their pensions and receive less. Yet a recently commissioned Government report written by ultra-Blairite ex-Labour Minister John Hutton revealed that public sector pensions would fall as a proportion of Britain's economy: in other words, they were set to become more affordable. In any case, the extra money raised was not intended to bolster pension funds, but to flow straight into the Treasury's coffers. This was in fact a deficit tax being imposed on public sector workers from dinner ladies to teachers.

Exploiting the fact that private sector pension coverage had collapsed over the previous decade, the government attempted to play divide-and-rule politics, a strategy amplified across the media. Why, the argument went, should private sector workers with comparatively meagre pensions subsidize the generous settlements of the public sector? There was no doubt that there had been a collapse in private sector pension provision. At the beginning of 2012, the Association of Consulting Actuaries warned that nine out of ten private sector–defined benefit schemes were closed to new entrants. But what was being proposed was a race to the bottom: public sector pensions should be dragged down, not private sector pensions dragged up.

The majority of public sector workers saw this rhetoric for what it really was: on 30 June 2011, hundreds of thousands of teachers and civil servants went on strike. But with the Government still refusing to make significant concessions, trade union ballots across the public sector delivered overwhelming support for industrial action. On 30 November, lollipop ladies, bin collectors, nurses and other workers went on strike. It was the biggest wave of industrial action since the 1926 General Strike. After all the many obituaries written about the trade union movement, the collective power of working people was back on the agenda.

Other movements, too, helped put class back on the agenda. In October 2011, anti-austerity protesters occupied Wall Street in the United States. They were, in part, inspired by the Spanish *indignados* (outraged) who had occupied Madrid's main square the previous May in protest at the Spanish government's response to the banking crisis; they, in turn, had followed the example of Egyptian revolutionaries who had taken Cairo's Tahrir Square. The New York protests spawned a global 'Occupy' movement, as similar camps were set up in hundreds of cities across the globe—including London, where tents were erected outside St Paul's Cathedral. The key slogan of the Occupy movement, 'We are the 99 per cent', reflected that the interests of the over-whelming majority of people conflicted with those of the elite 1 per cent at the top.

It may not have been an accurate figure, but that wasn't the point: the slogan tapped into a deep sense of injustice that had taken root since the collapse of Lehman Brothers in September 2008. Above all, it served as a reminder of who had caused the economic crisis and who was actually being made to pay for it. And it resonated. A poll con-ducted by ICM in October 2011 revealed that 38 per cent believed 'the protesters are naïve; there is no practical alternative to capitalism—the point is to get it moving again'. But another 51 per cent agreed that 'the protesters are right to want to call time on a system that puts profit before people'.

Britain remains in the middle of an apparently intractable crisis. As things stand, the position of the wealthy elite remains strong the world over, and the future looks incredibly bleak for millions of working people. But I passionately believe that hope lies in a return to class politics—that is, a rejection of the fiction that 'We're all in this together', and a recognition that while working people share basic common interests, they are on a collision course with the interests of those at the top.

Chavs wasn't about pity or nostalgia. It was about power. Above all else, it sought to highlight the central crisis of modern—the lack of working-class political representation. Only an organized movement of working people can challenge the economic madness that threatens the future of large swathes of humanity. But such a movement is impossible unless a number of myths are debunked: that we're all essentially middle-class; that class is an outdated concept; and that social problems are the failings of the individual.

My book is one contribution to taking on those myths. However, social change does not come through the scribblings of sympathetic writers, but through mass pressure from below. As an ideologically charged austerity programme inflicts hardship on communities across the country, there will surely be a growing determination to fight for an alternative. The Tories, unreconstructed Blairites and their wealthy backers would be reckless to imagine they have already won. There is still all to play for.

February 2012

Introduction

It's an experience we've all had. You're among a group of friends or acquaintances when suddenly someone says something that shocks you: an aside or a flippant comment made in poor taste. But the most disquieting part isn't the remark itself. It's the fact that no one else seems the slightest bit taken aback. You look around in vain, hoping for even a flicker of concern or the hint of a cringe.

I had one of those moments at a friend's dinner in a gentrified part of East London one winter evening. The blackcurrant cheesecake was being carefully sliced and the conversation had drifted to the topic of the moment, the credit crunch. Suddenly, one of the hosts tried to raise the mood by throwing in a light-hearted joke.

'It's sad that Woolworth's is closing. Where will all the chavs buy their Christmas presents?'

Now, he was not someone who would ever consider himself to be a bigot. Neither would anyone else present: for, after all, they were all educated and open-minded professionals. Sitting around the table were people from more than one ethnic group. The gender split was fifty-fifty and not everyone was straight. All would have placed themselves somewhere left-of-centre politically. They would have bristled at being labelled a snob. If a stranger had attended that evening and disgraced him or herself by bandying around a word like 'Paki' or 'poof', they would have found themselves swiftly ejected from the flat.

But no one flinched at a joke about chavs shopping in Woolies. To the contrary: everybody laughed. I doubt that many would have known that this derogatory term originates from the Romany word for child, 'chavi'. Neither were they likely to have been among the 100,000 readers of *The Little Book of Chavs*, an enlightened tome that describes 'chavs' as 'the burgeoning peasant underclass'. If they had picked it up from a bookshop counter for a quick browse, they would have learned that chavs tend to work as supermarket checkout cashiers, fast-food restaurant workers and cleaners. Yet deep down, everyone must have known that 'chav' is an insulting word exclusively directed against people who are working class. The 'joke' could easily have been rephrased as: 'It's sad that Woolworth's is closing. Where will the ghastly lower classes buy their Christmas presents?'

And yet it wasn't even *what* was said that disturbed me the most. It was *who* said it, and who shared in the laughter. Everyone sitting around that table had a well-paid, professional job. Whether they admitted it or not, they owed their success, above all, to their backgrounds. All grew up in comfortable middle-class homes, generally out in the leafy suburbs. Some were educated in expensive private schools. Most had studied at universities like Oxford, LSE or Bristol. The chances of someone from a working-class background ending up like them were, to say the least, remote. Here I was, witnessing a phenomenon that goes back hundreds of years: the wealthy mocking the less well-off.

And it got me thinking. How has hatred of working-class people become so socially acceptable? Privately educated, multi-millionaire comedians dress up as chavs for our amusement in popular sitcoms such as *Little Britain*. Our newspapers eagerly hunt down horror stories about 'life among the chavs' and pass them off as representative of working-class communities. Internet sites such as 'ChavScum' brim with venom directed at the chav caricature. It seems as though working-class people are the one group in society that you can say practically anything about.

* * *

You would be hard pushed to find someone in Britain who hates chavs as much as Richard Hilton. Mr Hilton is the chief executive of Gymbox, one of the trendier additions to London's flourishing fitness scene. Known for its creatively titled gym classes, Gymbox is unashamedly aimed at fitness freaks with deep pockets, demanding a steep £175 joining fee on top of £72 a month for membership. As Mr Hilton himself explains, Gymbox was launched to tap into the insecurities of its predominantly white-collar professional clientele. 'Members were asking for self-defence classes, as they were scared living in London,' he says.

In spring 2009, Gymbox unveiled a new addition to its already eclectic range of classes (including Boob Aerobics, Pole Dancing and Bitch Boxing): Chav Fighting. 'Don't give moody grunting Chavs an ASBO,' its website urged, 'give them a kicking.' The rest of the promotional spiel did not pull its punches either, in the voice of a vigilante with a good grasp of PR. 'Forget stealing candy from a baby. We'll teach you how to take a Bacardi off a hoodie and turn a grunt into a whine. Welcome to Chav Fighting, a place where the punch bags gather dust and the world is put to rights.' The leaflets were even more candid. 'Why hone your skills on punch bags and planks of wood when you can deck some Chavs ... a world where Bacardi Breezers are your sword and ASBOs are your trophy.'

There were some who felt that glorifying beating people up might be overstepping the mark. When the Advertising Standards Authority was called in, Gymbox responded with technicalities. It was not offensive, they claimed, because 'nobody in society would admit to being a Chav; it was not a group to which people wanted to belong.' Amazingly, the ASA cleared Gymbox on the basis that chav-fighting classes 'would be unlikely to condone or incite violence against particular social groups ...'

You would have to speak to Richard Hilton to appreciate the depths of hatred that inspired the class. Defining 'chavs' as 'young Burberry-clad street kids,' he went on to explain:

They tend to live in England but would probably pronounce it 'Enger-land'. They have trouble articulating themselves and have little ability to spell or write. They love their pit bull dogs as well as their blades. And would happily 'shank' you if you accidentally brush past them or look at them in the wrong way. They tend to breed by the age of fifteen and spend most of their days trying to score 'super-skunk' or whatever 'gear' they can get their sweaty teenage hands on. If they are not insti-tutionalized by twenty-one they are considered pillars of strength in the community or get 'much respect' for being lucky.

It is no surprise that, when asked if so-called chavs were getting a hard time in Britain, his response was blunt: 'No, they deserve it.'

Apparently the class was a hit with gym-goers. Describing it as 'one of the most popular classes we have ever run,' he claimed that: 'Most people related to it and enjoyed it. A few of the PC brigade were offended by it.' And yet, intriguingly, Mr Hilton does not think of himself as a bigot—far from it. Sexism, racism and homophobia, for example, were 'completely unacceptable'.

An extremely successful businessman, Richard Hilton has tapped into the fear and loathing felt by some middle-class Londoners towards the lower orders. It is a compelling image: sweating City bankers taking out their recession-induced frustrations on semi-bestial poor kids. Welcome to Gymbox, where class war meets personal fitness.

It is easy to gasp at Hilton's unembarrassed hatred, but he has crudely painted a widespread middle-class image of the working-class teenager. Thick. Violent. Criminal. 'Breeding' like animals. And, of course, these chavs are not isolated elements: they are, after all, regarded as 'pillars of strength in the community'.

Gymbox isn't the only British company to have exploited middle-class horror of large swathes of working-class Britain. Activities Abroad is a travel firm offering exotic adventure holidays with price tags often upwards of £2,000: husky safaris in the Canadian wilderness, Finnish log cabin holidays, that sort of thing. Oh, but chavs need not apply. In January 2009, the company sent a promotional email to the 24,000 people on its database, quoting a *Daily Mail* article from 2005 showing that children with 'middle-class' names were eight times more likely to pass their GCSEs than those with names like 'Wayne and Dwayne'. The findings had led them to wonder what sort of names were likely to be found on an Activities Abroad trip.

So, the team had a trawl through their database and came up with two lists: one of names you were 'likely to encounter' on one of their holidays, and one of those you were not. Alice, Joseph and Charles featured on the first list, but Activities Abroad excursions were a Britney, Chantelle and Dazza-free zone. They concluded that they could legitimately promise 'Chav-Free Activity Holidays'.

Again, not everyone was amused—but the company was unrepentant. 'I simply feel it is time the middle classes stood up for themselves,' declared managing director Alistair McLean. 'Regardless of whether it's class warfare or not, I make no apology for proclaiming myself to be middle class.'[1]

When I spoke to Barry Nolan, one of the company's directors, he was equally defiant. 'The great indignation came from *Guardian* readers who were showing false indignation because they don't live near them,' he said. 'It resonated with the sort of people who were likely to be booking holidays with us. It proved to be an overwhelming success with our client base.' Apparently, the business enjoyed a 44 per cent increase in sales in the aftermath of the furore.

Gymbox and Activities Abroad had taken slightly different angles. Gymbox were tapping into middle-class fears that their social inferiors were a violent mob, waiting to knife them to death in some dark alley. Activities Abroad exploited resentment against the cheap flights which allowed working-class people to 'invade' the middle-class space of the foreign holiday. 'You can't even flee abroad to escape them these days'—that sort of sentiment.

But both of them were evidence of just how mainstream middle-class hatred of working-class people is in modern Britain. Chav-bashing has become a way of making money because it strikes a chord. This becomes still more obvious when an unrepresentative story in the headlines is used as a convenient hook to 'prove' the anti-chav narrative.

When ex-convict Raoul Moat went on the run after shooting dead his ex-lover's partner in July 2010, he became an anti-hero for a minority of some of the country's most marginalized working-class people. One criminologist, Professor David Wilkinson, argued he was 'tapping into that dispossessed, white-working-class, masculine mentality, whereby they can't make their way into the world legitimately so behaving the way that Moat has behaved, as this kind of anti-hero, has, I think, touched a nerve.' White working-class men had, at a stroke, been reduced to knuckle-dragging thugs lacking legitimate aspirations. The internet hosted a vitriolic free-for-all. Take this comment on the *Daily Mail* site:

> Look around the supermarket, the bus and increasingly now on the road, you will encounter ever-growing numbers of tattooed, loud, foul-mouthed proles, with scummy brats trailing in their wake, who are incapable of acknowledging or even recognising a common courtesy, and who in their own minds can never, ever, be in the wrong about anything. These are the people who are getting sentimental about a vicious killer; they have no values, no morality and are so thick that they are beyond redemption. You are better off just avoiding them.[2]

This form of class hatred has become an integral, respectable part of modern British culture. It is present in newspapers, TV comedy shows, films, internet forums, social networking sites and everyday conversations. At the heart of the 'chavs' phenomenon is an attempt to obscure the reality of the working-class majority. 'We're all middle class now', runs the popular mantra—all except for a feckless, recalcitrant rump of the old working class. Simon Heffer is a strong advocate of this theory. One of the most prominent right-wing journalists in the country, he has often argued that 'something called the respectable working class has almost died out. What sociologists used to call the working class does not now usually work at all, but is sustained by the welfare state.'[3] It has given way to what he calls a 'feral underclass'.

When I asked him what he meant by this, he replied: 'The respectable working class has died out largely for good reason, because it was aspirational, and because society still provided the means of aspiration.' They had moved up the social ladder because 'they've gone to university, and they've got jobs in white-collar trades or professions, and they've become middle class.' Where the millions who remain in manual occupations, or the majority of the population who have not attended a university, fit into all this is an interesting question. According to Heffer, however, there are really two main groups in British society: 'You don't have families any more that live in sort of respectable, humble circumstances for generation after generation. They either become clients of the welfare state and become the underclass, or they become middle class.'

This is the model of society as seen through Heffer's eyes. Nice, middle-class people on one side; an unredeemable detritus on the other (the 'underclass' who represent 'that section of the working class that not only has no ambition, it has no aspiration'); and nothing in between. It bears no relation to how society is actually structured—but then why would it? After all the journalists producing this stuff have little, if any, contact with the people they disparage. Heffer has a thoroughly middle-class background, lives in the country, and sends his kids to Eton. At one point, he admits: 'I don't know a great deal about the underclass', a fact that has not deterred him from repeatedly slagging them off.

There are some who defend the use of the word 'chav' and claim that, actually, working-class people are not demonized at all; 'chav' is simply used to designate anti-social hooligans and thugs. This is questionable. To begin with, no one can doubt that those on the receiving end are exclusively working class. When 'chav' first appeared in the Collins

English Dictionary in 2005, it was defined as 'a young working-class person who dresses in casual sports clothing'. Since then, its meaning has broadened significantly. One popular myth makes it an acronym for 'Council Housed And Violent'. Many use it to show their distaste towards working-class people who have embraced consumerism, only to spend their money in supposedly tacky and uncivilized ways rather than with the discreet elegance of the bourgeoisie. Celebrities from working-class backgrounds such as David Beckham, Wayne Rooney or Cheryl Cole, for example, are routinely mocked as chavs.

Above all, the term 'chav' now encompasses any negative traits associated with working-class people—violence, laziness, teenage pregnancies, racism, drunkenness, and the rest. As *Guardian* journalist Zoe Williams wrote, ' "Chav" might have grabbed the popular imagination by seeming to convey something original—not just scum, friends, but scum in Burberry!—only now it covers so many bases as to be synonymous with "prole" or any word meaning "poor, and therefore worthless".'[4] Even Christopher Howse, a leader writer for the conservative *Daily Telegraph*, objected that 'many people use chav as a smokescreen for their hatred of the lower classes ... To call people chavs is no better than public schoolboys calling townies "oiks".'[5]

'Chavs' are often treated as synonymous with the 'white working class'. The BBC's 2008 *White* season of programmes dedicated to the same class was a classic example, portraying its members as backward-looking, bigoted and obsessed with race. Indeed, while the 'working class' became a taboo concept in the aftermath of Thatcherism, the 'white working class' was increasingly spoken about in the early twenty-first century.

Because 'class' had for so long been a forbidden word within the political establishment, the only inequalities discussed by politicians and the media were racial ones. The white working class had become another marginalized ethnic minority, and this meant that all their concerns were understood solely through the prism of race. They became presented as a lost tribe on the wrong side of history, disorientated by multiculturalism and obsessed with defending their identity from the cultural ravages of mass immigration. The rise of the idea of a 'white working class' fuelled a new liberal bigotry. It was OK to hate the white working class, because they were themselves a bunch of racist bigots.

One defence of the term 'chav' points out that 'Chavs themselves use the word, so what's the problem?' They have a point: some young working-class people have even embraced the word as a cultural identity. But the meaning of a word often depends on who is using it. When uttered by a heterosexual, 'queer' is clearly deeply homophobic; yet some gay men have proudly appropriated it as an identity. Similarly, although 'Paki' is one of the most offensive racist terms a white person can use in Britain, some young Asians use it as a term of endearment among their peers. In 2010, a controversy involving right-wing US shock-jock Dr Laura Schlessinger vividly illustrated this point. After using the word 'nigger' on-air eleven times in a conversation with an African-American caller, she attempted to defend herself on the grounds that black comedians and actors used it.

In all cases, the meaning of the word changes depending on the speaker. When uttered by a middle-class person, 'chav' becomes a term of pure class contempt. Liam Cranley, the son of a factory worker who grew up in a working-class community in Greater Manchester, describes to me his reaction when a middle-class person uses the word: 'You're talking about family: you're talking about my brother, you're talking about my mum. You're talking about my friends.'

This book will look at how chav-hate is far from an isolated phenomenon. In part, it is the product of a deeply unequal society. 'In my view, one of the key effects of greater inequality is to increase feelings of superiority and inferiority in society,' says Richard Wilkinson, co-author of the seminal *The Spirit Level*, a book that effectively demonstrates the link between inequality and a range of social problems. And indeed inequality is much greater today than it has been for most of our history. 'A widespread inequality is an extremely recent thing for most of the world,' argues the professor of human geography and 'inequality expert', Danny Dorling.

Demonizing people at the bottom has been a convenient way of justifying an unequal society throughout the ages. After all, in the abstract it would seem irrational that through an accident of birth, some should rise to the top while others remain trapped at the bottom. But what if you are on top because you *deserve* to be? What if people at the bottom are there because of a lack of skill, talent and determination?

Yet it goes deeper than inequality. At the root of the demonization of working-class people is the legacy of a very British class war. Margaret Thatcher's assumption of power in 1979 marked the beginning of an all-out assault on the pillars of working-class Britain. Its institutions, like trade unions and council housing, were dismantled; its industries, from manufacturing to mining, were trashed; its communities were, in some cases, shattered, never to recover; and its values, like solidarity and collective aspiration, were swept away in favour of rugged individualism. Stripped of their power and no longer seen as a proud identity, the working class was increasingly sneered at, belittled and scapegoated. These ideas have caught on, in part, because of the eviction of working-class people from the world of the media and politics.

Politicians, particularly in the Labour Party, once spoke of improving the conditions of working-class people. But today's consensus is all about *escaping* the working class. The speeches of politicians are peppered with promises to enlarge the middle class. 'Aspiration' has been redefined to mean individual self-enrichment: to scramble up the social ladder and become middle class. Social problems like poverty and unemployment were once understood as injustices that sprang from flaws within capitalism which, at the very least, had to be addressed. Yet today they have become understood as the consequences of personal behaviour, individual defects and even choice.

The plight of some working-class people is commonly portrayed as a 'poverty of ambition' on their part. It is their individual characteristics, rather than a deeply unequal society rigged in favour of the privileged, that is held responsible. In its extreme form, this has even led to a new Social Darwinism. According to the evolutionary psychiatrist Bruce Charlton, 'Poor people have a lower average IQ than wealthier people ... and this means that a much smaller percentage of working-class people than professional-class people will be able to reach the normal entrance requirements of the most selective universities.'[6]

The chav caricature is set to be at the heart of British politics in the years ahead. After the 2010 general election, a Conservative-led government dominated by millionaires took office with an aggressive programme of cuts, unparalleled since the early 1920s. The global economic crisis that began in 2007 may have been triggered by the greed and incompetence of a wealthy banking elite, yet it was working-class people who were—and are—expected to pay the price. But any attempt to shred the welfare state is fraught with political difficulties, and so the government swiftly resorted to blaming its users.

Take Jeremy Hunt, a senior Conservative minister with an estimated wealth of £4.1 million. To justify the slashing of welfare benefits, he argued that long-term claimants had to 'take responsibility' for the number of children that they had, and that the state would no longer fund large workless families. In reality, just 3.4 per cent of families in long-term receipt of benefits have four children or more. But Hunt was tapping into the age-old prejudice that the people at the bottom were breeding out of control, as well as conjuring up the tabloid caricature of the slobbish single mother who milks the benefits system by having lots of children. The purpose was clear: to help justify a wider attack on some of the most vulnerable working-class people in the country.

The aim of this book is to expose the demonization of working-class people; but it does not set out to demonize the middle class. We are all prisoners of our class, but that does not mean we have to be prisoners of our class prejudices. Similarly, it does not seek to idolize or glorify the working class. What it proposes is to show some of the reality of the working-class majority that has been airbrushed out of existence in favour of the 'chav' caricature.

Above all, this book is not simply calling for a change in people's attitudes. Class prejudice is part and parcel of a society deeply divided by class. Ultimately it is not the prejudice we need to tackle; it is the fountain from which it springs.

1

The Strange Case of Shannon Matthews

> Every middle-class person has a dormant class prejudice which needs
> only a small thing to arouse it … The notion that the working class
> have been absurdly pampered, hopelessly demoralised by doles, old-
> age pensions, free education, etc. … is still widely held; it has merely
> been a little shaken perhaps, by the recent recognition that unemploy-
> ment does exist.
>
> —George Orwell, *The Road to Wigan Pier*

Why does the life of one child matter more than another's? On the face
of it, the disappearances of Madeleine McCann in May 2007 and of
Shannon Matthews in February 2008 bore striking similarities. Both
victims were defenceless little girls. Both vanished without a trace:
Madeleine from her bedroom while she slept, Shannon on the way
home from a swimming class. Both cases featured tearful televised
appeals from the devastated mothers clutching the favourite toys of
their beloved daughters, begging for their safe return. It is true that
while Madeleine disappeared in an upmarket holiday resort in the
Portuguese Algarve, Shannon vanished from the streets of Dewsbury
in West Yorkshire. And yet, in both cases, the public was faced with the
same incomparable anguish of a mother who had lost her child.

But there were more than nine months and a few hundred miles separating the two cases. After a fortnight, British journalists had penned
1,148 stories devoted to Madeleine McCann. The stunning sum of £2.6

million had been offered as a reward to have her returned to her parents. Prominent donors included the *News of the World* and the *Sun* newspapers, Sir Richard Branson, Simon Cowell and J. K. Rowling. The missing infant quickly became a household name.

The McCann disappearance was no ordinary media circus. The case became a national trauma. Like some sort of macabre reality TV show, every little detail was beamed into the living rooms of a transfixed British public. News broadcasters sent their most celebrated anchors to report live from the Algarve. Posters with close-ups of her distinctive right eye went up in shop windows across the country, as though somehow the bewildered three-year-old would be found wandering the streets of Dundee or Aberystwyth. Members of Parliament wore yellow ribbons in solidarity. Multinational companies advertised the 'help find Madeleine' messages on their websites. The disappearance of one little girl had provoked the most extraordinary outpouring of media interest over such a case in modern times. The result was something approaching mass hysteria.

What a contrast with the pitiful response to Shannon Matthews's disappearance. After two weeks, the case had received a third of the media coverage given to McCann in the same period. There was no rolling news team from Dewsbury; no politicians wearing coloured ribbons; no 'help find Shannon' messages flashing up on company websites. The relatively paltry sum of £25,500 (though this later rose to £50,000) had been offered for her discovery, nearly all of which had been put up by the *Sun*. If money was anything to go by, the life of Madeleine McCann had been deemed fifty times more valuable than that of Shannon Matthews.

Why Madeleine? Some commentators were remarkably honest about why, of all the injustices in the world, it was the tragedy of this one little girl that provoked such anguish. 'This kind of thing doesn't usually happen to people like us,' lamented Allison Pearson in the *Daily Mail*.[1] What Pearson meant by people like her was people from comfortable, middle-class backgrounds. Kidnappings, stabbings, murders;

those are things you almost expected to happen to people living in Peckham or Glasgow. This sort of tragedy was not supposed to happen to folks you might bump into doing the weekly shop at Waitrose.

Pearson's distress at Madeleine's plight was matched only by her lack of sympathy for the case of Shannon Matthews. And it was for the same reason: the little girl's background. Even as police were losing hope of finding Shannon alive, Allison Pearson launched into a smug broadside about her family circumstances. 'Like too many of today's kids, Shannon Matthews was already a victim of a chaotic domestic situation, inflicted by parents on their innocent children, long before she vanished into the chilly February night.'[2] It was Pearson's only foray into the case. But when the McCanns came under fire for leaving their small children alone in the holiday flat from which Madeleine was abducted, she was one of their strongest defenders. 'The truth is that the McCanns were not negligent,' she said decisively. 'None of us should presume to judge them, for they will judge themselves horribly for the rest of their lives.'[3]

This middle-class solidarity was shared by India Knight at the more upmarket *Times*. 'The resort the McCanns went to belongs to the Mark Warner holiday group, which specialises in providing family-friendly holidays to the middle classes,' she confided. The joy of such a resort was that they 'were populated by recognisable types' where you could sigh in relief and think, 'Everyone is like us'. They were not places you would expect to meet 'the kind of people who wallop their weeping kids in Sainsbury's.'[4] These are revealing confessions. These columnists' undoubtedly sincere grief was not simply caused by the kidnapping of a little girl. They were distressed, basically, because she was middle class.

It's easy to see why the McCann family were so appealing to middle-class journalists. The parents were medical professionals from a smart suburb in Leicestershire. They were regular churchgoers. As a couple they were photogenic, well groomed and bursting with health. When pictured lovingly tending to their twin babies, they represented an almost idealized portrait of middle-class family life. Empathy for their plight came naturally to those like Allison Pearson and India Knight, because the McCanns' lives were similar to their own.

The contrast with the Matthews family could not have been greater. Shannon grew up on an impoverished estate in an old industrial northern town. Her mother, Karen, had seven children from relationships with five different men. She did not work, while her partner, Craig Meehan, was a supermarket fishmonger. Ms Matthews appeared to the world in unfashionable clothing, her hair pulled back, her face dour, without make-up and looking strikingly older than her thirty-two years. A slouching Mr Meehan stood next to her in a baseball cap, sweatshirt and tracksuit bottoms. They were definitely not 'people like us'.

The case simply could not provoke the same response among predominantly middle-class journalists. And it did not. Roy Greenslade, the former editor of the *Daily Mirror*, had no doubts about the dearth of media coverage: 'Overarching everything is social class.'[5] Was this unfair? It's difficult to explain why else, even in the first week of the Matthews disappearance, newspapers were still opting to give front-page coverage to possible sightings of Madeleine nine months after she had vanished.

Shannon's background was just too far removed from the experience of journalists who covered such stories. You don't need to indulge in psychobabble to understand why those who write and broadcast our news were so fixated with 'Maddie' while displaying scant interest in a missing girl from a northern backwater. 'Dewsbury Moor is no Home Counties idyll, nor is it a Portuguese holiday resort,' commented one journalist at *The Times* in an effort to explain why there was no media frenzy over Shannon. 'It is "up North", it is a bleak mix of pebbledash council blocks and neglected wasteland, and it is populated by some people capable of confirming the worst stereotype and prejudice of the white underclass.' He could hardly overlook the distress of some neighbours, but felt that others 'seemed only too ready to treat the drama of a missing child as a sort of exciting game that has relieved the monotony of life on the poverty line.'[6]

Such comments open a window into the minds of educated, middle-class hacks. They had stumbled into strange, unfamiliar territory. After all, they knew nobody who had grown up in these circumstances. It's no surprise that they found it difficult to empathize with them. 'I suspect in general a lot of national journalists, the people who will have gone up north to cover it, would have been entering an alien world,' says senior *Mirror* journalist Kevin Maguire. 'It'll have been as alien to them as Kandahar or Timbuktu. They just wouldn't know that Britain ... Because it's not *their* Britain, it's not the bit they live in, they come from.'

This is not baseless speculation. The occasional journalist even confessed as much. Melanie Reid in *The Times* argued passionately that 'us *douce* middle classes' simply did not understand the case 'because we are as removed from that kind of poverty as we are from events in Afghanistan. For life among the white working class of Dewsbury looks like a foreign country.'[7]

The working-class residents of Dewsbury Moor were certainly painfully aware of the reasons behind the lack of interest in Shannon Matthews. They knew that many journalists had nothing but contempt for communities like their own. 'Listen, we're not pissed out of our trees or high as a kite all the time, like they associate with council estates,' local community leader Julie Bushby angrily berated journalists. 'Ninety per cent of people here work. We've all taken money out of [our] own pockets for this.' Aware of the contrasting response to the disappearance of the girl who had become affectionately known simply as 'Maddie', she added: 'Two children have gone missing, that's the point. Everyone feels the same when that happens: rich, pauper, whatever. Good luck to Kate McCann. It's the kids we're looking for, isn't it? Not the mothers.'[8]

But, as it was to turn out, there was a big difference between the two cases. Unlike Madeleine McCann, Shannon was found alive on 14 March 2008. She had been kidnapped, tethered with a rope tied to a roof beam, hidden in a divan bed and drugged to keep her quiet. As far as the public was aware at that point, an estranged distant relative had snatched her. It was to be weeks before the true story emerged. Yet the knives were not out for the man believed to be the abductor, an eccentric loner who was the uncle of Karen Matthews's partner. In the firing line were Karen Matthews and, more importantly, the class she was taken to represent.

With Shannon safe, it was no longer considered tasteless to openly lay into her community. The affair became a useful case study into Britain's indulgence of an amoral class. 'Her background, a scenario that encompasses the awful, dispiriting and undisciplined face of Britain, should be read as a lesson in failure,' one columnist wrote in the *Birmingham Mail*. 'Karen Matthews, 32 but looking 60, glib hair falling across a greasy face, is the product of a society which rewards fecklessness.'[9]

Here was an opportunity to score fresh political points. Melanie Phillips is one of Britain's most notorious self-appointed moral arbiters and an aggressive champion of what she sees as traditional values. To her, the Shannon Matthews case was a gift, vindicating what she had been saying all along. Days after the girl was found, Phillips argued that the affair helped to 'reveal the existence of an underclass which is a world apart from the lives that most of us lead and the attitudes and social conventions that most of us take for granted.' In a hysterical tirade, the writer alleged that there were 'whole communities where committed fathers are so rare that any child who actually has one risks being bullied', and where 'boys impregnate two, three, four girls with scarcely a second thought'.[10] No evidence was given in support of these allegations.

In an increasingly poisonous atmosphere, some of the most extreme prejudices began to erupt into the open. In a debate on the case in March 2008, one Conservative councillor in Kent, John Ward, suggested that: 'There is an increasingly strong case for compulsory sterilisation of all those who have had a second child—or third, or whatever—while living off state benefits.' When challenged, Mr Ward was unrepentant about calling for the sterilization of 'professional spongers' who he claimed 'breed for greed'.[11] Sounds familiar? Local Labour councillor Glyn Griffiths thinks so, telling me it is 'effectively Nazi eugenics' which is 'unacceptable in a Western democracy'.

But his horror was not shared by the dozens of *Daily Mail* readers who bombarded the newspaper with messages in support of the Tory councillor. 'I fail to see the problem with his comments,' wrote one, adding: 'It is NOT a God-given right to mass-produce children.' 'What a great idea,' wrote another well-wisher. 'Let's see if the politicians are bold enough to adopt it.' More practical contributors suggested starting a petition in support, while another came up with the imaginative proposal to lace the entire water supply with an infertility drug and then offer an antidote only to 'suitable' parents. 'No doubt the liberal lefties will be up in arms,' added this perceptive contribution. 'After all, they rely on the unemployed "chavs" to vote them into power.' Yet another expressed their '100%' agreement with Ward's proposals: 'The country is sinking under the weight of these sponging bludgers.'[12]

Of course, class prejudice isn't always as crude as this. Unhinged though some of these comments are, they undoubtedly reflect an undercurrent of hatred in British society. But this was only the tip of the iceberg. When the dark truth of the Matthews affair came to light, open season was declared on working-class communities like Dewsbury Moor.

Over three weeks after her daughter had been found alive, Karen Matthews was dramatically arrested. In one of the most unimaginable crimes a mother could commit, she had kidnapped her own nine-year-old daughter to pocket the reward money, by then totalling £50,000. As if the case couldn't get any more surreal, Craig Meehan was charged with possessing child porn. 'Which one of you lot is going to be arrested next?' mocked the crowd gathered to watch the friends and relatives of Matthews as she appeared in court.[13]

Yet there was much more to the strange case of Shannon Matthews than an abusive parent who went to extraordinary lengths to use her own daughter for financial gain. The episode was like a flare, momentarily lighting up a world of class and prejudice in modern Britain. Of course, media intrigue was more than justified by the unique horror of the case and the perverse manner in which Karen Matthews had deceived her community, the police and the nation as a whole. And yet, for a whole host of media commentators and politicians, this was far from an isolated case, involving a depraved individual who shared guilt only with those who were directly complicit. 'The case seems to confirm many prejudices about the "underclass",' reflected one local newspaper.[14] It was as though everyone in the country from a similar background was crammed into the dock alongside her.

Acting as the nation's judges, juries and executioners, the tabloids turned on Dewsbury Moor. Local residents were fair game: after all, they had the audacity to live on the same street as Karen Matthews. The estate became a template for similar working-class communities up and down the country. 'Estate is like a nastier Beirut' was one thoughtful *Sun* headline. At first glance, this might appear rather tasteless. After all, Beirut was the epicentre of a particularly horrific civil war in which around a quarter of a million people died, reducing much of the city to rubble. But the *Sun* didn't lack evidence for its assertion. 'As the Press descended, people were pictured walking into the shops in their pyjamas up to MIDDAY ... even in the rain.' The estate 'is a real-life version of the smash hit Channel 4 series *Shameless*,' claimed this nuanced piece, referring to the hit show about the chaotic lives of a few families on a council estate in Manchester. Despite them having been tried and convicted by the *Sun*, the paper surprisingly found that 'local families refuse to admit it'.[15]

Journalists had to be more than a little selective to create this caricature. They didn't mention the fact that when the media became bored with some scruffy working-class girl vanishing 'up north', the local community had compensated by coming together to find her. Scores of volunteers had tramped from door to door with leaflets every night of her disappearance, often in pouring rain. They had booked coaches to take teams of people as far afield as Birmingham to hand out notices, while multilingual leaflets had been produced to cater for the area's large Muslim population. Many of the local people were poor, but they delved deep into their pockets to give some of the little they had to help find Shannon.

'I personally feel, and local councillors as a whole strongly feel, that the community demonstrated a unique strength,' reflects local councillor Khizar Iqbal. 'They all came together. Everyone was really concerned about the welfare of the child and wanted to see that child safe and well. I am very proud of the strength of community that was shown.' But this sense of a tightly knit working-class community, with limited resources, united behind a common cause, never became part of the Shannon Matthews story. It just didn't fit in with the *Shameless* image that the media was cultivating.

Nowhere in this coverage was the idea that someone could have the same background as Karen Matthews, or live on the same estate, without being horribly dysfunctional. 'What I thought was marvellous was some of the people round [Karen Matthews],' says former government minister Frank Field. 'One of her friends, when it came out that she had done all of this, said that when she met her, she was going to give her a good slapping and then a hug. I think that, sadly, what the press haven't done is answer more interesting questions: why is it that some of her neighbours are exemplary parents and why is she an old toe-rag who clearly can't look after herself, let alone any children?'

This was not a debate the media wanted to have. Far from it. Some journalists went as far as to suggest that people in these sorts of communities were somehow less than human. Take Carole Malone: a highly paid columnist and TV pundit who regularly indulges in angry rants against whoever has miffed her that week. Despite her wealth, she felt qualified to pass judgement on people living on council estates because she used to live 'next' to one. It was, she claimed, 'much like the one in

Dewsbury Moor. It was full of people like Karen Matthews. People who'd never had jobs, never wanted one, people who expected the state to fund every illegitimate child they had—not to mention their drink, drug and smoking habits.' Their 'houses looked like pigsties—dog crap on the floor (trust me, I've seen it), putrid carpets, piles of clothes and unwashed dishes everywhere.'

In case her attempt to strip these working-class communities of their humanity was too subtle for the reader, Malone spelt it out in black and white. Matthews, Meehan and Donovan, she declared, 'belonged to that sub (human) class that now exists in the murkiest, darkest corners of this country'. They were 'good-for-nothing scroungers who have no morals, no compassion, no sense of responsibility and who are incapable of feeling love or guilt.'[16] According to Malone these communities were filthy, subhuman and devoid of the basic emotions. They were crawling with the type of person who would stage the kidnapping of their own daughter for cash, or—as the *Daily Mail* put it more succinctly —the 'feral underclass'.[17]

Imagine that Carole Malone had been talking about people who were black, or Jewish, or even Scottish. There would have been the most almighty uproar, and rightly so. Malone's career would be over and the *Sun* would be facing legal action for printing material that incited hatred. But there was no outcry and no angry demands for her sacking. Why? Because the communities she was attacking are regarded as fair game. 'There is an ugly trend of bashing the less privileged developing in this country and I don't like it at all,' pleaded *Daily Star* columnist Joe Mott at the height of the hysteria over Karen Matthews. 'Let's stop using the situation as an excuse to take cheap shots at the working class.'[18] His was a lonely voice. As far as his fellow journalists were concerned, Karen Matthews wasn't a one-off. Britain was teeming with people like her.

They had created this impression through blatant manipulation of the facts. 'As with all these things, there are always some elements of truth in what is being said, but they are extrapolated for effect or exaggerated to create a better story from the media's point of view,' says Jeremy Dear, leader of the National Union of Journalists. 'It was almost like—what would you expect of these people?' Newspapers had directed their fire at 'her [Karen Matthews's] background and who she is: her class, more than her as an individual'.

Above all, underlying the coverage was the idea that the old working class had given way to a feckless 'chav' rump. 'What was once a working class is now, in some places, an underclass,' wrote Melanie McDonagh in the *Independent*. 'It is a decline that this unfortunate woman seems to embody.'[19] This was after all at the heart of the caricature: that we are all middle class, apart from the chav remnants of a decaying working class.

The Shannon Matthews affair was just one particularly striking example of the media using an isolated case to reinforce the 'chav' caricature: feckless, feral, and undeserving. But it was far from the last. Now that the ball was rolling, the media enthusiastically seized on other cases to confirm this distorted portrayal.

The news in November 2008 that a London toddler, initially known only as 'Baby P', had died as a result of horrific abuse at the hands of his mother and her partner provided one such case. Beyond the uproar at the systemic failures of the local council's child-protection agencies, the spotlight again fell on people who lived outside the cosy confines of 'Middle England'. 'Many of them will have had mothers with offspring by several different males,' claimed Bruce Anderson in the *Sunday Telegraph*. 'In the African bush, male lions who seize control of the pride often resent and kill the cubs fathered by their predecessors. In the London jungle, similar behaviour is not unknown.'[20] The Baby P horror fuelled what the Shannon Matthews affair had sparked in earnest: an attempt to dehumanize people living in poor working-class communities.

The few journalists who refrained from swelling the tide of bile were right to complain of 'cheap shots' at the working class. That is only half the story. It is rare for the media's eye to fall on working-class people at all; when it does, it is almost always on outlandish individuals such as Karen Matthews, or Alfie Patten—a thirteen-year-old boy wrongly alleged to have fathered a child born in early 2009. Journalists seemed to compete over finding the most gruesome story that could be passed off as representative of what remained of working-class Britain. 'They will look at the worst estate they can find, and the worst examples they can find,' objects *Guardian* columnist Polly Toynbee. 'They will point their camera at the worst possible workless dysfunctional family and say, "This is working-class life."'

That's not to pretend there aren't people out there with deeply problematic lives, including callous individuals who inflict barbaric abuse on vulnerable children. The point is that they are a very small number of people, and far from representative. 'Freakish exceptions—such as people with ten children who have never had a job—are eagerly sought out and presented as typical,' believes *Independent* journalist Johann Hari. 'There is a tiny proportion of highly problematic families who live chaotically and can't look after their children because they weren't cared for themselves. The number is hugely inflated to present them as paradigmatic of people from poor backgrounds.'

The media manipulation of the Shannon Matthews case was not itself the most worrying part of the story. Politicians recognize a bandwagon when they see one, and they hastily jumped on. Journalists' use of the Matthews case to caricature the supposed remnants of working-class Britain served a useful political purpose. Both the New Labour leadership and the Conservative Party were determined to radically cut the number of people receiving benefits. The media had helped to create the image of working-class areas degenerating into wholly unemployed communities full of feckless, work-shy, amoral, dirty, sexually debauched and even animal-like individuals. Conservative organs such as the *Daily Mail* had used the fact that Karen Matthews did not have a job as a reason to attack the welfare state (a bit rich coming from a newspaper which is a fervent champion of 'stay-at-home' mothers).[21]

The timing was perfect for politicians determined to give the welfare state a good kicking. Former Conservative leader Iain Duncan Smith, in charge of hashing out Tory social policy and founder of the curiously misnamed Centre for Social Justice, argued that with the revelations of the Matthews saga 'it is as though a door on to another world has opened slightly and the rest of Britain can peer in.'[22] You would think that millions of people were running around council estates, kidnapping their children in a crazed bid to cash in at the expense of the tabloid press. It was against this backdrop that the centre proposed that the ten million or so social housing tenants in Britain 'should be rewarded for decent behaviour by giving them a stake in their property'. This would help to break down the 'ghettos' of British council estates.[23] *Rewarded for decent behaviour.* It's the sort of language used when dealing with prison inmates, children or pets. A huge portion of Britain's population —all of them working class—was, in one fell swoop, implicated in Karen Matthews's actions.

To the Conservatives, Karen Matthews had become a convenient political prop. The Tory leader, David Cameron, himself used the affair to call for a drastic overhaul of the welfare state. 'The verdict last week on Karen Matthews and her vile accomplice is also a verdict on our broken society,' he argued in the *Daily Mail*. 'If only this was a one-off story.' As part of the reforms offered in response, Cameron pledged to 'end the something-for-nothing culture. If you don't take a reasonable offer of a job, you will lose benefits. No ifs, no buts.'[24] Here it was again: a link between Karen Matthews and much larger groups of working-class people. It was a clever political tactic. If the wider British public were led to believe that people who shared her background were capable of the same monstrous behaviour, they would be more likely to support policies directed against them.

Tory proposals even contemplated investigating the home lives of the long-term unemployed. Conservative work and pensions spokesperson Chris Grayling justified the plans by arguing that although the Matthews case 'was a horrendous extreme ... it raises the curtain on a way of life in some of our most deprived estates, of entire households who have not had any productive life for generations. It's a world that really, really has to change.'[25]

If these senior politicians were to be believed, Karen Matthews had demonstrated that there was a great layer of people below middle-class society whose warped lifestyles were effectively subsidized by the welfare state. 'The attribution of this to the welfare state is just bizarre,' comments Johann Hari. 'It's an inversion of the argument used against the welfare state in the late nineteenth century that the poor were inherently morally indigent and fraudulent, so there was no point giving them help.'

Of course, it is ludicrous to argue that a chronically dysfunctional individual like Karen Matthews was representative of working-class benefit recipients or council tenants, let alone the wider community. Those politicians who argued that she was failed to mention the horror felt by the community at her daughter's disappearance, and the way they united with such determination to find her.

Both journalists and politicians had used the reprehensible actions of one woman to demonize working-class people. Yet why did they consider the case to be such an insight into what life was like for so many communities outside the middle-class world? They claimed that the whole affair was a revealing snapshot of British society: and, in some ways, they had a point. But the case said a lot more about the people reporting it than about those they were targeting.

Imagine you're a journalist from a middle-class background. You grow up in a nice middle-class town or suburb. You go to a private school and make friends with people from the same background. You end up at a good university with an overwhelmingly middle-class intake. When you finally land a job in the media, you once again find yourself surrounded by people who were shaped by more or less the same circumstances. How are you going to have the faintest clue about people who live in a place like Dewsbury Moor?

The *Mirror*'s Kevin Maguire has no doubt that the background of media hacks has more than a little to do with the way they report on communities like Dewsbury Moor. 'I think it's bound to. You won't empathize or sympathize or understand and you might only bump into these people when they sell you a coffee or clean your house.' Increasingly, the lives of journalists have become divorced from those of the rest of us. 'I can't think of a national newspaper editor with school-age kids who has them in a state school,' he reflects. 'On top of that, most journalists at those levels are given private medical insurance. So you're kind of taken out of everyday life.'

Kevin Maguire is one of a tiny handful of senior journalists from working-class backgrounds. You will struggle to find anyone writing or broadcasting news who grew up somewhere even remotely like the Dewsbury Moor estate. Over half of the top hundred journalists were educated at a private school, a figure that is even higher than it was two decades ago. In stark contrast, only one in fourteen children in Britain share this background.[26]

More than anything, it is this ignorance of working-class life that explains how Karen Matthews became a template for people living in working-class communities. 'Perhaps it's because we're all middle class that we tut at the tragic transition of aspirational working class to feckless, feral underclass, and sneer at the brainless blobs of lard who spend their days on leatherette sofas in front of plasma TVs, chewing the deep-fried cud over Jeremy Kyle,' speculated commentator Christina Patterson. 'We've got a word for them too: "Chavs".'[27]

One effect of this is a belief that society has become dominated by a large middle class, increasingly subject to further internal hierarchies, with the rest consisting of a working class that has degenerated into the 'chav' caricature. Johann Hari often asked other media people what they thought the median income in Britain was. The reply was always dramatically above the actual figure. One senior editor estimated it at £80,000. This absurd figure is nearly four times higher than the true amount of £21,000. 'Of course if you never leave Zone One, if you've never met anyone from an estate, never been to one, then you live in a world of feverish fantasy.' Unlike many of his colleagues, Hari thought that it was nonsense to think of Karen Matthews as anything other than a 'pitiable freak'.

The journalists who reported on the Shannon Matthews affair are almost all from the same background, and hopelessly out of touch with ordinary life. So how has this happened? The reality is that it is more and more difficult for people from working-class backgrounds to get their foot in the door of newspapers or broadcasters. If more people in the media had grown up in communities like Dewsbury Moor, we might expect coverage to be more balanced when dealing with these issues. The odds of that happening as things stand are somewhere approaching nil. NUJ leader Jeremy Dear thinks the reason for this is simple. Increasingly, wannabe journalists have to pay for their own training, which usually means having *at least* one degree. That leaves a huge amount of debt on their shoulders when starting out in a profession with notoriously low wages for junior staff. 'The only people who can do that are those with financial support,' he says. 'That is, those whose parents can support them, which means the nature of those going into journalism has changed dramatically.'

The problem is not just the shortage of working-class people in journalism. Most newspapers discarded the old labour correspondents as trade union power declined precipitously. Local government journalists, who at least gave some account of ordinary life across the country, have also vanished. Over the past few years, regional newspapers, which traditionally reported on daily life in local communities, have either closed down or faced severe cuts. With the lives of ordinary people purged from the media, extreme cases such as Karen Matthews practically had a monopoly on the reporting of working-class life.

'Working-class people have completely ceased to exist as far as the media, popular culture and politicians are concerned,' argues Polly Toynbee. 'All that exists are nice middle-class people—nice people who own their own home, who the *Daily Mail* like. Then there are very bad people. You don't get much popular imagery of ordinary people of a neutral, let alone a positive kind.'

We've seen that prominent politicians manipulated the media-driven frenzy to make political points. Like those who write and broadcast our news, the corridors of political power are dominated by people from one particular background. 'The House of Commons isn't representative, it doesn't reflect the country as a whole,' says Kevin Maguire. 'It's over-representative of lawyers, journalists-as-politicians, various professions, lecturers in particular … there are few people who worked in call centres, or been in factories, or been council officials lower down.'

It's true to say that MPs aren't exactly representative of the sort of people who live on most of our streets. Those sitting on Parliament's green benches are over four times more likely to have gone to private school than the rest of us. Among Conservative MPs, a startling three out of every five have attended a private school.[28] A good chunk of the political elite were schooled at the prestigious Eton College alone, including Tory leader David Cameron and nineteen other Conservative MPs.

There was once a tradition, particularly on the Labour benches, of MPs who had started off working in factories and mines. Those days are long gone. The number of politicians from those backgrounds is small, and shrinks with every election. Fewer than one in twenty MPs started out as manual workers, a number that has halved since 1987, despite the fact that that was a Conservative-dominated Parliament. On the other hand, a startling two-thirds had a professional job or worked in business before arriving in Parliament. Back in 1996, Labour's then deputy leader John Prescott echoed the Blairite mantra to claim that 'we're all middle-class now', a remark that would perhaps be more fitting if he had been talking about his fellow politicians.

If these MPs do have an understanding of life in places like Dewsbury Moor, one wonders where they got it. 'The people who came here previously had been involved in many campaigns, had been involved in fighting for their communities, had been involved perhaps in sacrificing significant amounts personally to be involved in politics and to try and change the world,' argues Labour backbencher Katy Clark. 'That perhaps is far less true now.' Unlike senior Conservative MPs, she did not see Karen Matthews as representative of a wider group of people. 'I think Karen Matthews represented Karen Matthews.'

Just because a politician has a privileged background, it doesn't necessarily follow that they will lack sympathy for those who are less fortunate. Nonetheless, the odds of them understanding the realities of working-class communities are, unavoidably, considerably lower.

After all, how could someone like Prime Minister David Cameron even begin to understand a community like Dewsbury Moor? Even by the standards of most Conservative MPs, he's not exactly the sort of bloke you'd bump into in your local pub. He counts King William IV as an ancestor, his dad is a wealthy stockbroker, and his family have been making a killing in finance for decades. His wife, a senior director of one luxury goods business and owner of another, is the daughter of a major landowner and happens to be a descendant of King Charles II.

Now, it's true that as Leader of the Opposition Cameron famously hit back at those who challenged his privileged upbringing with the quip: 'It's not where you're from, it's where you're going.'[29] All well and good, but doesn't where he's *going* have an awful lot to do with where he's *from*? His belief that the Karen Matthews case is broadly representative makes sense when you look at his feelings towards people who share her background. When his messy daughter once emerged at a social gathering in his £2 million Notting Hill home, he reportedly groaned: 'You look like you've fallen out of a council flat.'[30] He's also admitted to regularly watching the TV comedy *Shameless*, which, as we've seen, has been compared to Dewsbury Moor by the tabloid press.[31] 'A lot of working-class people laugh at *Shameless*,' Kevin Maguire notes, 'but I sort of think they're laughing at it slightly differently than Cameron, who probably sees it as a drama-documentary.'

One of the Conservatives' few working-class MPs, Junior Transport Minister Mike Penning, admits that the lack of politicians from working-class backgrounds impinges on their ability to relate to people in communities like Dewsbury Moor. 'It's physically impossible for someone to have an understanding of and empathy with the problems that some are having: say, for instance, at the moment, there's a lot of people being made redundant. You don't know what that's like unless you've been made redundant.' Part of the problem, he argues, was the difficulties getting into the political world. 'It is without doubt, no matter what political party you come from, extortionately difficult to get into this great House unless you have some kind of leg-up the greasy pole.'

The fact that the British elite is stacked full of people from middle- and upper-middle-class backgrounds helps to explain a certain double standard at work. Crimes committed by the poor will be seen as an indictment of anyone from a similar background. The same cannot be said for crimes where a middle-class individual is culpable. The mass-murdering GP Harold Shipman might have gone down as a monster, but did anyone argue that his case shone a light on life in middle-class Britain? Where were the outraged tabloid headlines and politicians' sound-bites about middle-class communities that 'really, really have to change'?

And although cases such as the disappearance of Shannon Matthews are used as launch pads for attacks on so-called spongers, the wealthy do not receive anywhere near the same level of attention from the media or politicians. Welfare fraud is estimated to cost the Treasury around £1 billion a year. But, as detailed investigations by chartered accountant Richard Murphy have found, £70 billion is lost through tax evasion every year—that is, seventy times more. If anything, 'welfare evasion' is more of a problem, with billions of pounds worth of tax credits left unclaimed every year. The cruel irony is that poor people who live in communities like Dewsbury Moor actually pay more in tax as a proportion of their wage packets than many of the rich journalists and politicians who attack them. But where is the outcry over middle-class spongers? Given the media's distorted coverage, it's hardly surprising that people significantly underestimate the cost of tax avoidance and overestimate the cost of benefit fraud.[32]

Leading politicians and journalists had no interest in allowing the Shannon Matthews affair to go down in history as just another example of the capacity of some individuals for cruelty. A mother's grotesque ploy to use her vulnerable daughter for financial gain was deliberately inflated into something much greater, for the purposes of journalists and politicians determined to prove that traditional working-class communities had decayed into a morally depraved, work-shy rump.

But that's not to say that there are no wider lessons to be drawn from the case. On the contrary, it speaks volumes about class in Britain today. It would be dishonest to say that communities like Dewsbury Moor don't have their fair share of problems, even if they're not full of abusive unemployed parents running amok. The important question is, who is to blame: the communities, or the policies of successive governments over the last three decades? And how has Britain become so polarized that derision and contempt for 'chavs' has become so deeply ingrained in our society?

Neither the journalists nor the politicians who manipulated the affair of Shannon Matthews allowed pesky facts to get into the way of their wild claims. That the Matthews household was not a workless family—Craig Meehan had a job, after all—or that accomplice Michael Donovan was a computer programmer did not trouble right-wing pundits and politicians.

'I remember reading one comment about how many people in Southern England, maybe more middle-class England, were fascinated by what they saw as northern, subhuman, deprived communities,' remarks local Dewsbury vicar Reverend Simon Pitcher. 'I think there was an element of media porn. The whole of Dewsbury was portrayed as being particularly difficult and, in reality, it's not like that.' His statement could be applied to all communities suffering from poverty. In contrast to the sweeping assertions of British politicians and commentators, government figures show that nearly six out of every ten households in poverty had at least one adult in work.[33]

But this coverage was part of an effort to portray our society as divided into Middle England on the one hand and a pack of anti-social chavs living in places like Dewsbury Moor on the other. It's a myth. You wouldn't know it from the media coverage, but most of us think of ourselves as working class. As a poll published in October 2007 revealed, that's how over half the population described themselves. This figure has remained more or less steady since the 1960s.[34]

Of course, self-identification is an ambiguous, subjective business and people of all classes might, for various reasons, mischaracterize their place in the social pecking order. And yet the figure has an uncanny relation to the facts. In today's Britain the number of people employed in blue-collar manual and white-collar routine clerical jobs represents over half the workforce, more than twenty-eight million workers.[35] We're a nation of secretaries, shop assistants and admin employees. The lives of this majority are virtually ignored by journalists and politicians. Needless to say, over half the population has nothing in common with Karen Matthews. And yet the rare appearances made by working-class people on the public stage are more likely than not to be stories about hate figures—however legitimate—such as Karen Matthews.

Were politicians and journalists wrong to argue that communities such as Dewsbury Moor had particular social problems that set them apart from the rest of Britain? As with most stereotypes, there are grains of truth in the 'chav' caricature. It is undeniable that many working-class communities across Britain suffer from high levels of unemployment. They do have relatively large numbers of benefit recipients, and crime levels are high. Yet the blame has been directed at the victims rather than at the policies promoted by successive governments over recent decades.

Dewsbury Moor is a good example. The ward finds itself in the top 10 per cent for overall deprivation and child poverty. As we have seen with the bile spewed out by journalists during the Shannon Matthews affair, the detractors argue that this is largely due to the fecklessness of the people who live there. They're wrong. Governments have effectively socially engineered these working-class communities to have the problems that they have.

We've come a long way since Labour's Aneurin Bevan founded modern council housing in the aftermath of World War II. Above all, his aim was to create mixed communities. He reasoned that this would help people from different backgrounds to understand one another, breaking down the sort of prejudices we see today directed at chavs. 'It is entirely undesirable that on modern housing estates only one type of citizen should live,' he argued. 'If we are to enable citizens to lead a full life, if they are each to be aware of the problems of their neighbours, then they should all be drawn from different sectors of the community. We should try to introduce what was always the lovely feature of English and Welsh villages, where the doctor, the grocer, the butcher and the farm labourer all lived in the same street.'[36]

This laudable principle has been fatally undermined by policies introduced in the Thatcher era which New Labour have been happy to keep in place. Council estates like Dewsbury Moor now display the exact opposite result to that originally intended by Bevan. As the 1970s drew to a close, before the Thatcher government launched the 'right-to-buy' scheme, more than two in five of us lived in council housing. Today the figure is nearer one in ten, with tenants of housing associations and co-operatives representing half as many again.[37] Councils were prevented from building new homes and, over the last eleven years, the party of Bevan has refused to invest money in the remaining houses under local authority control. As council housing collapsed, remaining stock was prioritized for those most in need. 'New tenants coming in, almost exclusively in order to meet stringent criteria, will either be single parents with dependent children, [or] people out of institutions including prisons,' explained the late Alan Walter, a lifelong council tenant and chairman of the pressure group Defend Council Housing. 'And therefore they are, almost by definition, those without work.'

Many—but not all—of those who remained in council housing were too poor to take advantage of the right-to-buy scheme. 'A growing number of people who can afford to get out of social housing have done so, and it's then sold off to someone else not necessarily in a respectable family,' Polly Toynbee argues. 'The more people absent themselves from living in a council estate, the worse the divide gets: after all, there's virtually no rented sector.' The problems people faced had nothing to do with the fact they lived in council housing, and everything to do with the fact that only the most deprived were eligible to live on estates. The unsurprising result is that over two-thirds of those living in social housing belong to the poorest two-fifths of the population. Nearly half of social housing is located in the poorest fifth of neighbourhoods.[38] Things have certainly changed compared to thirty years ago, when a staggering 20 per cent of the richest tenth of the population lived in social housing.[39] If places like Dewsbury Moor have major social problems, it's because they have been *made* to have them.

Because of the sheer concentration of Britain's poorest living in social housing, council estates easily become associated with the so-called 'chavs'. While it is true that about half of Britain's poor own their homes, they too tend to live on estates. The increasing transformation of council estates into social dumping grounds has provided much ammunition for the theory that Britain is divided into middle-class society and a working-class chav rump, suffering from an epidemic of self-inflicted problems.

Government housing policies are not the only cause of the social disadvantages affecting working-class areas. Thatcherism unleashed a tsunami of de-industrialization, decimating communities such as Dewsbury Moor. Manufacturing jobs have collapsed over the last thirty years. When Thatcher came to power in 1979, over seven million of us earned a living in manufacturing. Thirty years later, this was true for less than half as many, a mere 2.83 million—not least because factories had relocated to developing countries where workers cost less.

The town of Dewsbury was once home to a thriving textile industry. Over the past three decades, these jobs have all but disappeared. At the bottom of the street where Karen Matthews once lived are dozens of disused lock-ups, including abandoned textile mills and expansive industrial estates. 'This was known as the heavy woollen area of West Yorkshire. There were also lots of engineering and manufacturing jobs,' Reverend Pitcher explains. 'Those jobs have all gone; there's virtually no manufacturing industry. So what do people do? What choices do people have for work? People depend on the big supermarkets for their jobs. There's no other place to work for any significant job.' The impact on local people has been devastating. 'This has had a destabilizing effect on the community—the sense of community we once had has evaporated.' The lack of large manufacturing firms made it very difficult for those who had not succeeded in education to find a job.

The impact of this industrial collapse can be seen on the Matthews family. Both the grandparents and parents worked in local industry, particularly in textiles. And yet, as Karen Matthews's mother put it: 'The town has changed now. The textiles have gone and there aren't the same jobs as there were.'[40] Manufacturing in areas like Dewsbury Moor used to provide secure, relatively well-paid, highly unionized jobs that were passed down from generation to generation.

'The decline of the British manufacturing and industrial base has decimated communities up and down the country,' says Labour MP Katy Clark. 'If you just talk about the constituency I represent [North Ayrshire and Arran], we used to have large-scale industrial and manufacturing industries which employed on occasion tens of thousands of people. All those jobs have gone and in their place, low-paid usually service-sector and public-sector jobs have come.'

Industry was the linchpin of local communities. Its sudden disappearance from places like Dewsbury Moor caused massive unemployment during the 1980s. Today, the official unemployment rate in the area is only a percentage point above the national average. But this statistic is deeply deceptive. If you exclude people engaged in full-time study, well over a quarter of the people in Dewsbury West are classed as 'economically inactive'. That's around 10 per cent over the average. The main reason is that many of those who lost their jobs were officially classified as ill or incapacitated, in a process common to all the areas that, like Dewsbury, lost their industries in the 1980s and 1990s. It is difficult to argue that this is because they are lazy scroungers. In late 2008, the government announced plans to push 3.5 million benefit recipients into jobs. At the same time they estimated that there were only around half a million vacancies. That's the lowest on record. People are out of work in places like Dewsbury Moor quite simply because there are not enough jobs to go around.

It is clear that the 'chav' caricature epitomized by Karen Matthews has sunk deep roots into British society. More and more of us are choosing to believe that the victims of social problems are, in large part, responsible for causing them. Three-quarters of us, for example, thought that the gap between high and low incomes was 'too large' in 2006—but only slightly over a third supported spending more on welfare benefits for the poor. While nearly half of us felt that an unemployed couple should be classed as 'hard up' in 1986, that level declined to just over a third by 2005. Even more strikingly, while only 19 per cent felt that poverty was caused by laziness or a lack of willpower in 1986, the figure had increased to 27 per cent twenty years later.[41]

What is remarkable about these figures is that they have come at a time when inequality has grown as sharply as social mobility has declined. The Gini coefficient—used to measure overall income inequality in Britain—was rated as 26 in 1979. Today it has risen to 39. It is not simply that this growing social division renders those at the top more likely to be ignorant of how other people live their lives. As we have seen, demonizing the less well-off also makes it easier to justify an unprecedented and growing level of social inequality. After all, to admit that some people are poorer than others because of the social injustice inherent in our society would require government action. Claiming that people are largely responsible for their circumstances facilitates the opposite conclusion. 'We're developing a culture where it's acceptable and indeed normal to speak of the white working class in very dehumanized language, and this is a common symptom of a highly unequal society,' Johann Hari warns. 'If you go to South Africa or Venezuela—or other Latin American countries with a tiny wealthy elite—it's common for them to speak of the poor as if they're not quite normal or somehow subhuman.'

The Shannon Matthews affair casts a disquieting light on modern Britain. It didn't spark contempt for working-class people. It simply exposed prejudices that have become rampant in our society. The hysteria around the case shows that it is possible to say practically anything about those caricatured as chavs. Somehow a huge part of Britain has been made complicit in crimes they had nothing to do with. With neither middle-class politicians nor journalists showing any willingness to give a platform to the reality of working-class communities, the pitifully dysfunctional lives of a tiny minority of individuals have been presented as a case study of modern life outside so-called Middle England. 'Chavs' have become more despised than practically any other group of people.

Where has this hatred come from? There is certainly nothing new about venting spite against those at the bottom of the pile. Theologians of the seventeenth century deplored the 'indiscreet and misguided charity' extended to poor people who were 'the very scabs, and filth, and vermin of the Common-wealth'.[42] In the nineteenth century, the harsh Poor Laws threw the destitute and unemployed into workhouses where they toiled in hellish conditions, and commentators debated whether the respectable working class was giving way to a debauched rump they labelled the 'residuum'. The rise of eugenics in the early twentieth century led even some who considered themselves left-wing to argue for the sterilization of the 'unfit' poor—or even for their extermination.

Chav-bashing draws on a long, ignoble tradition of class hatred. But it cannot be understood without looking at more recent events. Above all, it is the bastard child of a very British class war.

2

Class Warriors

...one of the worlds is preaching a Class War, and the other
vigorously practising it.

—George Bernard Shaw, *Back to Methuselah*

The Tories have, in modern times, been at pains to present themselves
as standing above class and sectional interests. 'One Nation' was one of
their most treasured phrases throughout much of the twentieth century.
When David Cameron was elected leader of the Conservative Party in
2005, the Tories were, to begin with, full of fluffy rhetoric about understanding marginalized young people (Cameron wants us to 'hug a
hoodie', mocked New Labour), and even about narrowing the gap
between rich and poor.

But as soon as they are safely behind closed doors, away from the
cameras, the cuddly PR-speak can abruptly disappear. I witnessed the
mask slip myself, when in my final year as an undergraduate. An
extremely prominent Tory politician from the moderate wing of the
party had come to deliver an off-the-record speech to students. So that
he could speak candidly, aspiring student journalists were barred from
reporting on the speech and we were sworn to preserve his anonymity.
It soon became clear why. As the logs crackled in the fireplace on
a rainy November evening, the Tory grandee made a stunning
confession.

'What you have to realize about the Conservative Party,' he said as though it was a trivial, throwaway comment, 'is that it is a coalition of privileged interests. Its main purpose is to defend that privilege. And the way it wins elections is by giving *just* enough to *just* enough other people.'

Here was an analysis that could have dropped out of the pages of *Socialist Worker*. A doyen of the Conservative Party had more or less confessed that it was the political arm of the rich and powerful. It was there to fight the corner of the people at the top. It was waging class war.

Asked to picture a 'class warrior', perhaps most people would see a chubby union leader in a flat cap, becoming progressively redder in the face as he denounces 'management' in a thick regional accent—not well-bred men with sleek suits and clipped accents.

When I asked former Labour leader Neil Kinnock if the Conservatives were the class warriors of British politics, he shook his head gravely. 'No, because they've never had to engage in a class war,' he said. 'Largely because we signed the peace treaty without realizing that they hadn't.'

The demonization of the working class cannot be understood without looking back at the Thatcherite experiment of the 1980s that forged the society we live in today. At its core was an offensive against working-class communities, industries, values and institutions. No longer was being working class something to be proud of: it was something to escape from. This vision did not come from nowhere. It was the culmination of a class war waged, on and off, by the Conservatives for over two centuries.

This is certainly not the way the Conservative Party has sought to present itself in public. Whenever the interests of its 'coalition of privileged interests' have been menaced by even the most moderate arguments for social reform, it has decried them as attempts at 'class war'. After six years spent resisting reforms introduced by the post-war Labour government, such as the National Health Service and the welfare state, the Tories denounced Labour in those exact terms. 'Of all impediments the class war is the worst,' declared the 1951 Conservative Manifesto, accusing Labour of hoping to 'gain another lease of power by fomenting class hatred and appealing to moods of greed and envy'.

But a cursory look at its history uncloaks a party that has always defended 'privileged interests', particularly against the threat posed by working-class Britons. Throughout the nineteenth century the Tories were fervent opponents of allowing any but the richest to vote. When the 1831 Reform Bill was presented to Parliament, proposing to extend suffrage to as many as one out of every five adult males, the Tory reaction was hysterical. One Tory MP sensationally alleged that the Bill represented 'a revolution that will overturn all the natural influence of rank and property.' Lord Salisbury, the future Tory prime minister, sulked about the expanding suffrage with dark predictions that 'first-rate men will not canvass mobs, and mobs will not elect first-class men.'

It was in the twentieth century that the Tories and their coalition of privileged interests would face their greatest political threat. Working-class people had organized themselves into trade unions by the million. These unions went on to found the Labour Party with the specific mission of representing working-class interests in Parliament for the first time. Well before Thatcher, the Tories launched rearguard actions against this menace. The governments of Lord Salisbury and Arthur Balfour stood enthusiastically by the infamous Taff Vale legal judgement of 1901, which hit at the unions by making them liable for profits lost in strikes. Looking back on the episode, the future Tory Prime Minister Stanley Baldwin later confessed: 'The Conservatives can't talk of class war. They started it.'

When trade unions launched a general strike in 1926, the Tory government warned of red revolution and mobilized the armed forces. After the strike was broken, senior conservative and irreconcilable class warrior Arthur Balfour boasted: 'The General Strike has taught the working class more in four days than years of talking could have done.' As part of this lesson, mass picketing and any strikes launched in

41

support of other workers were banned, and union links with Labour were weakened. The working class was put back in its box.

In view of all this one may well wonder how, in an age of mass democracy, the Tories could ever have hoped to win an election. But the Conservatives are the most successful political party in the Western world. They governed Britain for two thirds of the twentieth century. The former head of Margaret Thatcher's policy unit, Ferdinand Mount, gives short shrift to the senior Tory's 'privileged coalition' theory, dismissing it to me as 'the kind of show-off cynicism which old politicians like to indulge in. I should have thought it would be quite hard to score consistently twelve to fourteen million votes at general elections if you did not have some genuine sympathy with the less privileged majority.' It is a compelling point. If everyone has the vote, then why would working-class people vote for a political gravy train for the rich?

That old class warrior Lord Salisbury was himself surprised to discover that up to a third of manual workers voted Tory in the early twentieth century. It all goes back to the second part of our anonymous politician's thesis: that Conservatives win by 'giving *just* enough to *just* enough other people'. The Tories have always sought to weaken the collective power of working-class people as a group in society. But they also knew how to win elections by courting working-class voters as individuals, by methods which were frequently ingenious.

One common ploy was moderate social reform with conservative ends. It was a method used to great effect by Benjamin Disraeli, Conservative prime minister in the late nineteenth century, who continues to be fondly regarded by the ever-diminishing band of 'One Nation' Tories as their founding father. His government introduced limited progressive measures such as reducing the maximum working day to ten hours and banning children from working full-time. His calculation was that it would 'gain and retain for the Conservatives the lasting affection of the working classes'. Indeed, some trade union leaders hated the Liberals more in this period, and Thatcher herself looked to the laissez-faire capitalism of nineteenth-century Liberal leader William Gladstone for inspiration.

Of course, the whole point of Disraelian Toryism was to preserve the existing social order. As the relatively moderate Tory Michael Heseltine put it a century later, it was 'good enlightened capitalism—paternalism if you like. *Noblesse oblige.* I believe strongly that those with power and privilege have responsibilities.'

After all, no Tory would ever think of the party as out to hammer the working class. All politicians, no matter how reactionary, feel a need to rationalize their policies for a greater good. Many undoubtedly had—and have—noble, paternalistic ideas of public service. It is a deeply held and sincere Conservative belief that what is good for business is good for the country. But there is no escaping the fact that the Tory leadership has always been dominated by the wealthiest elements of society, determined to thwart reforms offered first by the Liberals and then by the Labour Party. Sticks alone could not contain the working class in a democratic system: carrots had to be offered too.

The Tories have long used populism as a trump card to win working-class support. From the late nineteenth century they tapped into a growing backlash against Irish and Jewish immigration, culminating in the introduction of the restrictive Aliens Bill in 1904. Promised crackdowns on immigration have been a mainstay of Tory electioneering ever since. Flying the flag in a range of ways has invariably aided the Conservative cause: for example, appealing to nationalist sentiments by opposing self-rule for Ireland at the turn of the twentieth century. And, of course, popular fear of crime has long been fertile political territory for a party with a tough law-and-order message.

They have lost their salience today, but religious allegiances once played a major role. Before 1914, if you were staunchly Church of England (once derided as the 'Tory Party at prayer') you were pretty likely to vote Conservative. Today's Liverpool may be the most solidly Labour city in Parliament, but religious sectarianism and Tory anti-Catholicism once made it a hub of working-class Toryism.

Social aspiration has been another fruitful vote-catcher, as well as a means of undermining working-class identity. There was room at the top, ran the promise: you could improve your lot by edging up the social ladder. In areas devoid of a strong middle class—Scotland, Wales and most of Northern England—this had limited appeal. But where there was a solid middle class, people from working-class backgrounds were always more likely to opt for the Tories. It was a way of keeping up with the Joneses—and even, so they thought, of joining them. 'What you find is that Labour is strong in the mining seats, even in the interwar years, or in the East End of London—because there's no middle class, basically,' says political historian Ross McKibbin. 'It doesn't take much of a middle-class presence to affect the way that working-class people are prepared to vote.'

Above all, the Tories have been able to win working-class support through ruthless pragmatism. After World War II, the Tories and their supporters were forced on to the back foot. Recent memories of the Great Depression seemed to have permanently discredited free-market capitalism, and the Tories had no option but to accept the welfare state, higher taxation and a strong union movement. Tony Crosland, a senior post-war Labour politician, noted that the Conservatives had no choice but to fight elections 'largely on policies which twenty years ago were associated with the Left, and repudiated by the Right'.[1] But with the Conservatives in power throughout the 1950s and the unions and Labour taking a moderate direction, some Tories could not resist speculating that they had the upper hand. 'The class war is over and we have won it,' declared Tory Prime Minister Harold Macmillan in 1959.

This ceasefire did not last long. The new consensus unravelled in the 1970s as company profits went into free fall and trade unions flexed their muscles once more. Suddenly it looked as if the class war was back on. This time, a new generation of Tories intended to win it—for good.

Few men can claim to have had as much influence over modern Britain as Keith Joseph. The son of a construction magnate, Joseph was the most prominent figure of the Tory right in the early 1970s. When the Conservatives were defeated in two successive general elections in 1974, Joseph became one of the leaders of a new breed of Tory who rejected the post-war consensus of welfare capitalism that had been upheld by earlier Conservative governments. Instead, they wanted to curb union power, sell off state-owned industries and return to nineteenth-century principles of laissez-faire capitalism. For Joseph the road to Damascus moment came when Tory Prime Minister Edward Heath was booted from office, after having taken on the miners and lost. 'It was only in April 1974 that I was converted to Conservatism,' he later claimed. 'I had thought I was a Conservative but I now see that I was not really one at all.'

Keith Joseph and his laissez-faire cabal were supporters of American free-market guru Milton Friedman. When, in 1974, the Labour Party returned to Downing Street with a promise 'to bring about a fundamental and irreversible shift in the balance of power and wealth in favour of working people and their families', Friedman's ideas were still largely confined to the textbooks. The exception was Chile, where in 1973 General Augusto Pinochet, with US backing, had removed the elected socialist President Salvador Allende in one of the most brutal coups in Latin America's tortured history. Pinochet shared one of the main aims of his ideological soulmates in Britain: to erase the working class as a concept. His goal, he declared, was to 'make Chile not a nation of proletarians, but a nation of entrepreneurs'.

But Keith Joseph blew his chance to lead a similar project through the ballot box in Britain. In a speech in October 1974, he expressed some of the attitudes towards 'the lower orders' that were once common among middle-class eugenicists. He argued that 'a high and rising proportion of children are being born to mothers least fitted to bring children into the world and to bring them up. They are born to mothers who were first pregnant in adolescence in social classes 4 and 5 ... Some are of low intelligence, most of low educational attainment.' But the killer line was this: 'The balance of our population, our human stock is threatened.' Joseph's message was clear. The poor were breeding too fast, and the danger was they were going to swamp everybody else.

Though Joseph was only repeating prejudices long held among many wealthier Britons, his mistake was to repeat them in public. His hopes of becoming Conservative leader were over. But all was not lost. In his place his protégée, Margaret Thatcher, the MP for Finchley, stood and won. Joseph's influence was evident in much of the intellectual underpinning of what became known as Thatcherism, leading critics to call him the Iron Lady's 'Mad Monk'. Following her election victory in 1979, the Conservatives would launch the country's most audacious experiment in social engineering since the Puritans ruled England over three hundred years earlier. 'We have to move this country in a new direction, to change the way we look at things, to create a wholly new attitude of mind,' Thatcher urged her party.

To understand Thatcherism's attitude to working-class Britain, it is important to start by looking at Thatcher herself. Some of her warmest admirers have often been at pains to portray her—wrongly—as a person of humble origins. As the staunchly Thatcherite Tory MP David Davis told me: 'Margaret was always a bit more middle class than she made out.' It is almost a cliché to describe her as a grocer's daughter, but it was this that coloured her entire political outlook. Growing up in the Lincolnshire market town of Grantham, her father had instilled in her a deep commitment to what could be called lower-middle-class values: individual self-enrichment and enterprise, and an instinctive hostility to collective action. Her biographer, Hugo Young, noted that she had little if any contact with working-class people, let alone the trade union movement.

Her attitudes were undoubtedly cemented when in 1951 she married a wealthy businessman, Denis Thatcher, who believed that trade unions should be banned altogether. She surrounded herself with men from privileged backgrounds. In her first Cabinet, 88 per cent of ministers were former public school students, 71 per cent were company directors and 14 per cent were large landowners. No wonder, then, that one of her Cabinet ministers told a journalist just before the 1979 election: 'She is still basically a Finchley lady ... She regards the working class as idle, deceitful, inferior and bloody-minded.'[2]

If Thatcher had one aim, it was to stop us thinking in terms of class. 'Class is a Communist concept,' she would later write. 'It groups people as bundles and sets them against one another.'[3] She wanted to erase the idea that people could better their lives by collective action, rather than by individual self-improvement: that is, 'pulling yourself up by your bootstraps'. Just months after her election victory in 1979, she had intended to spell this out to the country in stark terms.

'Morality is personal. There is no such thing as collective conscience, collective kindness, collective gentleness, collective freedom,' she planned to argue. 'To talk of social justice, social responsibility, a new world order, may be easy and make us feel good, but it does not absolve each of us from personal responsibility.' It was clearly too much for her speechwriters and did not make the final cut. However, they were not able to stop her infamous declaration several years later (in lifestyle magazine *Woman's Own*, of all places): 'There's no such thing as society. There are individual men and women and there are families.'

The Tories might be a party rooted in Britain's class divisions, but they are at pains to deflect any reminders of this fact. Indeed, for right-wing ideologues in the Thatcher mould, any talk about class is subversive for a host of reasons. It implies that one group possesses wealth and power in society, while others do not. If you accept that much, it is only a step to concluding that this is something that needs to be rectified. It suggests that a group of people live by working for others, which raises questions of exploitation. It encourages you to define your own economic interests against those of others. But, above all, it conjures up the notion of a potentially organized bloc with political and economic power, and one that could wage war against wealth and privilege. That made the existence of the working class *as a concept* the mortal enemy of Thatcher's everyone-for-themselves model of capitalism.

Thatcher had not the slightest ambition to get rid of social classes, she just didn't want us to perceive that we belonged to one. 'It's not the existence of classes that threatens the unity of the nation, but the exis-tence of class feeling,' as an official Conservative Party document put it in 1976.[4] And yet, at the same time, Thatcherism fought the most aggressive class war in British history: by battering the trade unions into the ground, shifting the tax burden from the wealthy to the working class and the poor, and stripping businesses of state regula-tions. Thatcher wanted to end the class war—but on the terms of the upper crust of British society. 'Old-fashioned Tories say there isn't any class war,' declared Tory newspaper editor Peregrine Worsthorne. 'New Tories make no bones about it: we are class warriors and we expect to be victorious.'

At the centre of this crusade was a concerted attempt to dismantle the values, institutions and traditional industries of the working class. The aim was to rub out the working class as a political and economic force in society, replacing it with a collection of individuals, or entrepreneurs, competing with each other for their own interests. In a new, supposedly upwardly mobile Britain, everyone would aspire to climb the ladder and all those who did not would be responsible for their own failure. Class was to be eliminated as an idea, but it was to be bolstered in practice.

There has been no greater assault on working-class Britain than Thatcher's two-pronged attack on industry and trade unions. It was not just that the systematic trashing of the country's manufacturing indus-tries devastated communities—though it certainly did, leaving them ravaged by unemployment, poverty and all the crippling social prob-lems that accompany them, for which they would later be blamed. Working-class identity itself was under fire.

The old industries were the beating hearts of the communities they sustained. Most local people had worked in similar jobs and had done so for generations. And of course the unions, whatever their faults and limitations, had given the workers in these communities strength, solidarity and a sense of power. All of this had sustained a feeling of belonging, of pride in a shared working-class experience.

For those who, like myself, grew up in a country without strong unions, it is easy to understate the significance of Thatcherism's war on the organized working class. Such was Thatcher's legacy that when Labour came to power in 1997, Tony Blair could boast that even after his proposed reforms, trade union laws would remain 'the most restrictive' in the Western world. When working-class people were demonized before the advent of Thatcherism, it was almost always because of fear of the unions. 'I recall in the 60s, 70s and 80s, strikers—and most of the strikers then were working class—were treated pretty badly in the media, always in a very hostile way,' recalls *Mirror* journalist Kevin Maguire. Aggressive picketers and 'unions holding the country to ransom' were mainstays of newspaper copy. At the heart of the Tory strategy was their clever manipulation of a series of strikes by largely low-paid public sector workers in 1978 and 1979—or, as it became known, the Winter of Discontent.

Even today, over thirty years later, the Winter of Discontent remains a kind of right-wing folk story used to bash unions whenever there is even a murmur of industrial unrest. Scenes of uncollected rubbish rotting in the streets and the dead going unburied are recounted in almost apocalyptic tones.

Yet the strikes were almost completely avoidable. James Callaghan's Labour government had imposed years of effective pay cuts on public sector workers in order to keep down inflation. But this approach was based on the myth that union pay claims caused price rises, rather than the other way round. Inflation was rampant across the Western world at the time, regardless of how strong unions were. 'What really kicked things off in the late 1960s was the start of economic liberalization and the removal of credit controls, leading to excessive credit growth,' says former City economist Graham Turner. Another factor was the printing of huge sums of money by the US government to pay for the

Vietnam War, which unleashed a tidal wave of inflation across the West. Low-paid workers like refuse collectors went on strike in the winter of 1978–9 because their living standards were in free fall, and they were being made to pay for an inflationary crisis that they had had no part in creating.

Tony Benn was a minister in the Labour Cabinet during the Winter of Discontent. 'It was a conflict, an economic conflict between working people on the one hand and their employers on the other, and the government supported the employers, in effect,' he recalls. 'And it led to a great deal of disillusionment.'

There is no doubting that the Winter of Discontent fuelled popular frustration with unions. Right-wing tabloids went into overdrive, making it look like Britain was descending into chaos. Members of the public faced inconvenience because of cancelled services. The increasingly impoverished workers who had been forced to strike did not get a hearing.

Thatcher's government relentlessly manipulated these memories. Its goal was to crush the unions forever. New laws allowed employers to sack strikers, reduced dismissal compensation, forbade workers to strike in support of others, repealed protections preventing courts seizing union funds, and made unions liable for huge financial penalties. Changing the law was not, however, enough: examples had to be made. As industrial relations expert Professor Gregor Gall puts it, the government inflicted 'a series of defeats on unions in set-piece battles with the public sector, and encouraged private sector employers to take on the unions'. The first to face Thatcher's iron fist were the steelworkers in 1980, who lost a thirteen-week strike battle and would pay the price with thousands of jobs. Three years later, striking workers on picket lines at the *Stockport Messenger* were charged by 3,000 riot police and beaten up in neighbouring fields. Their union, the National Graphical Association, had its assets seized by the government.

In the face of this onslaught, you might have expected the trade unions to rally together and fight back. But they didn't. Unions—and the Labour Party for that matter—were hopelessly divided. Their leaders were caught disastrously off-balance by the determination and ferocity of the Thatcherite crusade. The government took note of the weakness of its enemies, and picked off those workers who dared to fight back. But all the laws and set-piece battles combined did not have the same crushing effect as another of Thatcher's weapons: Britain's ever-growing dole queues.

The Tories had made a big deal out of the fact that unemployment had reached a million under Labour in 1979, employing ad firm Saatchi & Saatchi to design their famous 'Labour Isn't Working' poster. But under Thatcher, some estimates put the number out of work as peaking at four million. The terror of losing your job suppresses any temptation to fight back. 'The *major* catalyst for Thatcher's alterations in labour law was unemployment,' says former Labour leader Neil Kinnock. 'Stupid bourgeois people, like the ones who write the newspapers, say that four million unemployed means an angry, assertive workforce. It doesn't. It means at least four million other very frightened people. And people threatened with unemployment don't jeopardize their jobs by undertaking various acts of labour militancy—they just don't do it.'

When I asked Thatcher's first chancellor of the exchequer, Geoffrey Howe, if mass unemployment had a role in restraining union power, he agreed. 'I think it had in demonstrating the emptiness of continuing to behave as they were behaving.' But, he was quick to add, his policies were not 'a conscious medicine to achieve that'. Even so, one of the great achievements of Thatcherism, as far as Howe was concerned, was crushing 'trade union tyranny'.

Others involved with the Tory governments put it rather more bluntly. When Sir Alan Budd was the Treasury's chief economist in the early 1990s, he suspected that the government 'never believed for a moment that this was the correct way to bring down inflation. They did, however, see that it would be a very, very good way to raise unemployment, and unemployment was an extremely desirable way of reducing the strength of the working classes.'

Regardless of the government's motives, 'the legacy of Geoffrey Howe is the de-industrialization of our economy,' in the words of economist Graham Turner. Within three months of sweeping to power in 1979, the Tories dramatically abolished exchange controls, allowing financial companies to make huge profits from currency speculation. This allowed the City to thrive at the expense of other parts of the economy, like manufacturing. But above all, it was allowing the value of the pound to soar that did for industry, making its exports far more expensive than overseas competitors. By 1983—after just five years— nearly a third of manufacturing had vanished from Britain's shores. Once-thriving working-class communities lay in ruin.

Now, at a time of economic crisis caused by overdependence on the City and a depleted manufacturing base, even leading Tory figures today are talking about the need for Britain to start making things again. Many of the old industrial communities remain in pieces. But remorse for Thatcherism's scorched-earth policies is difficult to come by. I asked Thatcher's chancellor if he regretted the use of a blunt instrument like raising interest rates. 'It was inescapable,' says Geoffrey Howe. 'Most things we were grappling with were part of unconscious, suicidal management ... So it was uncomfortable for industry—but no one was really arguing for an escape route. It would have been nice. But then there were other things that would have gone wrong.' As far as Howe is concerned, manufacturing only has itself to blame. 'Everyone regrets it, yes. It was so much caused by the behaviour of industry itself ... I've often questioned the suicide note of much of British industry at that time.'

Senior Tory MP and one-time Conservative leadership contender David Davis is less repentant still. 'Well, was it avoidable?' he demands, visibly agitated. 'What would you have done? Tell me what you would have done. Put money into manufacturing? That's what stuffed it up in the first place! What *could* they have done?' He goes as far as to argue that Thatcher's government 'did quite a lot for the communities, in terms of, you know, sorts of schemes to try and retrain and so on. No, no, I think they did a lot there. The truth of the matter is it just may not work, that's the problem … the truth of most public policy is that you've got about a 50 per cent success rate if you're lucky in economic areas of public policy.' Even Howe admits that many of their initiatives in that regard, like 'Business Start-Up Schemes and things like that … turned out to be tax avoidance societies.'

As far as Davis is concerned, manufacturing had been kept alive by 'props' which Thatcher had no option but to kick away. 'And also, there is an extent to which you are acting like King Canute, trying to stop the tide, trying to stop manufacturing going to China,' he argues. 'Ironically, since it's very often socialists who argue against this—it's actually a part of material redistribution going on. The market redistributing income from the wealthy West to the poor East. And in many ways I approve of that.' He is quick to add that this 'doesn't mean I want us to give away jobs'—though it is difficult to see any other conclusion to what he is arguing.

'I think that's a grotesque rewriting of history,' retorts *Guardian* economics editor Larry Elliott. 'The Tories came into power and made a series of catastrophic economic blunders, sending the pound shooting up on the foreign exchanges, which made our exports highly uncompetitive. They allowed inflation to get to 20 per cent, and pushed interest rates up to 17 per cent, which made borrowing expensive—which was crucial for manufacturing.' He dismisses out of hand the idea that the 15 per cent of British industry that went to the wall in the early Thatcher years was 'ripe for the kill'.

In other words, industry had been stripped from Britain because of government policy, not because of the onward march of history. No other Western European nation saw the obliteration of manufacturing in such a brutally short period. Just consider the contrast with the response to the financial crisis that exploded in 2008. While Thatcherism left manufacturing to bleed to death in the 1980s, the New Labour government pumped billions of pounds of taxpayers' money into banks whose greed and stupidity had left them teetering on the edge of collapse. The reason? The banks were too big to fail. 'You could say the same about manufacturing,' says Graham Turner. 'The world eventually recovered, and had you supported manufacturing more, we might not have lost so many manufacturing jobs.'

All of this prompts the question: did the Tories have any interest in saving manufacturing, crocodile tears or no? As far as Thatcher and her acolytes were concerned, finance and services were the future; making things belonged to the past. In his memoirs John Cole, a former BBC political correspondent, recalls asking Thatcher how this 'service' or 'post-industrial' economy would work. 'She cited an entrepreneur she had met the previous week, who wished to take over Battersea power station and turn it into what we both knew as a "Disneyland", but subsequently learned to call a theme park.' The following day, he put this anecdote to the economic attaché at the United States Embassy. 'He looked at me in genuine astonishment, thoughtfully laid down his fork, and exclaimed: "But gee, John, you can't all make a living opening doors for each other!"'[5] However, an economy based on everyone 'opening doors for each other' was exactly what Thatcher had in mind.

Thatcher's attacks on unions and industry dealt body blows to the old, industrial working class. Well-paid, secure, skilled jobs that people were proud of, which had been a linchpin of working-class identity, were eradicated. All the things people associated with working-class Britain were disappearing. But even after Thatcher won again in 1983, Britain's working class was not quite dead as a political and social force. The decisive battle was still to come.

'The interesting thing people haven't recognized quite,' observes Geoffrey Howe, 'is that the Thatcher government is in fact the Heath government given a second chance, with very much the same personnel.' It is a point worth underlining. The Tories under Ted Heath had been swept from office by a national miners' strike in 1974. Heath had asked the electorate: 'Who governs Britain?' The answer came back: 'Not you, mate!' It was a humiliating defeat, and the first time that unions had effectively overthrown a government. Thatcher had not forgotten it. Her response must rank as one of the most callous acts of revenge in British history.

Retribution wasn't the only motive. The miners had been the vanguard of the union movement in Britain throughout the twentieth century. Britain's only general strike had been called in support of the miners in 1926. They had the capacity to single-handedly bring the country to a standstill by cutting off its energy supply, as they had demonstrated in the 1970s. If you could see off the miners, what other group of workers could stop you? That's why the defeat of the Miners' Strike was the turning point in the history of modern working-class Britain.

'Mining communities were vibrant communities, but they were built around the pit. The pit was the heart of the community, it was the pit that bound everyone together,' recalls one National Union of Mineworkers (NUM) leader, Chris Kitchen. 'The code of honour that existed underground was part of the fabric of the community as well. You didn't get young lads going off the rails at the weekend. You wouldn't upset an old guy because he would be the same one you'd rely on in the pit to protect your life at work, so why would you upset him at the weekend over a few pints?'

When Thatcher's government unveiled its pits closure programme in 1984, many of these tightly knit communities faced oblivion. Strikes spontaneously broke out in the Yorkshire coalfields and spread across the country. NUM leader Arthur Scargill declared these strikes a national strike and called all miners out, a decision ratified by a national Conference in April that year. Of the major pits, only the Nottinghamshire miners—who wrongly, as it turned out, thought their jobs were safe—refused to strike, a cause of great bitterness among the wider mining community.

As Tony Benn recalls, the struggle 'electrified the labour movement. I did 299 public meetings in a year, and wherever you went there was tremendous support and activity.' But in the national media and among Thatcher's supporters, Scargill became a hate figure. There was also fear, not least at the excitement generated by the miners' struggle. When I discussed it with Simon Heffer, the arch-Thatcherite *Daily Telegraph* journalist, he was moved to make parallels with the Nazis:

> I think Scargill's mentally ill, actually. I was present at the 1984 Labour Party Conference when Scargill made this speech, which was devastating in its impact. I mean, I'd never before been in a room where he has spoken, or where anyone has spoken with such effect. And it was his orthodox Stalinist critique. I think it included the phrase—and I'm remembering this from twenty-five years ago—'Margaret Thatcher is fighting for her class, I am here fighting for my class.' I've seen Hitler on television, and it reminded me of the sort of demagoguery that Hitler engaged in. It was terrifying, because while I was able to stand removed from it, there were people in there who were all getting incredibly excited about it, and probably do get excited about it to this day.

Unlike most Nottinghamshire miners, Adrian Gilfoyle went on strike until the bitter end. Above all, he remembers the comradeship of working down the pit. 'The strike were important because of saving jobs,' he says. 'I've got two lads—obviously I wouldn't have wanted them to go down pit if they could get another job, but at least, when they grew up, there was that opportunity if there weren't any other jobs, to go there, and it was a good apprenticeship. It was worth fighting for.'

At times, the struggle felt like class war in the most literal sense. 'You used to wake up at around five o'clock in morning, and there were these police from London, and they were banging their shields at five in the morning, waking everybody up,' Gilfoyle recalls. 'You wouldn't have believed it, honestly. Horrible, it was. But it made me even more determined, when you got all that, you see.'

Yet all that was nothing compared to the Battle of Orgreave. On 18 June 1984, up to 6,000 miners attempted to blockade a coking plant in Orgreave, South Yorkshire. Adrian Gilfoyle was among them. They were met by thousands of police officers, including several on horseback, from ten counties across Britain. Suddenly, the police charged.

That day, when the trouble started, they all made out it was the miners responsible ... There were all the pickets, doing nothing, and all of a sudden the police just charged with horses, and that's when all the trouble started. And I remember, me and my brother stood there watching and couldn't believe it, and next thing, this copper was chasing us on a horse, and we just managed to get out his way, and he hit this other lad straight across the back of head with a truncheon and split his head open ... We ran and got into Asda, and the manager stopped police coming in, and he said to us: 'Just get a basket, put in what you want, and get off and I'll support you.' It was horrible, though.

All the trials of the picketers arrested by the police collapsed, and hundreds of thousands of pounds were paid out in compensation.

Like many striking miners, Gilfoyle depended on the support of his wife. 'She was in the Women's Action Group and all sorts. She went to marches all over the place, and she went to Ollerton when that lad got killed [twenty-three-year-old Yorkshire miner David Jones who died on a picket line in suspicious circumstances], she went to his funeral. I've got a photograph of her stood round the grave.' One day he told her, 'Oh, I'm going back to work tomorrow, duck.' 'You go back to work and I'll break your legs!' she responded. It was not only miners like Adrian Gilfoyle making sacrifices: his wife came back one day 'sobbing her heart out' after losing her job as a primary school assistant, following a complaint by a miner who had returned to work.

Not long after the strike ended, she came home feeling unwell. 'She said "phone the doctors for me", and I'd cancelled my phone in the strike, so I had to go to a neighbour's, and she collapsed and had a heart attack and died within a few minutes.' She was only thirty-three, leaving him with two sons aged five and ten.

The Miners' Strike collapsed on 3 March 1985, after a titanic year-long struggle. Brass bands and union banners accompanied the miners as they marched defiantly back to work. 'Maggie had her way, didn't she?' says Gilfoyle. 'And we went back with our tails between our legs, really.' Unlike in 1974, the government had made detailed preparations. It had stuck by the Ridley Plan, a Conservative Party document leaked in 1978 which was a blueprint for taking on the unions, and the miners in particular, including the stockpiling of coal.

Other unions and the Labour leadership refused to back the miners, because they had not held a national ballot. 'It divided the labour movement from the Labour leadership really, because the Labour leadership was giving virtually no support to the miners,' says Tony Benn. Whatever the reasons adduced to avoid backing the miners, the fate of the labour movement was bound up with the Strike. The defeat was a crippling blow from which it never recovered. The miners had been the strongest unionized force in the country: if they could be routed, what hope for anyone else?

Scargill was denounced for his supposedly hysterical claims that the government was determined to destroy the mining industry. Today, virtually nothing remains of it. As even Thatcher's lieutenant, Norman Tebbit, recently admitted: 'Many of these [mining] communities were completely devastated, with people out of work turning to drugs and no real man's work because all the jobs had gone. There is no doubt that this led to a breakdown in these communities with families breaking up and youths going out of control. The scale of the closures went too far.'[6]

The one thing that both supporters and opponents of the Strike agree on is that it taught the unions a lesson they would not forget. 'It was the turning point of the government,' says Robert Forsythe, a retired miner in West Lothian. 'When they beat the miners, they could beat anyone.' Simon Heffer concurs. 'I think that the miners' strike remains a wet dream for various leftists ... I think the only legacy it's had really has been to say to other great forces of organized labour, you take on the government at your peril.' Even today, a quarter of a century later, trade union leaders still feel haunted by the Strike. Trade union leader Mark Serwotka says that its 'legacy was years of despondency and defeatism'.

Many miners and their supporters vilified Neil Kinnock for refusing to support the Strike. Today, he sticks to his 'plague on both your houses' attitude towards Scargill and Thatcher, but reserves most of his vitriol for the miners' leadership. But even he is under no illusions as to the consequences, describing it as a 'salutary' defeat for the labour movement. Trade unions 'saw that if the Tory government could pulverize the coal mining industry, they could do it to anybody. And that changed the mentality of organized labour, understandably. I couldn't blame *anybody*!' He adds:

> The ambition of the Thatcher government related in some degree to the defeat of Ted Heath. But it had much to do with the determination, to put it at its mildest, to put the labour movement in its place. And the most obvious [way to do] that strategically is to take on and defeat the miners. Because they understood—as anybody who thought about it would understand—the repercussive effects of defeating the miners would be very substantial in the rest of the labour movement, as it turned out to be.

To many people at the time, the Miners' Strike looked like the last hurrah of the working class. Their most ferocious phalanxes had been crushed and sent back to their pit villages, to face a lingering decline. The popular historian David Kynaston remembers the atmosphere after the Strike. 'It basically meant that people assumed that the old working class no longer had the power, no longer had the clout, which was a huge change in thinking,' he recalls. 'And there were people living in sort of middle-class suburbia like me, who felt well-disposed —but it suddenly seemed relatively unimportant in all honesty.'

On the eve of the Thatcherite crusade, half of all workers were trade unionists. By 1995, the number had fallen to a third. The old industries associated with working-class identity were being destroyed. There no longer seemed anything to celebrate about being working class. But Thatcherism promised an alternative. Leave the working class behind, it said, and come join the property-owning middle classes instead. Those who failed to do so would have no place in the new Britain.

When the newly elected Thatcher government unveiled its Housing Bill in 1979, it could barely contain its excitement. 'This bill lays the foundations for one of the most important social revolutions of this century,' Michael Heseltine claimed triumphantly. At the heart of the legislation was what became popularly known as 'right-to-buy'. Council housing tenants were now able to buy their own homes at knock-down prices. If you had been a tenant for twenty years, for example, you could have half the market price taken off. One hundred per cent mortgages were offered. Home ownership was to be promoted by government like never before.

The policy was undoubtedly popular with many working-class people. A million council homes were sold in a decade. Former tenants would mark their entry into home ownership by giving their properties a lick of paint. By 1985, the Labour Party had dropped its opposition to the policy. Even so, it was not always as voluntary as it sounds. At the end of the 1980s, the Conservative government introduced legislation that aimed to strangle councils financially and force them to sell off their housing.

Owning a home did not catapult a person into the middle class. To be paying off a mortgage instead of paying rent did not change the fact that you had to work for a living. Looking back at his lifetime, Neil Kinnock remembers that 'in the 1950s, 60s and 70s, the people in the streets from which I came bought their houses from their private landlords, and it didn't change their affiliations, or their commitment, or their sense of identity at all.' British car workers had long been homeowners, yet had been among the most militant trade unionists in the 1970s.

But the policy was part and parcel of Thatcher's determination to make us think of ourselves as individuals who looked after ourselves above all else. Only that would make people feel responsible for their successes and failures. Thatcherism was fostering a new culture where success was measured by what you owned. Those who did not adapt were to be despised. Aspiration was no longer about people working together to improve their communities; it was being redefined as getting more for yourself as an individual, regardless of the social costs.

The social costs were high indeed. The 'left-behinds', the council tenants who had the audacity not to jump on the property ladder, faced the consequences of official disapproval. Before Thatcher came to power, the average rent of a council tenant was £6.20 a week; a decade later, it was nearly four times higher. Spending on housing dropped by a stunning 60 per cent under Thatcher. But it was to be the next generation that would suffer most. The government prevented councils from building social housing to replace the stock that was being sold off.

Housing charity Shelter opposed right-to-buy at the time. 'The critical reason was a recognition of the impact that the policy would have over the long term on the availability of social housing stock,' says Shelter's Mark Thomas. 'The concern was that we'd be selling off these homes at a discount and that the proceeds that were realized wouldn't actually be reinvested in building replacement social homes, and in fact that turned out to be the reality. We've only just very recently moved to a situation where we're building more social homes per year than we're losing under the right-to-buy.'

Rising demand for housing pushed prices up, encouraging disastrous house-price bubbles. Housing became increasingly unaffordable for huge swathes of the population. Millions of people were condemned to languish for years on council housing waiting lists. Little wonder that the number of homeless Britons soared by 38 per cent between 1984 and 1989 alone.[7]

The policy also drove a wedge through working-class Britain, creating a divide between homeowners and council tenants. Right-to-buy meant that the best housing stock was sold off; and it was the relatively better-off council tenants who were becoming homeowners. Those who remained council tenants tended to be poorer and in the worst homes. By 1986, nearly two-thirds of tenants were from the bottom 30 per cent in terms of income, and only 18 per cent were from the richest half. Yet, just seven years earlier, a fifth of the richest 10 per cent were council house dwellers. Council housing became increasingly reserved for those who were most deprived and vulnerable. It was in the 1980s that council estates got their bad name as dilapidated, crime-ridden, and deeply poor: exaggerations in part—and any elements of truth were the direct result of government policies.

Encouraging home ownership was not the only tool for redefining the idea of aspiration. In Thatcher's Britain, wealth (and to *be* wealthy) was to be glorified. The Conservatives promoted the idea that people were rich because of their own hard work and talent, along with the implication that those who did not become so were somehow lacking. 'I believe the person who is prepared to work hardest should get the greatest rewards and keep them after tax, that we should back the workers and not the shirkers,' was Thatcher's clarion call.

The rich were idolized as never before, not least the City men. The so-called Big Bang, or deregulation of financial services, not only made Britain even more dependent on the City: it also turned spivs and speculators into heroes. 'Every man a capitalist,' declared Thatcher: an unattainable goal, but it showed the route that people were now expected to march along.

For the first time in generations, it was a blatant government aim to shovel as much money in the direction of the rich as possible. In the first Budget, top bracket taxes of 83 per cent on earned income and 98 per cent on unearned income were slashed to 60 per cent, and corporation tax went from 52 to 35 per cent. In 1988 the then-chancellor Nigel Lawson went even further: the top rate of tax was reduced to 40 per cent. Geoffrey Howe is unrepentant about what he calls 'changing the tax structure to make it incentivized and not obstructive of enterprise'.

Yet the reality of this part of Thatcher's class war is that it shifted the tax burden from the rich to everybody else. 'Whether or not it had the right impact on distribution of wealth or income, I can't tell,' Howe says. 'But it certainly did liberalize, enhance the chances of making money, saving money, expanding business ...'

As Howe puts it, the Conservatives had 'to find the resources with which to reduce the burden of direct taxes'. So they put up VAT, a tax on consumer goods. The poorer you are, the more of your income goes on VAT. But it was springtime for the rich. By the end of the Tories' reign, in 1996, the richest 10 per cent of families with three children were over £21,000 a year richer on average than when Thatcher had come to power.[8] The wealthiest decile's incomes shot up by 65 per cent for each married couple. Their taxes went from over half to just above a third of their income.[9] Film director Stephen Frears remembers when Lawson cut the top rate to 40 per cent. 'It was as if Lord Lawson knocked on my door and said, "Well, we'll give you a cheque for fifty grand!"'

For everyone else, taxes went from 31.1 per cent of their income in 1979 to 37.7 per cent by the end of 1996, courtesy of the 'party of low taxes'. The real income of the poorest tenth collapsed by nearly a fifth after housing costs.[10] The slice of the nation's wealth they owned nearly halved.[11] A family with three children in the bottom 10 per cent of the population was £625 a year poorer in 1996 than when Thatcher arrived in No. 10. There were five million people in poverty in 1979; by 1992, the number was closer to fourteen million. And while the top 1 per cent saw income growth of just under 4 per cent a year under the Conservatives, if you were on a median income it went up by an average of only 1.6 per cent.[12]

Geoffrey Howe was a little uncomfortable when I read him statistics showing that the living standards of the poor had actually declined. 'I haven't often considered it in that form because ... No, I don't, I don't sort of leap around at that, it's ... at the end of the period they've got better off, I think?'

According to Richard Murphy, a chartered accountant and leading tax specialist, 'Thatcher shifted the burden of taxation from those who were best off in society to those who were least well off in society. Part of the increasing gap between rich and poor in the Thatcherite years was the result of her fiscal policy. I've got no doubt at all that that was deliberate.' Why deliberate? 'Because her philosophy was, those who were at the top of the pile generated the wealth that she wanted to be created; she viewed the rest as the also-rans, and it didn't matter.' The tax system had been reconfigured to reflect people's supposed worth.

How could a government-backed wealth grab by the rich be justified? Thatcherites talked about trickle-down, as if the growing wealth sloshing around at the top would eventually drip down to the bottom. But this clearly was not happening. So, instead, Thatcherism attacked the victims of its failed economic policies. If they were suffering, then it must be their own fault.

At the centre of Thatcher's philosophy was the idea that poverty did not really exist. If people were poor, it was because of their own personal failings. 'Nowadays there really is no primary poverty left in this country,' she once said. 'In Western countries we are left with the problems which aren't poverty. All right, there may be poverty because they don't know how to budget, don't know how to spend their earnings, but now you are left with the really hard fundamental character-personality defect.'[13]

At the 1981 Conservative Party Conference, Norman Tebbit famously said that his father 'got on his bike and looked for work, and he went on looking until he found it'. Now that industrial Britain was in meltdown, this was what the swelling ranks of the unemployed were supposed to do. 'Get on your bike' became a national cliché, summing up Thatcherism in a nutshell: that the unemployed (among others) must take personal responsibility for the problems that the government had foisted upon them. In line with this thinking, unemployment benefits were cut and no longer rose with people's earnings. That government policies had landed people in this situation did not even get a hearing. The irony, of course, was that when workers fought for their jobs—as the miners had—they were demonized even more.

The Conservatives remain prone to launching regular broadsides against so-called welfare dependency. But it was under Thatcher that public spending on benefits soared to historically unprecedented levels —because of the permanent loss of secure jobs in the old industrial heartlands. Thatcher has robustly defended herself against accusations that her policies were responsible. When it came to people on welfare, she proclaimed, their 'poverty is not material but behavioural'. She even insisted that 'welfare dependence is the classic manifestation of a still-too-socialist society.'[14] Perhaps, then, Thatcher brought the country closer to socialism than has previously been recognized.

The explosion of crime was another striking example of how Thatcherite ideology worked in practice. The British Crime Survey, launched in 1981 to gauge the level of violent crime, reported just over two million incidents at its inception. By the end of Conservative rule, the rate had doubled. The areas hardest hit were poorer communities where jobs had vanished. The link between crime and the social damage wrought by mass unemployment and poverty was indisputable—except for people like Thatcher. 'It is often said and I have had it said to me in the House that unemployment is the cause of crime. I have said: "No it is not, it most certainly is not."'[15]

Thatcher was determined to deal with the symptoms of her scorched-earth economic policies, not the causes. The Criminal Justice Bill in 1986, which provided for longer sentences and limited defence challenges to jurors, appealed to a popular fantasy that the solution to crime was simply to lock up more criminals. In the same year, the Public Order Act granted the police sweeping new powers. Thatcherism's attitude was that crime was an individual choice, not one of the many social ills that thrive in shattered communities.

The attitude to drug users was much the same. The number of registered drug addicts soared under Tory rule: from less than 3,000 in 1980 to 43,000 by 1996. In contrast to the predominantly middle-class drug misusers of the 1960s, the addict of the 1980s was young, often out of work, single, with few or no qualifications and living in a deprived area. Drugs specialist Dr Julian Buchanan found de-industrialization to be a root cause as opportunities for unskilled young people disappeared: 'For the first time, drug-taking became associated with working-class youth living in disaffected and isolated communities.'[16]

Martin Barnes, chief executive of DrugScope, has no doubt that the collapse of the old industries is in large part to blame. 'I'm old enough to remember the recessions of the 1980s and 1990s, and they ripped the guts out of a lot of communities, and families and individuals,' he says.

> With communities and families and individuals impacted by unemployment, it wasn't just that they lost their jobs, it wasn't just the communities being impacted by the businesses moving out. It was also that their incomes were simply inadequate. If you can buy some heroin or pinch some stuff to buy it—the first time you take it, the experience is apparently almost indescribable, you couldn't imagine how good it feels. Is it any wonder then that's what some people used to feel better?

But Thatcher's response was to declare: 'We are at war against drugs.' By 1995, nearly a hundred thousand people were being charged with drug-related offences, around four times more than just a decade previously.

Other vulnerable working-class groups faced attack. Single parents, who largely lived in poverty, were characterized as feckless, benefit-addicted and work-shy. By 1991, there were twice as many as there had been just twenty years ago. The increase had been greater in poorer areas, particularly those hardest hit by unemployment. But there was no sympathy for often desperately poor women struggling to raise a child alone.

When Peter Lilley, then Cabinet minister in charge of Social Security, attacked single mothers in a speech at the 1992 Conservative Party Conference, he was merely articulating years of prejudice against them. To the tune of a song by Gilbert and Sullivan, he sang: 'I've got a little list, I've got a little list of young ladies who get pregnant just to jump the housing list.' It had got to the point where government ministers were singing songs on public platforms to taunt poor people who were utterly voiceless. This was Thatcherism at its basest.

Did this bile go down well with some working-class people? Undoubtedly it did, and it became a fixture of politics to play groups of working-class people against each other. Thatcherism aimed to separate the working-class communities most ravaged by the excesses of Thatcherism from everybody else. This was old-fashioned divide-and-rule, as practised by conquerors throughout the ages. Those working-class communities that suffered most from Thatcher's ruinous class war were now herded into an 'underclass' whose poverty was supposedly self-inflicted.

All this hammering of working-class culture, communities and identity would have lethal consequences. Football had long been the key leisure interest of working-class people. As scriptwriter Jimmy McGovern has put it:

> The popular image of the working class is inextricably tied up with football, the sole surviving mass working-class pursuit in an era that has seen all other vestiges of working-class pride, from the traditional industries of coal mining, textiles and engineering to the historic links between organized labour and the political party that bore its name, swept away.[17]

Football fans had become demonized as hooligans and thugs because of the actions of a small, violent minority. The manner in which working-class people had become not just demonized, but even dehumanized, had a stomach-churning role in the worst tragedy in the history of British football: the 1989 Hillsborough Disaster.

On a sunny spring day, before kick-off at the FA Cup semi-final between Liverpool and Nottingham Forest at Sheffield's Hillsborough Stadium, huge numbers of Liverpool fans congregated outside the stadium. The central pens were already crammed with enthusiastic fans waiting for the referee to blow his whistle, but, disastrously, the police opened an exit gate to allow more through. Protocol dictated that when the central pens had reached capacity, police would direct fans to the side pens. Inexplicably they failed to do so. A crush ensued. As had become standard practice in football stadiums across the country, Liverpool supporters were caged in like animals by metal fences. As suffocating fans spilled out on the pitch in a desperate bid for survival, the police tried to drive them back because they presumed it was a pitch invasion.

Even as fans administered the kiss of life to those dying on the pitch, the police formed a cordon to prevent Liverpool fans reaching the Nottingham Forest supporters on the other side of the stadium. Fans trying to break through the cordon to carry the injured to ambulances were forcibly turned away because the police were reporting 'crowd trouble'. Although forty-four ambulances had arrived at the stadium, police only allowed one to enter. Of the ninety-six Liverpool fans killed by the events of 15 April 1989, only fourteen even made it to hospital. The youngest victim was a ten-year-old boy.

A subsequent inquiry held the police, under the command of Chief Superintendent David Duckenfield, responsible because of 'a combination of inadequate safety procedures and defective crowd management'. But the police had no intention of accepting responsibility. So, instead, they attacked the victims. Police spread misinformation that the disaster was caused by the drunkenness of Liverpool fans. Duckenfield claimed that the locked gate had been forced open by Liverpool fans, and his officers were encouraged to manufacture evidence to prove their responsibility.

On the Wednesday after the tragedy, the *Sun* newspaper launched a savage attack on the victims on the basis of lies circulated by the police. Fans picked the pockets of the dead and dying, it claimed. Police officers, fire-fighters and ambulance crew were attacked by hooligans. Liverpool supporters urinated on the bodies of the dead. A police officer giving the kiss of life was beaten up. A dead girl had even been 'abused'. Even today the *Sun* remains widely boycotted in Merseyside, despite an apology for these lies fifteen years after the issue was published. In a decade of attacking and denigrating working-class Britain, Hillsborough plumbed new depths.

How did the new, aggressive Tory class warriors win time and time again? As Geoffrey Howe boldly puts it, 'the case against us when we were doing it was never really very frightening.' The reasons have long been shrouded in myth. It is routinely claimed that Thatcher won record working-class support because of council house sales and populist law-and-order policies. It is true that such measures did push some working-class voters into the Tory fold, particularly in the south of the country.

According to Howe, the Tories won them over because they 'have a respect for success and the desire to achieve it themselves. And so more naturally see our approach as being more favourable to that. And they're less concerned with tackling poverty, in a way.' This has always been at the heart of Tory strategy: to drive wedges between better-off and poorer working-class voters, while peddling the idea that there is 'room at the top' for those with the grit and determination.

And yet the reality is that Thatcher came to power in 1979 with a smaller share of the vote than any winning party since World War II, excepting the two general elections of 1974. More people voted for Labour in 1979 (when they lost) than in 1974 (when they had won). It was the defection of Liberal voters to the Conservative camp that had enabled Thatcher's victory. Under the old One Nation leaders such as Anthony Eden, the Tories had regularly won around the 50 per cent mark: but the most Thatcher ever got was less than 44 per cent. When you factor in the number of people who actually voted—with the Labour-inclined poor being less likely to do so—Thatcher never won the support of more than a third of eligible voters.

Indeed, Thatcher sank to third place in some opinion polls during the first phase of her premiership. Then the Argentinean military junta came to her rescue. When they invaded the Falklands in 1982, barely anyone had even heard of the islands: but British victory in the war led to a wave of patriotic fervour. Even so, that was far from the most important reason she triumphantly returned to Downing Street in 1983, in spite of her ruinous policies.

As Labour shifted to the left following Thatcher's victory, the party split, with the right forming the Social Democratic Party and making an Alliance with the Liberals. Reflecting on the catastrophe of 1983, Michael Foot believed that 'the main reason was the breakaway of the so-called Social Democrats. Their treachery brought the country Thatcherism.'[18] Thatcher had lost half a million votes since 1979, but her fragmenting opposition allowed the Tories to come through the middle in constituencies across the country, giving her a landslide.

Labour maintained its lead among unskilled working-class voters even in the ill-fated election of 1983. Among skilled and semi-skilled working-class voters, however, it did not regain its lead over the Tories until 1992—when almost all of those who were Alliance voters returned to their old political home. If Thatcher kept winning, it was primarily because the 60 per cent of skilled and semi-skilled workers who voted against her were hopelessly split.

Yet Labour's repeated drubbing had consequences of its own. The idea that Labour gave a voice to working-class people, that it championed their interests and needs, was severely weakened during the 1980s. On issue after issue, Labour under Kinnock capitulated to Thatcher's free-market policies. Any who resisted were sidelined.

Above all, though, it was the party's acute demoralization in the face of Thatcherite triumphalism that paved the way to this surrender. For example, when I asked Kinnock how he managed to win what he called his 'tussle' with the unions to make them accept that Labour would not reverse Thatcher's union laws, he replied: 'It was made easier by the defeat, the size of the defeat in 1987, and the way in which I was determined to exploit that. And I exploited it mercilessly, because by 1988, I heard myself saying more and more and more, "It's the only offer you're going to get."' Even before the advent of New Labour, Thatcherism had ensured that the working class would be bereft of political champions. 'The real triumph was to have transformed not just one party, but two,' as Howe was later to put it.

In only a decade or so, Thatcherism had completely changed how class was seen. The wealthy were adulated. All were now encouraged to scramble up the social ladder, and be defined by how much they owned. Those who were poor or unemployed had no one to blame but themselves. The traditional pillars of working-class Britain had been smashed to the ground. To be working class was no longer something to be proud of, never mind to celebrate. Old working-class values, like solidarity, were replaced by dog-eat-dog individualism. No longer could working-class people count on politicians to fight their corner. The new Briton created by Thatcherism was a property-owning, middle-class individual who looked after themselves, their family and no one else. Aspiration meant yearning for a bigger car or a bigger house. As miners' leader Chris Kitchen put it: 'Forget the community spirit and all that. If you can't make a profit, then it has to be stopped. That's always what Thatcher's ethos was about.'

Those working-class communities who had been most shattered by Thatcherism became the most disparaged. They were seen as the left-behinds, the remnants of an old world that had been trampled on by the inevitable march of history. There was to be no sympathy for them: on the contrary, they deserved to be caricatured and reviled.

There was a time when working-class people had been patronized, rather than openly despised. Disraeli had called working-class people 'angels in marble'. 'Salt of the earth' was another phrase once associated with them. Today, they are more likely than not to be called chavs. From salt of the earth to scum of the earth. This is the legacy of Thatcherism—the demonization of everything associated with the working class.

3

Politicians vs Chavs

Now the working classes are no longer feared as a political peril they
no longer need respect, and the uppers can revel in their superiority as
if this were the eighteenth century.

—Polly Toynbee[1]

Conservative Prime Minister David Cameron cannot be said to lack
courage. When he trekked up to Glasgow East to support the Tory
candidate in a 2008 by-election, there were a number of suitable obser-
vations he could have made given the facts on the ground. Glasgow has
twice as many people out of work as the national average. More than
half of the city's children live in poverty. The city tops Scottish league
tables for drug addiction, overcrowded housing and pensioner poverty.
Life expectancy in Glasgow's Calton neighbourhood is fifty-four years
—well over thirty years less than men in London's Kensington and
Chelsea district, and lower than in the Gaza Strip.

'I come here to apologize for the destruction of industry under
Thatcher's rule during the 1980s,' Cameron could have said. 'Today's
modern Conservatives recognize the effect this has had on jobs, on
communities and on people's hopes and aspirations. It will never happen
again.' Surely admitting the damage wrought by the policies of previous
Conservative administrations could only have bolstered the electoral
propects of a Tory candidate facing a stiff challenge in hostile territory.

But David Cameron was more interested in reinforcing middle-class prejudice than in boosting the Tory vote in an unwinnable seat. 'We talk about people being at risk of poverty, or social exclusion: it's as if these things—obesity, alcohol abuse, drug addiction—are purely external events, like a plague, or bad weather. Of course, circumstances—where you are born, your neighbourhood, your school and the choices your parents make—have a huge impact. But social problems are often the consequence of the choices people make.'

With the help of Tory briefings, newspapers left their readers in no doubt as to what Cameron was getting at. 'David Cameron tells the fat and the poor: take responsibility,' as *The Times* put it. 'Fat or poor? It's probably your own fault, Cameron declares,' was how the evidently delighted *Daily Mail* reacted. Cameron was tapping into sentiments that Thatcherism had made respectable: the idea that, more often than not, less fortunate people had only themselves to blame.

Glasgow's working class *had* actually suffered from what David Cameron so breezily dismissed as 'external events': the collapse of British industry. The Tory leader was asking people to take responsibility for what happened when these jobs disappeared. The steelworks, which employed 30,000, had been the first to go; then the Templeton carpet factory; and, finally, Arrol's engineering works. Many smaller industries and suppliers dependent on these industrial hubs had disappeared along with them. But Cameron made no mention of these inconvenient truths; instead he resorted to criticizing the victims.

What made David Cameron's speech all the more remarkable is his own ultra-privileged background. There is no evidence that he has ever had any real contact with the people he was haranguing. Unlike the average Glaswegian, he owes everything to his family's wealth, power and connections. 'My father was a stockbroker, my grandfather was a stockbroker, my great-grandfather was a stockbroker,' as he once boasted to a gathering of City types.

As a boy, Cameron attended Heatherdown Preparatory School in Berkshire, which counts Princes Andrew and Edward among its former pupils. At the precocious age of eleven he travelled by Concorde to the US with four classmates to celebrate the birthday of Peter Getty, the grandson of oil billionaire John Paul Getty. A former tutor, Rhidian Llewellyn, recalled seeing Cameron and his friends tucking into caviar, salmon and beef bordelaise. Cameron cheerfully raised a glass of Dom Perignon '69, toasting: 'Good health, Sir!'

It is well known that he spent his teenage years at Eton College, the traditional training ground of Britain's ruling elite. But before Cameron had even started university, he worked as an adolescent parliamentary researcher for his godfather, the Tory MP Tim Rathbone. A few months later, after his father pulled a few strings, Cameron went to Hong Kong to work for a multinational corporation. Following his graduation from Oxford University, where he was a member of the infamous toffs' drinking society the Bullingdon Club, he was para-chuted into a job at Conservative Central Office, which had received a mysterious phone call from Buckingham Palace that can't have ruined his chances. 'I understand that you are to see David Cameron,' a man with a grand voice told a Central Office official. 'I've tried everything I can to dissuade him from wasting his time on politics but I have failed. I am ringing to tell you that you are about to meet a truly remarkable young man.'

When Cameron left Central Office a few years later, his rarefied circle helped yet again to push him up the ladder. Annabel Astor, the mother of his equally privileged fiancée Samantha Sheffield, suggested to her friend Michael Green, chairman of Carlton Television, that he should hire him. 'She's a very formidable lady,' he later recalled. 'When she says to me, "Do something", I do it!'[2] As Cameron himself put it: 'I have the most corny CV possible. It goes: Eton, Oxford, Conservative Research Department, Treasury, Home Office, Carlton TV and then Conservative MP.' For an idea of just how disconnected Cameron is from the way the majority of us live, Dylan Jones's *Cameron on Cameron* has him describing his wife's upbringing as 'highly uncon-ventional'—because 'she went to a day school'.

There is one trait that Cameron shares with working-class people in Glasgow. He, like them, is a prisoner of his background. It was not inevitable that he would become prime minister, but whatever happened, it was pretty certain that he would die as he was born: in the lap of wealth and privilege. For hundreds of thousands of Glaswegians, it is equally likely that they will grow up with the same risks of poverty and unemployment as their parents.

According to one of his old schoolmates, Cameron is an unrepentant social elitist. 'I think there's something very unconservative about believing that because of who you are, you are the right person to run the country. It's the natural establishment which believes in power for power's sake, the return of people who think they have a right to rule.' Or as another contemporary from Eton put it: 'He's a strange product of my generation … He seems to represent a continuation of, or perhaps regression to, *noblesse oblige* Toryism. Do we really want to be ruled by Arthurian knights again?'³

But Cameron has indeed surrounded himself with privileged 'Arthurian knights', a point forcefully put to me by a rather unexpected source. Rachel Johnson is no firebrand leftist. She is the sister of the better-known Conservative mayor of London, the floppy-haired, bumbling Boris. Her father, Stanley, was a Conservative member of the European Parliament, and her brother, Jo, is a City journalist-turned-Tory MP. She is a success story in her own right as editor of the *Lady*, a rather frumpy magazine that seems to be largely read by posh women out in the shires. Indeed, the classifieds for nannies and domestic staff are among its big selling points. 'NANNY REQUIRED for delightful girls in West Byfleet,' reads one typical advert.

And yet, despite being the sister of a senior Eton-educated Tory politician (although she argues that Boris Johnson's background is 'very different' from that of David Cameron), she expressed her disgust to me before the 2010 general election that 'the prospect is Old Etonians bankrolled by stockbrokers … It's back to the days of Macmillan and Eden.' She has a point. All in all, twenty-three out of twenty-nine ministers in Cameron's first Cabinet were millionaires; 59 per cent went to private school, and just three attended a comprehensive.

No wonder that, as one poll revealed, 52 per cent of us believe that 'a Conservative Government would mainly represent the interests of the well-off rather than the ordinary people.' It is a sentiment you will often hear expressed in working-class communities. As East Londoners Leslie, a home carer, and Mora, a pensioner, put it to me: 'The Conservatives, they're all for themselves ... They look after the rich people, but not the poor people.'

At the centre of Cameron's political philosophy is the idea that a person's life chances are determined by behavioural factors rather than economic background. 'What matters most to a child's life chances is not the wealth of their upbringing but the warmth of their parenting,' Cameron claims. Despite a grudging acceptance of 'a link between material poverty and poor life chances', it is clear that he believes the main driving force in an individual's life is personal behaviour. This is, of course, politically convenient. If you think the solution to poverty is parents being nicer to their kids, then why would it matter if you cut people's benefits?

No one has endorsed this Cameronian attitude to class inequalities more than former Tory leader Iain Duncan Smith. After Cameron became prime minister, he appointed Duncan Smith as secretary of state for work and pensions—effectively the guardian of the British welfare state. Through his think-tank, the Centre for Social Justice (CSJ), Duncan Smith has developed the idea that poverty is not about lacking money: it is due to problems like lack of discipline, family break-up, and substance abuse.

As the darling of the Tory grass roots, right-wing Conservative MEP Daniel Hannan, put it: 'It follows that you do not end poverty by giving money to the poor: a theory that British welfarism has amply demonstrated over 60 years.'[4] David Cameron himself welcomed one CSJ report with a highly questionable statement: 'Families matter because almost every social problem that we face comes down to family stability.' Not lack of jobs, or class division: 'family stability' explains all. If you are less well off, then it is your behaviour that has to be changed, according to this Tory vision.

These ideas are the foundation stones of Cameron's semi-apocalyptic vision of 'Broken Britain'. Social problems affecting particular poor working-class communities are first exaggerated and then portrayed as representative. Each time a tragic incident hit the headlines, Cameron seized on it as evidence.

For example, the nation was shocked in 2009 by the torture and attempted murder of two little boys, aged nine and eleven, by two other young boys in the former mining village of Edlington in South Yorkshire. The aggressors had themselves endured years of abuse. But for Cameron, the attacks were proof that the country had collapsed into what he described as a 'social recession'. 'On each occasion, are we just going to say this is an individual case?' Cameron thundered. 'That there aren't links to what is going on in our wider society, in terms of family breakdown, in terms of drug and alcohol abuse, in terms of violent videos, in terms of many of the things that were going wrong in that particular family?'

Or take the case of thirteen-year-old Alfie Patten. In early 2009, it was claimed that his girlfriend had conceived when he was aged just twelve. Newspapers splashed pictures of this baby-faced, four-foot-tall alleged father across their front pages. Iain Duncan Smith could not resist making political capital out of the episode, claiming it underlined the Tories' point about 'Broken Britain'. 'Too many dysfunctional families in Britain today have children growing up where anything goes,' he said, warning that the sense of right and wrong was collapsing in some parts of society. The Tories were strangely silent when, in the end, it turned out that Alfie was not the father after all.

But the Tories are quick to cultivate middle-class fears of rampaging hordes of state-subsidized barbarians just outside the gates. Months before the 2010 general election, then-Shadow Home Secretary Chris Grayling made an astonishing comparison between Moss Side, a working-class district of south Manchester, and the US drama *The Wire*, which focuses on the war between police and drug gangs in Baltimore. Moss Side, too, was experiencing an 'urban war', Grayling claimed. Locals were outraged —and no wonder. In 2007, there were 234 murders in Baltimore, a city of 630,000 people. In Britain as a whole there were 624 violent killings in the same year, while figures for 2010 reveal thirty-one murders in the whole of Greater Manchester. Baltimore had 1 per cent of the UK's population, but its murder rate was around a third of the UK's.

In their effort to create caricatures of depraved working-class communities, the Tories were not above citing blatantly false information. In a propaganda leaflet entitled *Labour's Two Nations* published in early 2010, they released some astounding figures that suggested a teenage pregnancy pandemic was sweeping through Britain's poor communities. The document repeatedly affirmed that women under eighteen were 'three times more likely to be pregnant in the most deprived areas compared to the least deprived areas. In the most deprived areas 54 per cent are likely to fall pregnant before the age of 18, compared to just 19 per cent in the least deprived areas.'

It was a real wake-up call: over half of all teenage girls in some areas were falling pregnant! It turned out the Tories had put the decimal points in the wrong place, making figures wrong by a multiple of ten. The real figure for the ten most deprived areas was actually just 5.4 per cent. The document also failed to mention a decline in under-eighteen conceptions of over 10 per cent in these areas—reversing a trend that had been going up under previous Tory governments.[5] By 2007, 11.4 per cent of conceptions were to women under the age of twenty—about the same level as that conservative golden age of family values, the 1950s.[6] Now, no doubt this howler was an honest mistake. But it says much about the Tories' view of these communities that they were not sufficiently startled by such outlandish figures to double-check them before press-releasing their document.

Indeed, the Tories have shown even more aggressive ways of tapping into middle-class prejudices against teenage pregnancy, which, undeniably, is far more common in working-class communities. Following in the footsteps of Peter Lilley and his stigmatizing 'little list' of teenage mothers, the Tory shadow children's minister, Tim Loughton, hinted at locking them up. 'We need a message that actually it is not a very good idea to become a single mum at 14,' he said. '[It is] against the law to get pregnant at 14. How many kids get prosecuted for having underage sex? Virtually none. What are the consequences of breaking the law and having irresponsible underage sex? There aren't any.' When asked if they should be prosecuted, he dodged the question. 'We need to be tougher,' he insisted.[7]

What the Tories are doing is placing the chav myth at the heart of British politics, so as to entrench the idea that there are entire communities around Britain crawling with feckless, delinquent, violent and sexually debauched no-hopers. Middle England on the one hand and the chavs on the other. This was taken to its logical conclusion by a report published in 2008 by the Tory leadership's favourite think-tank, Policy Exchange. The document reckoned that northern cities such as Liverpool, Sunderland and Bradford were 'beyond revival', had 'lost much of their raison d'être' because of the decline of industry, and their residents should all be moved south. 'Regeneration, in the sense of convergence, will not happen, because it is not possible.'

The report provoked a firestorm and David Cameron had no choice but to repudiate it. Yet this think-tank is at the heart of the modern Conservative Party: it was founded by the current Cabinet ministers Michael Gove and Francis Maude (who described being a co-founder as his proudest political achievement) as well as Nicholas Boles, now an MP and a key figure of Cameron's 'Notting Hill set'.

The echoes of this breathtaking plan could be perceived in proposals unveiled by Iain Duncan Smith in the early days of the Conservative-led coalition following the 2010 general election. While the government was cutting jobs and help for those without work, Duncan Smith suggested that council tenants could be taken out of unemployment black spots and relocated, hundreds of miles away if necessary. Millions were 'trapped in estates where there is no work,' he lamented, without suggesting that the government might consider bringing jobs to these areas. The message was clear: these were communities without hope or a future, and nothing could be done to save them. As the pro-Conservative *Telegraph* newspaper put it, the parallels with Norman Tebbit's 1981 call for the unemployed to 'get on your bike' were uncanny.[8]

Even before they came to power nationally, the Tories were already undertaking a spot of what you might call 'social cleansing'. In 2009, Conservative-run Hammersmith and Fulham Council came under fire for apparently planning to remove poor residents from council houses. The council proposed to demolish 3,500 council properties and to build upmarket homes to attract middle-class residents in their place. According to council leader Stephen Greenhalgh, an advisor to David Cameron, council housing was 'warehousing poverty' and entrenching welfare dependency. Documents released under the Freedom of Information Act described a council estate as a 'barracks for the poor' and included plans to increase rents from £85 to £360 a week.[9] Hammersmith and Fulham is often mentioned as Cameron's favourite council. It certainly showcases some of the Tories' least constructive attitudes to working-class people. Many of the Tories' ideas about social inequality—such as blaming people for their circumstances—have a firmly Thatcherite pedigree. But they can also be traced back to a right-wing pseudo-political scientist, the American Charles Murray. Murray is perhaps most famous for his controversial (to say the least) 1994 book, *The Bell Curve*, which suggested that inherent racial differences had an impact on IQ levels. Like today's Tories, Murray claimed that family breakdown had triggered the rise of an 'underclass' in British society. He argued 'that the family in the dominant economic class—call it the upper middle class—is in better shape than most people think, and is likely to get better. Meanwhile, deterioration is likely to continue in the lower classes.'

Rising illegitimacy in 'the lower classes' had produced what Murray called the 'New Rabble', marked by growing crime, 'dropout from work', child neglect and so on. One of the solutions, Murray argued, was for childbearing to entail 'economic penalties for a single woman. It is all horribly sexist, I know. It also happens to be true.'[10]

Rather than financial sanctions for childbearing single women, the Tories promoted a £150 tax break for married couples in the 2010 general election campaign. Their first Budget scrapped Labour's health-in-pregnancy grant, made it compulsory for single parents to seek work when their child reached the age of five (down from ten), froze child benefit, and introduced tough welfare cuts and penalties that would disproportionately affect single mothers. Nonetheless, Murray and the Cameron Conservatives share a basic underlying philosophy. Social problems in working-class communities are magnified and then blamed on the personal characteristics and lifestyles of the inhabitants. The logical next step is to withdraw state financial support from such communities and, instead, focus on changing individual behaviour.

To get a better idea of the Tory approach to social division in British society, I had a chat with senior MP David Davis. Davis is often feted as a rare working-class Tory, but he prefers to play down his roots. 'People seem to think my background was underprivileged,' he says. 'It wasn't. It was just normal.' Indeed, after graduating from Warwick University, Davis spent seventeen years working for Tate & Lyle, ending up as a senior director. When I asked Davis if the privileged backgrounds of Tory frontbench ministers made it difficult for them to connect with the electorate as a whole, he was refreshingly honest. 'Truthfully, it's partly true of me too! You know, it's a long time since I lived on a council estate, and the only thing that you have that pulls you back to earth, really, is the constituency surgery, where you're dealing with people on a Friday night and Saturday morning with their problems.'

Davis is certainly no more sympathetic towards the plight of working-class people than other Tories. 'There have been a couple of TV programmes recently. One in which they went down to what in the old days would have been called a dole queue ... and said: "Would you like a job?" Chap said yes, and was told: "It's picking squash on a farm." They won't do that, you know. And something similar happened a week or two ago showing the work rate of a British worker against some Polish workers—and the Polish workers were working twice as fast. This is a surmise, I don't know this to be true, but my instant reaction to that sort of thing would be: we are probably facing a work ethic problem, which is worse than welfare dependency.'

Davis is quite keen to contrast what he depicts as the unmotivated British worker with 'the large number of immigrants who've probably got a stronger work ethic ... And so from the point of view of the employer, they're relatively cheap and work quite hard, so if you want to be hard-nosed about it, why employ a not so hard-working Brit who's demanding a higher salary?'

What struck me was his willingness to make an intellectual argument in defence of inequality. 'I wouldn't try and do anything about correcting the inequalities,' he explained, 'because the *inequalities* are widened by people getting richer, not by the poor getting poor—but by the rich getting richer. And frankly, so long as they generate wealth for the economy, so long as they generate tax income and so on, then I'm comfortable with it.'

I pointed out the recent groundbreaking research by academics Richard Wilkinson and Kate Pickett in their book, *The Spirit Level*. They used irrefutable statistics to show that the more unequal a society is, the more social problems it has—like crime and poor health, for example. In other words, more equal societies were happier societies. David Davis gave the book short shrift. 'It's bullshit,' he said. 'It's *bullshit* ... I think it's one of these fashionable, stupid ideas. It's easy to sell a book, but I don't think it stands up.'

In political historian Ross McKibbin's opinion, the Tories are 'there to defend inequality, always have been. It's like all conservative parties anywhere—they're designed to defend inequality and social privilege.' Davis's comments vindicate Ross's analysis; if anything, perhaps, it doesn't go far enough. Davis is, in effect, celebrating inequality as a *good thing.* The Tory demonization of working-class communities must be seen in this light. It is difficult to justify a grossly uneven distribution of wealth on grounds of fairness. But what if the people at the top are entitled to be there because of their entrepreneurial flair, while those at the bottom are deeply flawed and so deserve what they get? Davis's attitude towards British working-class people is shaped by the idea that people's lot in life is determined by their personal characteristics. The crux of his argument is that they just don't work as hard as workers from other countries—which, he says, partly explains issues like unemployment.

Criticizing working-class people is politically useful for a Conservative-led government determined to drive through cuts that will disproportionately hurt the same group. Some of the first programmes to face the axe after the 2010 general election included free school meals and help for the young unemployed. The first Budget unleashed the biggest cuts to public services in a century and—just like the Tory government of the early 1980s—upped the rate of VAT, a tax that hits those on low incomes the hardest. Despite ministers' claims that they were serving in a 'progressive government', economists estimated the poorest would be hit six times harder than the richest.[11] When Tory minister Bob Neill was asked why northern cities were losing millions of pounds compared to southern cities, his shameless response was: 'Those in greatest need ultimately bear the burden of paying off the debt.'[12]

So much for the Tories: after all, most of their leading lights were born into privilege and are ideologically committed to defending grossly uneven distributions of wealth and power. What about Labour's record? Even a politician as New Labour through-and-through as former Cabinet minister Hazel Blears is clear that Labour's purpose was 'to ensure that, first of all, working-class people have a voice in Parliament. That's why it was set up, because before then, you didn't.' Labour governments introduced all of the major reforms of the post-war period that have improved the lot of the working class, from the NHS to workers' rights.

The tragedy is that New Labour bears much of the responsibility for the negative light in which the working class is now seen.

History will remember two TV moments from the 2010 general election. The first was the novelty of televised debates between the party leaders, which led to a surge in Liberal Democrat support that had dissipated by the time the electorate cast their ballots. But just as memorable, and far more revealing, was when Labour Prime Minister Gordon Brown bumped into Gillian Duffy, a sixty-five-year-old pensioner, in the streets of Rochdale.

If you were looking for a representative Labour voter, Mrs Duffy would surely fit the bill. Before retirement she had spent thirty years working with disabled kids for Rochdale Council. Her late father used to sing Labour's anthem, 'The Red Flag', when he was a teenager. Mrs Duffy shared his commitment and had voted Labour all her life.

When Mrs Duffy spotted Gordon Brown on a walkabout around her home town, she demanded answers to the sorts of concerns shared by millions of working-class people. She told Brown that the three main things 'I had drummed in when I was a child was education, health service and looking after people who were vulnerable'. She was worried that her two grandchildren would struggle to afford to go to university when they were older. Finally, she expressed fairly mild concerns about the levels of immigration. The conversation ended amicably as Brown told Mrs Duffy: 'You're a very good woman, you've served your community all your life.'

And that might have been all there was to it. But Brown had forgotten to remove his TV microphone. As soon as he stepped into the waiting car, he let his annoyance rip. 'That was a disaster. Should never have put me with that woman... whose idea was that?' When an aide asked what she had said, Brown uttered words that, for many, represented the last nail in his political coffin. 'Ugh, everything— she's just a sort of bigoted woman, said she used to be Labour. It's just ridiculous.'

The scandal (inevitably christened 'Bigotgate') summed up the contempt many felt New Labour had towards working-class people. 'Working-class people are sort of seen as a problem. They drink too much, they smoke too much, they don't look after their kids properly, they're feckless, they're work-shy. Racist. Essentially, that's how they're seen,' says *Guardian* economics editor Larry Elliott, who contends that one of the big reasons Labour lost the 2010 election was because it lost touch with its working-class base. 'They didn't really like these people very much,' he argues. 'They thought they didn't have the right sort of raspberry-wine vinegar to put on their radicchio and so on. There was a growing contempt for the working class, not just among the parties of the right, but also among the parties of the left. And I think that's a really big part of what's changed in Britain in the last thirty years.'

Bigotgate was an accidental bubbling to the surface of New Labour's private contempt for Labour's working-class electoral base. Yet it appeared in the form of intentional policy announcements, too. There are four million overwhelmingly working-class social housing tenants in Britain. While 30 per cent of voters overall opted for Labour and 37 per cent voted Tory in the 2010 general election, it was 47 and 24 per cent respectively among people living in social housing. New Labour did not reciprocate their loyalty. In early 2008, the then housing minister Caroline Flint sneered at the levels of unemployment among council-house tenants. Referring to the culture of 'no one works around here', Flint suggested that those who did not get a job could lose their home. New tenants would sign 'commitment contracts' before moving into a property, and it was hinted that the measure could eventually also apply to those already living in council homes.

The housing charity Shelter expressed dismay, claiming that Flint would send Britain back to the Victorian era. 'The Government wants to return Britain's unemployed to the workhouse by throwing them on the streets,' said Adam Sampson, Shelter's chief executive. 'What is being proposed would destroy families and communities and add to the thousands who are already homeless.'[13]

'You've got to ask: what would happen to those people told that they had to leave their current properties?' adds Shelter's Mark Thomas. 'Where would they actually end up? And what would be the cost to the taxpayer associated with that? And the government really didn't seem to have answers to that sort of question.'

Caroline Flint's proposals could never have been implemented, because they were illegal under existing laws: councils were not permitted to make people homeless. But she had fuelled the now widespread political sentiments that council tenants were freeloaders.

Flint expressed surprise at how social mixing in council housing had declined and levels of unemployment had shot up on estates over the last thirty years. Unless she was grossly incompetent at her job, she would have known that this was the legacy of right-to-buy. The least disadvantaged tenants had bought their homes, while the Tories—followed by New Labour—had refused to build any more. That meant that the remaining, ever-diminishing stock was prioritized for those most in need.

According to the late Alan Walter, a lifelong council tenant and former chairman of Defend Council Housing, this demonization also has political purposes. 'They promote this idea that anyone who wants to get on aspires to be a homeowner, and only those who can't do any better will live in council housing.' Walter saw a two-fold purpose: 'One, to make people who live on council estates feel inadequate; and two, to force those who can afford or might afford it to think they have to get out.' It was all part of New Labour's strategy of encouraging those working-class people who had resisted the Thatcherite property-owning dream to surrender.

The Flint episode illustrates a real change in the attitudes of what could be called 'Old Labour' and 'New Labour' towards working-class people. Yes, 'Old Labour' is a problematic term. As the avowedly New Labour former Cabinet minister James Purnell told me: 'Old Labour was one of those terms which was clearly a construct, and insofar as it meant anything really, it was the sort of things that "you the voters" happen not to like about us now, and because of the things that we've done in your memory.'

But what was known as the 'Old Labour Right', the old social democratic leadership of the party, was remarkably different from New Labour as represented by figures like Purnell. (Indeed, one right-wing Conservative MP privately expressed to me the Tories' deep regrets at Purnell's decision to stand down as an MP at the 2010 general election. There was a bit of an overlap in political views between them and Purnell, I suggested. 'Oh, *massive* overlap. *Massive*. I would have loved for him to have become Labour leader.')

Former prime minister James Callaghan was a classic example of Old Labour: a working-class politician whose power base was the trade unions. Old Labour still celebrated, or at least paid tribute to, working-class identity. Although Callaghan was on what was then the right of the party, he still felt obliged to couch policies in class terms. As chancellor in the late 1960s, for example, he confronted the devaluation camp head-on by accusing: 'Those who advocate devaluation are calling for a reduction in the wage levels and the real wage standards of every member of the working class.'

That is not to deny Old Labour's flaws. It was top-down and bureaucratic, and its celebration of working-class identity did not adapt to the entry of women and ethnic minorities into the workforce. 'Basically, what the London left was doing [in the 1970s and 1980s] was rebelling against that Old Labour culture because it was quite sexist and racist,' recalls former London Labour mayor Ken Livingstone. 'It had huge weaknesses, and in a sense so much of what we were doing in the 1970s and 1980s was forcing the labour movement in London to recognize that it had to organize women and ethnic minorities.' Yet Old Labour remained committed to the idea of raising the conditions of the working class as a *class*, even if this sometimes amounted to mere lip service.

In contrast, New Labour's philosophy is not rooted in improving the lot of the working class; it is about *escaping* the working class. New Labour was very open about this project. For example, Gordon Brown fought the 2010 general election on creating 'a bigger middle class than ever before'.

According to Matthew Taylor, Blair's former head of strategy, New Labour made a distinction between the 'aspirational working class … who felt that Labour was anti-aspiration' and a 'non-aspirational working class'. The 'non-aspirational working class' had no place in New Labour. They were ignored on the grounds that they had nowhere else to go and, in any case, were less likely to vote. 'So,' says Taylor,

> I think Labour's strategy was: 'How do we appeal to the aspirational working class?' Does that mean that they took for granted whatever it is we mean by the 'non-aspirational working class'? Well, maybe partly took for granted, maybe partly those people are in constituencies that Labour are going to win anyway. So, whether you might consider that to be callous, but in a first-past-the-post [electoral] system you don't focus your energies on people who are in constituencies where they don't make a huge difference. And partly those people are also less likely, or least likely, to turn out.

But what did New Labour mean by aspiration? 'If you look at the discourse around aspiration, it's a very restricted notion of what it is,' says influential Labour backbencher and former advisor to Tony Blair, Jon Cruddas. 'If you … compare and contrast the Middle England of Blair and Brown, located somewhere in the South East, everyone's relatively prosperous, growth is guaranteed—it's a very atomized notion of aspiration. You aspire to own more material things.'

To Cruddas, aspiration has a very different meaning. He refers to *Everytown*, a book written by philosopher Julian Baggini in which he searches for the real 'Middle England': that is, a community containing all the characteristics of the country as a whole. He ends up in the predominantly working-class, Northern English town of Rotherham. 'It was more fraternal, it was more solidaristic, it was more neighbourly,' says Cruddas. 'And in that lies, I think, a tale about how we can completely misconstrue this notion of aspiration ...' In other words, real aspiration means much more than simple self-enrichment. 'As Alan Milburn [New Labour minister and one of Blair's key allies] used to say, when he was asked what was the essence of the Labour project, he said: "It is to help people to earn and own." Well, was it? Was it? It never was for me.'

In New Labour's eyes, being aspirational working class meant embracing individualism and selfishness. It meant fighting to be a part of Brown's 'bigger middle class than ever'. As Stephen Pound, a loyalist Labour MP, argues: 'I think part of the problem is that people in the working classes have been sold the line that they shouldn't be there, and you can somehow drag yourself up ... The old socialist motto is "rise with your class, not above it". The reality of this country is that to rise, you rise above your class.'

What does 'non-aspirational working class' mean, then? 'I think *everyone's* aspirational,' says Ken Livingstone. 'I think that what the Blairites have patronizingly called non-aspirational, I suppose, is those people who still had a sense of community and still recognized that the whole community does better together or they all do badly together.' The non-aspirational working class are, as their label suggests, frowned upon: because they have failed to jump on the Thatcherite, property-owning, endlessly acquisitive bandwagon. According to the New Labour lexicon, only self-enrichment counts as aspiration. Unless you're determined to climb up the class ladder, you are devoid of aspiration.

There are few more devout Blairites than former New Labour Cabinet minister Hazel Blears. But she is affronted by the notion of a 'non-aspirational working class'. 'It's not an analysis that I would ever subscribe to,' she says. 'I have yet to meet a young person who isn't aspirational, irrespective of their background, and I think in some ways that writes people off. And I object to that, I object to that really quite significantly. It's a bit like the Tory division between the deserving poor and the undeserving poor—and that takes us back to Victorian times ... I don't think the Labour Party has time for people who can work but won't. But, neither do you write off their children and their whole families on that basis.'

It is not just adults who are lumped into the non-aspirational category. New Labour politicians frequently diagnose a 'poverty of aspiration' in working-class kids to explain things like poor school results or why poverty is transmitted from generation to generation. For example, former New Labour education secretary Alan Johnson once railed against 'a corrosive poverty of aspiration which is becoming particularly prevalent amongst today's generation of working-class boys'. It is not the lack of jobs and apprenticeships following the collapse of industry that is to blame, but rather the attitudes of working-class children.

In this spirit, a government report published in December 2008 highlighted the alleged 'under-ambition' of working-class people living in the old industrial heartlands. The question of what these kids are supposed to aspire to in areas lacking well-paid jobs is never addressed. But this approach was fully in the Thatcherite mould: that responsibility for the social problems facing working-class people should be placed squarely on their shoulders.

The notion of 'aspirational' versus 'non-aspirational' was just one way that New Labour attempted to exploit fissures in the working class that had emerged under Thatcherism. Another was to win the support of what New Labour politicians called 'hard-working families' (a term Blears also resisted, because 'there was always the presumption that if you didn't somehow fit in that, then the devil take you, and you were left to your own devices') as opposed to millions of supposedly idle people dishonestly claiming benefits. It is true that bashing 'welfare scroungers' may be more likely to attract the support of a low-paid worker than a millionaire. After all, if you work hard for a pittance, why wouldn't you resent the idea of people living a life of luxury at your expense?

The reality is that attacks on welfare have been directed at the working-class communities most devastated by the collapse of industry.

The old industrial heartlands contain the highest levels of people without work and dependent on benefits. The root cause is a lack of secure jobs to replace the ones that disappeared. As Iain Duncan Smith has admitted, rather than creating new jobs, successive governments encouraged unemployed people to claim disability benefits, in order to massage the employment figures.

Yet New Labour's approach was to stigmatize and demonize these vulnerable working-class people. The then-government's welfare advisor David Freud—who, appropriately enough, later defected to the Tories—claimed in 2008 that two million people should be pushed off benefits and into work. And yet the government claimed at the time that there were only half a million job vacancies, and this was before the full force of the recession had hit. 'I mean, that was a figure that David Freud just kind of plucked out of the air,' admits his former boss, James Purnell.

Until an abortive attempt to overthrow Gordon Brown in 2009, James Purnell had overall charge of New Labour's so-called welfare reform programme. He had promised to create 'a system where virtually everyone has to do something in return for their benefits'. It was right to 'penalize' people who, he claimed, were not trying to get work. 'If there is work there for people, we believe they should do it. We can't afford to waste taxpayers' money on people who are playing the system.'[14] That £16 billion worth of benefits were in fact going unclaimed each year—around two and half times the amount of money the government was trying to save—went unmentioned. So did the fact that the majority of people in poverty were in work. Purnell was presenting work as an automatic gateway out of poverty but, in low-pay Britain, that's hardly the case.

One of Purnell's proposals was that people could be made to work in exchange for benefits. Given that Jobseeker's Allowance at the time was worth only £60.50, if you were made to work a forty-hour week, for example, you would end up being paid just £1.50 an hour. Those unlucky enough to find themselves in the most devastated communities were not only accused of 'playing the system'. They faced being made to work for a fraction of the minimum wage.

When speaking to me, Purnell markedly softened his rhetoric. 'All of the conditionality in the system was there to make sure that people helped themselves,' he argued. It was consistent with long-established Labour traditions, he reassured me. But what about the fact that there were more people on benefits in certain communities because all the old industrial jobs had vanished, leaving only scarce, low-paid, insecure service sector jobs? 'I wouldn't buy the argument that it's better to be on IB [Incapacity Benefit] than to be in a supermarket job or in a call centre job,' he responded, referring to evidence that prolonged jobless-ness is unhealthy both for the individual and their family. 'I totally recognize that going from a job which was a highly skilled industrial job into something which people not necessarily would have wanted is a step down, but it's certainly less of a step down than ending up on Incapacity Benefit.'

It is safe to say that Mark Serwotka is not a fan of Purnell. Serwotka is the leader of the 300,000-strong civil service union, the Public and Commercial Services (PCS) union. Agitated to even hear his name, he described Purnell as 'the worst social security secretary in the history of this country' and 'a shameful man who professes to be a Labour politi-cian'. He was particularly angered by Purnell's attitude to places like Merthyr, where Serwotka grew up. Recently, Hoover closed its factory there after sixty-one years of providing work for the community. 'There's no mines, there's no pits, there's real deprivation—and Purnell essentially says: "You're not trying hard enough to get work, and therefore we need sanctions to force people into work." '

Serwotka repeatedly clashed with Purnell when he was in office. The minister demanded to know how he was stigmatizing people, so Serwotka quoted back at him a *New Statesman* article in which Purnell speaks of people on benefits 'having miserable lives where their universe consists of a trip from the bedroom to the living room'.[15] Serwotka says that Purnell claimed he was 'only quoting someone else', although there is no evidence of this in the article. 'If we think about that for a moment,' says Serwotka, 'it is absolutely blaming the victims of all this, when they're the *victims*, not the *problems*.'

As Serwotka says, the 'absurdity' of the whole policy is that it was 'the same for the whole country, as if the labour market in the South East was the same as the labour market in the South Wales Valley, and clearly it's not. But if you introduce the same policy, what you do is stigmatize the areas where there's no work.' The 'welfare reform' programme fuelled still further the demonization of the poorest working-class communities. It magnified the problems it purported to address and failed to explain the real reasons behind them. It also cleared the ground for the Tories—who went out of their way to praise James Purnell and his welfare policies—to go even further after they formed a government in May 2010.

Looking at the whole welfare debate, Jon Cruddas thinks that 'even if it's unacknowledged, it still is premised on the notion of "the mob" that we have to control.' Cruddas saw the promotion of what he calls 'the mob at the gates' being 'reproduced culturally through forms of representation on TV—you know, the whole language around "chav" '. This is an absolutely fundamental point. New Labour, through programmes like its welfare reform, has propagated the chav caricature by spreading the idea that people are poor because they lack moral fibre. Surveys show that attitudes towards poverty are currently harder than they were under Thatcher. If people observe that *even* Labour holds the less fortunate to be personally responsible for their fate, why should they think any different? No wonder the image of communities teeming with feckless chavs has become so ingrained in recent years.

This spectre of the 'the mob at the gates' conjured up by Cruddas has heavily featured in the government's crackdown on anti-social behaviour. Again, huge numbers of working-class people support action to combat anti-social behaviour. It is, after all, more likely to affect someone living on a council estate than a professional out in the suburbs, and has a real impact on the quality of people's lives. But the government's response has been to stigmatize working-class youth rather than address the root causes.

Take Anti-Social Behaviour Orders (ASBOs), introduced under New Labour but now facing abolition under the Conservative-led government. They could be imposed for minor incidents and restrict the individual's behaviour in various ways: like banning them from a street, or forbidding them from swearing. If the ASBO was violated, the culprit could be sent to prison for up to five years. Originally, New Labour promised that under-eighteens would only have ASBOs served under exceptional circumstances but, as it turned out, year on year around half were imposed on the young. Overwhelmingly, those on the receiving end were both poor and working class—and, according to a survey in 2005, nearly four out of every ten ASBOs went to young people with mental health problems such as Asperger's Syndrome. In one case, a child with Tourette's was given an ASBO for his compulsive swearing.

Whether or not you agree with ASBOs, it is difficult to deny that they have increased the bad reputation of young working-class kids and popularized the chav caricature. After all, members of the Bullingdon Club—whose great tradition is to smash up pubs and restaurants—were never likely to be awarded an ASBO. Even New Labour's own youth justice 'tsar', Professor Rod Morgan, criticized the measures for 'demonizing' a whole section of British youth and criminalizing them for offences that once would have been regarded as 'high jinks'. It is difficult to disagree with author Anthony Horowitz when he says that ASBOs 'add up to create a cumulative vision of a Britain full of yobs, with crack houses on every inner-city estate; drunken youths running amok in provincial towns, and so on'.[16]

Taken together, New Labour policies have helped to build a series of overlapping chav caricatures: the feckless, the non-aspirational, the scrounger, the dysfunctional, and the disorderly. To hear this sort of rhetoric from Labour, rather than the Tories, has confirmed the stereotypes and prejudices many middle-class people have about working-class communities and individuals. But it can be far subtler than out-right attacks. Many of New Labour's underlying philosophies were steeped in middle-class triumphalism. They were based on the assumption that the tattered remnants of the working class are on the wrong side of history—and must be made to join 'Middle England' like the rest of us.

'The new Britain is a meritocracy,' declared Tony Blair upon assuming office in 1997. If New Labour had an official religion, it would surely be meritocracy. But there is a dark irony in how celebrated this concept became. 'Meritocracy' was not originally intended to describe a desirable society—far from it. It was meant to raise the alarm at what Britain could become.

Michael Young, who penned Labour's 1945 Manifesto, coined the phrase in his 1958 book, *The Rise of the Meritocracy*. As he later explained, this was 'a satire meant to be a warning (which needless to say has not been heeded) against what might happen to Britain between 1958 and the imagined final revolt against the meritocracy in 2003.' He warned that its consequences would mean 'that the poor and the disadvantaged would be done down, and in fact they have been ... It is hard indeed in a society that makes so much of merit to be judged as having none.'[17]

In a meritocracy, those who possess the most 'talent' will rise naturally to the top. Social hierarchy will therefore be arranged according to 'merit'. Society would remain unequal, but those inequalities would reflect differences of ability. Matthew Taylor understands the dangers, but believes this is the best cause on offer. 'I think that meritocracy is not a bad rallying call because we're so far away from it, you know what I mean? To have a genuine meritocracy we'd have to abolish inherited wealth, we'd have to abolish private schools ... So when people say to me: "Well, meritocracy, isn't that kind of a reactionary concept and shouldn't we argue for more than that?", I can say: "Well, yeah, fine, but we're so far away from even having that."'

Of course, New Labour never had any intention of abolishing inherited wealth or private education. It argued for 'meritocracy' within a society rigged in favour of the middle class. Meritocracy ends up becoming a rubber stamp for existing inequalities, re-branding them as deserved. When I interviewed Simon Heffer, the right-wing *Telegraph* columnist, he argued: 'I think we are still largely a meritocracy, despite the destruction of the grammar schools, and I think class is a state of mind in that sense.' Meritocracy can end up being used to argue that those at the top are there because they deserve to be, while those at the bottom are simply not talented enough and likewise deserve their place. It is used in education to belittle vocational subjects in favour of the academic. All this before even examining the criteria for what counts as 'merit': for example, does a multi-millionaire advertising consultant deserve to be above a hospital cleaner in the pecking order of things?

The natural companion of meritocracy is 'social mobility', which New Labour put at the heart of its 2010 general election campaign. A few years before, Alan Milburn, one of Tony Blair's closest allies, had spoken of Labour's crusade to ensure 'that more people get the opportunity to join the middle class'. Rather than improve the conditions of the working class as a whole, social mobility is offered as a means of creaming off a minority of working-class individuals and parachuting them into the middle class. It underlines the notion that being working class is something to get away from.

It does not mean abolishing or even eroding classes, but just making it easier for individuals to move between them. It would not have any impact on the conditions of the majority of working-class people. Social mobility can mean offering an escape route from poverty, rather than attempting to abolish poverty. Sociologist John Goldthorpe disputes the consensus that there has been a decline in social mobility but, in any case, regards it as a red herring: 'The reason why there's been all this emphasis on social mobility is that all the political parties prefer to talk about social mobility and equality of opportunity rather than equality of conditions.'

Surprisingly, Blairite Hazel Blears is equally critical. 'I've never really understood the term "social mobility" because that implies you want to get out of somewhere and go somewhere else because you're mobile! And I think that there is a great deal to be said for making who you are something to be proud of. And if you're working class, not to wear that as a kind of chip on your shoulder, or even a burden that you carry around with you, but actually something that is of value, for its own sake, that says something about who you are, what your values are, where you come from.'

If the officially sanctioned route to improving your lot in life is to become middle class, what about the people left behind? Clearly not everyone can become a middle-class professional or a businessperson: the majority of people still have to do the working-class jobs in offices and shops that society needs to keep ticking. By putting the emphasis on escaping these jobs rather than improving their conditions, we end up disqualifying those who remain in them. We frown upon the supermarket checkout staff, the cleaners, the factory workers—slackers who failed to climb the ladder offered by social mobility.

Another way that New Labour skirted the issue of inequality was by following in Thatcher's footsteps and pretending that class no longer existed. At the end of the 1990s, the government appointed a committee to revisit the official social classifications used for national statistics— then known as 'Social Class based on Occupation'. John Goldthorpe was delighted that it would be based on his own research, but was intrigued to discover that it had been renamed the 'National Statistics Socio-Economic Classification'. When he asked a member of the committee, he was told that New Labour had vetoed any reference to class. It illustrated New Labour's dogged determination to scrub class from the country's vocabulary.

Hazel Blears traces the disavowal of class to Labour's experience in the 1980s and early 1990s when, she says, the party 'had been identified with quite an adversarial class politics'. In part, she believes this was because Labour's reputation had been tarred by the memory of once-mighty trade unions abusing their power. That, she claims, gave Thatcher legitimacy to say 'something must be done' to curb them. 'I think as a reaction to that, the Labour Party then both in economic terms and class terms was absolutely determined to prove its credentials, that it wasn't an extreme, adversarial party that was simply divisive.' In her own way, Blears has accepted that the retreat from class was the product of the repeated defeats suffered at the hands of Thatcherism triumphant.

With 'class' no longer an option to describe inequality and disadvantage in society, New Labour invented new terms. 'Social exclusion' and the 'socially excluded' was the code for 'poverty' and 'the poor'. New Labour launched a Social Exclusion Unit after it first came to power. It even had a minister for social exclusion. The term strips away the more unpleasant connotations of poverty, like poor housing, low pay and so on. In essence it was a less pejorative way of saying 'underclass', with the same implications of a group of people who have been cut off from society. It was the New Labour take on the chav phenomenon: a dysfunctional, excluded group at the bottom, and then the happy rest of us.

'You never knew how these people were being defined,' says John Goldthorpe, 'or what numbers you could put on it, what proportion they were. But then you said, "What exactly are they socially excluded *from*?" And you were told, "The mainstream of British society." But that's ridiculous! In a society that's as stratified and unequal as ours, there is no mainstream ... Again, it was this New Labour thing, they wanted to do something about the very bottom, and then pretend that apart from that, there wasn't a problem. But that's wrong! ... As I see it, the socially excluded is largely made up of people who are the most disadvantaged within the working class.'

'Exclusion' did not have to mean being excluded by society—but rather being excluded by your own actions. When I asked Matthew Taylor whether one of the legacies of Thatcherism was that politicians now regarded social problems as the result of individual behaviour, he thought it was complex but, overall, felt that was the case.

There has been a general view which is—and it is in the move from 'class' to 'exclusion' as conceptions—that exclusion is something which kind of suggests that 'I am excluding myself', that there is a process, that my own behaviour is replicated in my social status. Class is something which is *given* to me. Exclusion is something which *happens* to me and in which I am somehow an agent. And so I think, yeah, absolutely, there was a sense not that you should blame the poor for being poor, although there was a bit of that as well, but that poverty was a process in which people were active in one way or another ... not simply the result of great impersonal social forces.

As one of Tony Blair's most senior advisors, and a very perceptive and astute political commentator, Matthew Taylor's honest inside look at some of the philosophies that shaped New Labour is revealing. Rather than simply being the result of social forces, your place in society was partly determined by your behaviour.

Jon Cruddas is in no doubt that politicians of all colours have a vested interest in denying the existence of class. It has proved an effective way of avoiding having to address working-class concerns in favour of a small, privileged layer of the middle classes. 'They devise ever more scientific methods of camping out on a very small slice of the electorate ... those who are constituted as marginal voters in marginal seats.' Working-class voters were taken for granted as the 'core vote' who had nowhere else to go, allowing New Labour politicians to tailor their policies to privileged voters.

No New Labour politician personified this attitude more than Tony Blair. Matthew Taylor offers an interesting insight into Blair's political approach. 'I worked for Tony Blair, and the point about Tony is that Tony would always say when I would say to him, or other people would say to him: "What about a bit more kind of *leftism* in all of this? What about a bit more about poverty and justice and blah blah blah? ..."' Blair's response was blunt, to say the least:

Tony would always say: 'Fine, but I don't need to worry about that, because that's what everybody else in the Labour Party wants, and that's what everybody else in the Cabinet wants, and that's what Gordon [Brown] wants, and that's kind of fine. And I'll leave them to do that, because I know that's how they'll spend all their time. They don't want to do public service reform, they don't want to do wealth creation, they're not interested in any of that, they'll just kind of hammer away at that agenda. My job is to appeal to the great mass of people on issues that the Labour Party generally speaking is just not interested in.

The near-obsession with ignoring working-class voters meant inflating the importance of a very small tranche of wealthy voters who were mis-leadingly construed as Middle England. After all, an individual in the very middle of the nation's income scale only earns around £21,000. 'You're probably right that we did misportray Middle England,' admits Matthew Taylor, 'but that again, I'm afraid, is not just a Labour charac-teristic. It's characteristic of the middle classes as a whole.'

This distortion sometimes reached absurd levels. Stephen Byers is a former New Labour Cabinet minister and one of Blair's closest allies. In 2006 he floated the idea of abolishing inheritance tax in order to win back 'Middle England', despite the fact that only the wealthiest families in Britain were liable to pay it.

'There's a particular strand of uber-Blairism which basically is kind of just fucking mad,' says Matthew Taylor, 'and I'm afraid Stephen—who I like personally, I haven't seen him for years—he, I'm afraid, was probably more guilty than anybody else of occasionally floating these kind of mad Blairite ideas.' New Labour never did adopt Byers's grovellingly pro-wealthy inheritance tax proposal. Nonetheless, his thinking represented a deeply influential strain of Blairism that side-lined working-class people in favour of the concerns of a tiny but gilded section of the population.

It is not just the fetishizing of the demands of the wealthy and power-ful that has rendered the working class invisible. The promotion of multiculturalism in an era when the concept of class was being abandoned meant that inequality became almost exclusively understood through the prism of race and ethnic identity. Dr Gillian Evans, a leading anthropologist and expert on social class, argues that while 'the struggle for class equality was said to have either been squashed or won, depending on your perspective', the battle for racial equality continued through multiculturalism. 'This saw black and Asian people struggling for greater ethnic and cultural respect and this has been, relatively speaking, a fantastic resistance movement that is to be celebrated.'

But because multiculturalism became the only recognized platform in the struggle for equality, Dr Evans argues that, on the one hand, we fail to acknowledge 'the existence of a multi-racial working class', and on the other, the white working class is 'forced to think of themselves as a new ethnic group with their own distinctive culture'. Most dangerously of all, middle-class people have ended up 'refusing to acknowledge anything about white working class as legitimately cultural, which leads to a composite loss of respect on all fronts: economic, political and social.'

We are rightly encouraged to embrace and celebrate ethnic minority identity, not least as a counterweight to continued entrenched racism. But a racialized 'white' working class is not seen as having a place in this classless multiculturalism. There are, after all, no prominent, respected champions for the working class in the way that there are for many minority groups. The interests of working-class ethnic minority people end up being ignored too, because the focus is on building up the ethnic minority middle class by ensuring diversity within the leading professions.

Yet, as New Labour lurched from crisis to crisis under Gordon Brown, it became increasingly difficult simply to pretend the working class did not exist. The racist BNP was growing in working-class communities in, for example, East London and North-West England. But New Labour politicians took the rising working-class backlash against immigration at face value, instead of examining underlying causes such as lack of affordable housing or secure, well-paid jobs. Rather than focusing on the *economic* ills shared by the working class of all creeds and colours, New Labour redefined them as *cultural* problems affecting the *white* working class. The white working class became one marginalized ethnic minority among others.

For example, back in 2009 New Labour launched a £12 million project specifically designed to help white working-class communities. Of course it is true that there are many working-class—and yes, largely white—communities that have been neglected or even abandoned by New Labour, and are in urgent need of help. But this approach takes us further down the road of linking the problems of working-class communities to their ethnic identity, rather than to their class. More dangerously, it encourages the idea that working-class people belonging to different ethnic groups are in competition with each other for attention and resources.

The thoughtless comments by New Labour minister Margaret Hodge in 2007 epitomized this view. Her cack-handed response to the rise of the BNP in her constituency was to complain that migrant families were being given priority for homes over people with a 'legitimate sense of entitlement'. Instead of demanding her government do something about its shoddy record on social housing, she made the interests of white working-class people and of immigrants seem pitted against each other.

'White working-class people living on estates sometimes just don't feel anyone is listening or speaking up for them,' was how Hazel Blears put it in 2009, when she was New Labour's communities secretary. Blears was absolutely correct: millions of white working-class people did feel unrepresented and voiceless. But for Blears, their concerns were almost entirely defined by immigration. 'Whilst they might not be experiencing the direct impact of migration, their fear of it is acute … Changes in communities can generate unease and uncertainty.'[18]

Only when the BNP was breathing down its neck did New Labour start talking about the working class again—and even then it was in a racialized form, and restricted to the immigration issue. Above all, it was an exception to New Labour's repudiation of working-class values, and its emphasis on everyone joining the middle class.

If you want to explode the myth that class is dead in modern Britain, and that anyone can rise to the top through their own efforts, the Palace of Westminster is a good place to start. MPs swan in and out of meetings with lobbyists and constituents, occasionally popping to the Chamber to speak or vote when called by the piercing division bell. Overwhelmingly from middle-class, professional backgrounds, the combined salary and expenses of the average backbencher comfortably puts them in the top 4 per cent of the population.

Scurrying around after them, or gossiping over lattes in Portcullis House, is an army of fresh-faced, ambitious parliamentary researchers. With unpaid internships (often, quite unlike their bosses, without even expenses provided) almost always a prerequisite for making it on to an MP's staff rolls, Parliament is a middle-class closed shop. Only those able to live off the financial generosity of their parents can get their foot in the door.

At the service of MPs and hacks alike are the cleaners and catering staff. Many of them trek across London on night buses to arrive in the House at the crack of dawn. Their wages place them easily in the bottom 10 per cent of the population. Until a fight for a living wage was successful in 2006, the cleaners of the 'Mother of All Parliaments' were subsisting on the minimum wage in one of the most expensive cities on the planet. Watching middle-aged women trundling around trolleys containing the leftovers of roast chicken and chocolate gateaux, you can be forgiven for feeling as though you had walked into a Victorian aristocrat's manor.

It would be easy, but lazy, to portray Parliament as a microcosm of the British class system. It isn't, but it certainly showcases the gaping divides of modern society. When I interviewed James Purnell just before the May 2010 election that brought the Tories and their Lib Dem allies to 10 Downing Street, I put to him how unrepresentative Parliament was: two-thirds of MPs came from a professional background and were four times more likely to have attended a private school than the rest of the population. When I referred to the fact that only one in twenty MPs came from a blue-collar background, he was genuinely shocked. 'One in *twenty*?'

When I asked him if this had made it more difficult for politicians to understand the problems of working-class people, he could hardly disagree. 'Yes, indeed. I think it's become very much a closed shop ...' For Purnell, this middle-class power grab was the result of a political system that has become closed to ordinary people.

In the build-up to the 2010 general election, a number of excited headlines claimed that trade unions were parachuting candidates into safe seats. 'Unions put their candidates in place to push Labour to the left,' bellowed *The Times*. And yet, in the end, only 3 per cent of new MPs were former trade union officials. There was no similar outrage about the number of prospective candidates with careers in the City— the sector that, after all, was responsible for the biggest economic crisis since the 1930s. One in ten new MPs had a background in financial services, twice as many as in the 1997 landslide that brought Labour to power. Politics has also increasingly been turned into a career rather than a service: a stunning one in five new MPs already worked in politics before taking the Parliamentary oath.

When you look back at the 1945 Labour Cabinet that constructed the welfare state after the ravages of World War II, the contrast is almost obscene. The giants of Clement Attlee's government were Ernest Bevin, Britain's representative on the global stage; Nye Bevan, the founder of the National Health Service; and Herbert Morrison, Attlee's number two. All were from working-class backgrounds, starting life as a farm boy, miner, and grocer's assistant, respectively. It was the trade unions and local government that had provided them with the ladders to climb, enabling them to end up as towering political figures and respected statesmen.

But take a look at today's treatment of John Prescott, one of the few working-class members of New Labour. You don't have to agree with his politics to flinch at the class-based ridicule heaped on him. The son of a railway signalman, Prescott went on to fail his eleven-plus and became a waiter in the Merchant Navy. His impressive rise from such roots to the post of deputy prime minister was rarely applauded, however. Tory MP Nicholas Soames, a grandson of Winston Churchill, used to shout drinks orders at him in the House of Commons whenever he rose to speak. Tory MPs and journalists who have benefited from hugely expensive private educations mocked his occasionally garbled English.

When he entered the House of Lords, that retirement home for the ruling elite, the *Telegraph*'s chief leader writer scoffed: 'I'm not sure ermine suits John Prescott.' The comments left by *Telegraph* readers on the newspaper's website were a class war free-for-all. One passed on a friend's hilarious description of him as 'the builder's bum-crack of the Labour Party'. 'Baron Pie & Chips' and 'Prescott is a fat peasant' were other witticisms, as was 'John "here's a little tip" Prescott'. 'Someone has to serve the drinks between debates!' guffawed another. Prescott was ridiculed because some felt that by being from lowly working-class stock, he sullied the office of deputy prime minister and then the House of Lords.

Working-class people once rose in politics through the mighty institutions of trade unions and local government. But today the trade unions are on their knees and local government has been stripped of many of its powers. Former London mayor Ken Livingstone regrets the

> abolition of the traditional council structure where working-class people got elected, learned via committees how things are run, and then went to Parliament. That's gone ... There's a lot of people that used to be on Lambeth Council or Camden Council who weren't terribly good in terms of literacy and numeracy, but loved representing their area, and

could work the machine and the council. They didn't have to have bloody A-levels or degrees to do it. In that sense the barriers against the working class are stronger now, not because an aristocratic elite is keeping them out, but because a sort of middle-class layer has introduced too many qualifications, rules, and regulations.

You are more likely to make it to Parliament if you are a middle-class, Oxbridge-educated former special advisor these days.

When I spoke to Peter, a leisure centre worker in East London, he summed up the scepticism many working-class people feel towards the political establishment. 'I think they're on a different wavelength. I think most of the politicians are very rich and don't understand the normal problems of people, because they come from a different background. And, you know, you see them all on television, most of them are very wealthy, so they wouldn't understand our problems, you know.'

It was his firm belief that 'they would never know what normal people go through.' This is a fundamental point in understanding politicians' demonization of working-class communities. It is, of course, largely down to the legacy of Thatcher's assault on working-class Britain, and the establishment of a consensus that individual salvation can only be achieved through joining the middle class. But this consensus has established itself so easily in Westminster because our increasingly privileged political elites were—and are—fertile ground for these kinds of ideas. They are largely disconnected from working-class communities, and cannot imagine anyone not sharing their middle-class values and aspirations. They find it easy to explain working-class problems as the consequences of personal behaviour, not the social structure of the country. Above all, stereotypes about the working class have found a sympathetic hearing from overwhelmingly middle-class politicians who have rarely mixed with people with less privileged backgrounds.

The shadow of Thatcher's class war and the demonizing of working-class communities by both the Tories and New Labour have had drastic consequences. Political trends always exert a profound influence on the culture. The repercussions of the attack on working-class values and institutions have fanned out through society. Like Westminster, our media and entertainment are dominated by the most privileged sectors. They have been all too ready to put working-class people down in the crudest possible ways.

4

A Class in the Stocks

Treorchy in the Rhondda is chav-infested. Although here, people don't even know what a chav is!! The reason being that everyone is a chav! There are no posh folk, as the place is working class and unemployment is rife!

—ChavTowns website

There has never been an age when the working class were properly respected, let alone glorified. From the Victorian era to World War II, working-class people were barely mentioned in books. When they appeared at all, they were caricatures. As one expert on Victorian literature put it, even a middle-class supporter of reform like Charles Dickens presented working-class people as having 'the two-dimensional qualities of cartoon figures'.[1] George Orwell observed: 'If you look for the working classes in fiction, and especially English fiction, all you find is a hole ... the ordinary town proletariat, the people who make the wheels go round, have always been ignored by novelists. When they do find their way between the corners of a book, it is nearly always as objects of pity or as comic relief.'[2]

And yet things did change after World War II. Labour, the party created by working-class people to represent them in Parliament, had won a landslide victory and was there to stay as one of the country's two major political forces. Sweeping social reforms were introduced to address working-class concerns. Trade unions enjoyed influence at the highest levels of power. Working-class people could no longer be ignored.

'The war changed everything,' says Stephen Frears, a film director who often weaves class themes into his work (from early television serializations of Alan Bennett plays to the 1985 classic, *My Beautiful Laundrette*). 'Novels started being about the working classes. Plays started being about the working classes. I found all of that very, very interesting.' For someone from a middle-class background like Frears, this was a profoundly liberating experience –what he refers to as his 'emancipation'. 'There was suddenly a whole group of people who'd never been heard before, really … The focus before had been on such a narrow range of subjects in Britain, which was those who live the life of the upper classes or middle classes, whatever. So suddenly the world became more interesting.'

A real milestone was the launch of *Coronation Street* on ITV in 1960. For the first time a TV series revolved around sympathetic, realistic working-class characters and looked at how they lived their lives. It struck a chord and within months attracted over 20 million viewers. It rode the wave of so-called Northern Realism, a new genre of film that explored the realities of working-class life. *Saturday Night and Sunday Morning*, *A Taste of Honey*, *Room at the Top* and *Cathy Come Home* were classic examples. While working-class people were the stars of favourites such as *The Likely Lads*, it was middle-class people who could find themselves the butt of jokes in *The Good Life* and other series. There was even a popular sitcom in the 1970s—*The Rag Trade*—about female trade unionists who took on their bosses and always won. As late as the 1980s there were classic TV shows being written around likable working-class characters, such as *Only Fools and Horses* and *Auf Wiedersehen, Pet*.

That is not to say that the portrayal of working-class life was always completely realistic. 'I think there was an awful lot of romanticization of the working class and their communities, say thirty, forty, fifty years ago,' says historian David Kynaston. 'If you think about the portrayals of the working class in the films of the immediate post-war period, often they show working-class people as sort of buffoons, but not as villains or unpleasant. It was more kind of one-dimensional. They might be uncouth, but nevertheless not *bad* people.' Former Labour leader Neil Kinnock agrees. 'For a very, very long time, certainly in much of the twentieth century, the working class was idealized by a small number of very influential intellectuals, people in the arts and education. Otherwise it was patronized.'

There was a big leap from being patronized to being despised. The shift would come with the advent of Thatcherism and its assault on what you could call *working-classness*—working-class values, institutions, industries and communities. 'The big shift in portrayal is surely —and it's an obvious point but it's surely a true point—that from about the 80s, it became possible in the media to, as it were, disparage the working class … in a disrespectful and wholly unkind way,' as David Kynaston puts it.

Among the earliest examples of these sentiments filtering into popular culture were two characters invented by comedian Harry Enfield, Wayne and Waynetta Slob. First appearing in 1990, they could be regarded as 'proto-chavs': feckless, foul-mouthed, benefit-dependent and filthy. When Waynetta (a 'nightmare prole', as one journalist put it in 1997)[3] becomes pregnant, for example, the couple debate calling their unborn child 'Ashtray'. Even today, the media enthusiastically use Waynetta Slob as a template when attacking groups of working-class people. 'Rising toll of "Waynettas" with three times as many women as men signing onto sickness benefits under New Labour' screamed one recent *Daily Mail* headline. Underneath a photo of a greasy-looking Waynetta Slob holding her baby was the thoughtful caption: 'The type of people mocked by Harry Enfield's character Waynetta Slob have [*sic*] increased.'[4]

But it was the emergence of the 'chav' phenomenon that brought together previously disparate prejudices against working-class people.

The website 'ChavScum' was launched at the end of 2003, with a tagline reading: 'Britain's peasant underclass that is taking over our towns and cities'. In its current incarnation ('ChavTowns') contributors compete over attacking chavs: entries can be simple, like 'shitty council scum people' living in 'shitty council / ex-council housing', for example. Another targets the chavs of the town of Leek who 'spend their days on the checkout at Aldi or working in the delightful Kerrigold cheese factory. The most ambition ever seen in the town made the front page of the Leek Post and Times when one 15 year old mother of 17 made a passing comment about maybee [*sic*] working on the deli counter at Morrisons one day.'

Supermarket employees in Winchester don't come off much better. According to one account: 'Even when they are on the checkout, the customer is always invisible as they chat about pregnancies at fourteen, and how "Cristal got drunk on Friday night, and went home with Tyrone—the bastard" etc etc ad nauseam.'

There are entire books dedicated to this genre. For a long time, Lee Bok's *The Little Book of Chavs* was perched on the counters of the now-defunct bookshop chain Borders. Its most recent edition boasted that it had sold over 100,000 copies and had been reprinted eight times. It even contains a list of 'Chav occupations' to aid identification. If you were a female chav (or 'Chavette'), you would be a trainee hairdresser, a trainee beautician, a cleaner or a barmaid. Chav men work as cowboy builders, roofers or plumbers; they may also be market stall traders, mechanics or security guards. Both sexes could be spotted at a checkout in low-price supermarket chains like Lidl, Netto or Aldi, or toiling in a fast-food restaurant.[5] The equally poisonous follow-up book, *The Chav Guide to Life*, revealed that as well as being 'loud and lower class', 'Most Chavs come from not well-off, working-class families on council estates, and get their money from the dole.'[6]

The creators of the Chavscum website published their own literary contribution to chav-hate. In *Chav!: A User's Guide to Britain's New Ruling Class*, Mia Wallace and Clint Spanner offer tips for 'Spotting a chav in the wild'. Chavs, you see, are like animals. 'Cutting-edge, fake designer fashion, branded sportswear and accessories to die for, fabulously extravagant 9-carat-gold "bling" (jewellery), it's all here in this fun-for-all-the-family, point-scoring game!' A 'chavette' was regarded 'as an infertile freak by her immediate community' if she had not had a child before the age of seventeen. The chav television channel of choice was 'ITV Chav … where a chav knows they will never get stimulated or challenged or *anyfing*.' Unless they are watching *This Morning*, because 'with its slightly middle-class aspirations it can be a bit scary.' Worst of all, chav kids were in danger of swamping decent children at schools across the country:

> There used to be a stigma attached to receiving free school meals and some poorer families would send their kids in with a packed lunch rather than accept such a benefit. However, as the balance has shifted in schools and many of the pupils now come from a chav background, getting the free meal is *de rigueur*. Non-chav children are now embarrassed to pay for a meal, and may be set about as the 'posh kid' if they do.[7]

As chav-hate began to emerge as a force in mainstream culture in 2004, it found supporters in the mainstream press. Jemima Lewis, a *Telegraph* journalist, responded to the Chavscum website with a column entitled 'In defence of snobbery'. 'Both varieties of snobbery—traditional or inverted—have their perils, but on balance, I prefer the former,' she wrote, without satire. 'This is partly because I am middle class and would prefer not to be mocked for it. But it is also because traditional snobbery at least aspires towards some worthy goals: education, ambition, courtesy.'[8] Hating the lower orders was good for them, was the crux of her argument: it made them aspire to escape their woeful circumstances and get some manners.

For those of its readers who were bewildered by the chav phenomenon, the *Daily Mail* published a handy 'A to Z' of chavs. 'A' was for

'A-Level'—'Something no Chav has ever possessed.' 'U' was for 'Underage': 'What every Chavette is at the time of her first sexual experience.' The sexual promiscuity of chav women, one of the big obsessions of chav-haters, is encapsulated in the *Mail*'s 'joke' offering: 'What's the difference between a Chavette and the Grand Old Duke of York? The Grand Old Duke of York only had 10,000 men.' And, of course, chavs were to be taunted for their low-paid jobs. 'What do you say to a Chav when he's at work? Big Mac and fries, please, mate.'[9] Another article by the same journalist suggested that Britain was being overrun by chavs. 'Some people call them scum. Sociologists call them the underclass. But call them what you like, they're taking over the country.'[10]

Those labelled 'chavs' became frequently ridiculed for failing to meet lofty middle-class standards in what they wore, or how they ate. Celebrity chef Jamie Oliver was rightly applauded for his crusade to bring healthy food to the British school dinner menu. But it was a campaign marred by tut-tutting at the eating habits of the lower orders. On his Channel 4 programme, Oliver referred to parents who failed to sit around a table for dinner as 'what we have learned to call "white trash"'. Indeed, his TV series *Jamie Oliver's School Dinners* focused on poor estates where mothers struggled to feed their kids with what little money they had.[11] Jonathan Ross asked him on BBC1: 'Well, do you ever think that some people shouldn't be allowed to be parents? Like people from council estates?' It was a 'joke' met with cheers.[12]

The same goes for alcohol consumption. When the government's chief medical officer, Sir Liam Donaldson, issued guidelines recommending that children under the age of fifteen should not drink at all, *Daily Telegraph* journalist James Delingpole became hot under the collar. Sir Liam had had the temerity to suggest that offering young kids small amounts of wine was a 'middle-class obsession'. But Delingpole thought he was aiming at the 'wrong target': 'We all know where Britain's most serious child-drinking problems lie: on sink estates and among broken homes where rudderless urchins are routinely downing alcopops and cans of super-strong lager before they've reached their teens.'

The middle classes had been attacked because they were a 'soft target', while the real culprits had been let off because even if they 'were capable of reading a newspaper, they wouldn't give a stuff'. Never mind that a study by the National Centre for Social Research found that children from affluent backgrounds were the biggest drinkers, and teenagers with unemployed parents were less likely to have even tried alcohol. 'This seems to indicate that young people of very low social position may be less likely to try alcohol, possibly because it is less likely to be available in the home,' said the researchers.[13] But Delingpole was merely fleshing out the stereotype that, while the middle classes consumed alcohol in a respectable, cultured way, the lower orders spent their time rolling around in a drunken stupor. It was *their* lifestyles that needed regulating, not those of the civilized middle class.

Middle-class journalists were also affronted by the bad manners of the chavs. So much so, in fact, that they used their well-paid columns to launch snooty attacks against people who lack a platform to defend themselves. The *Daily Telegraph*'s Janet Daley has a particular distaste for the unwashed masses. She cannot even go to the theatre without 'a gang of boisterous, inebriated chavs who will disrupt the performance and may threaten you with assault if you upbraid them.' Meanwhile, the National Gallery had been overwhelmed by a 'human barricade of dossers and fun-loving exhibitionists'.

Of particular concern to Daley were the 'yobs' who by going on holiday forced her to 'flee to those parts of Abroad which the louts ignore'. What perturbed her most was that these people were 'neither poor nor unemployed. Indeed, most of them had the sorts of jobs that would once have been described as "respectable working class".' The truth was that rude working-class people were ruining the holidays of sensitive, superior people like herself. Daley wanted the middle classes to civilize the lower orders—but they were prevented from doing so. 'It is bourgeois guilt that prevents those who would impose standards from acting: the socially privileged simply cower and refuse to intervene, for fear of appearing contemptuous of those less fortunate than themselves.'[14] Manners belonged to the middle classes: and it was high time that they sorted out the impertinent chavs.

Not that the born-and-bred middle classes are the only guilty parties. Some who hail from working-class roots and have achieved wealth and success against the odds have told themselves: 'If I can make it, then anyone with the talent and determination can too'. Take John Bird, the founder of the *Big Issue*. 'I'm middle class. I got out of the working class as quickly as I could,' he once said. 'The working class is violent and abusive, they beat their wives and I hate their culture.'[15] John Bird is far from the only example of a wealthy, formerly working-class individual who spits at those they have left behind. You have 'escaped' purely because of your own exceptional talents and abilities, you can think to yourself—and those who have not got ahead have only themselves to blame.

It would be nice to dismiss chav-hate as a fringe psychosis confined to ranting right-wing columnists. But there is a type of chav-hate that has become a 'liberal bigotry'. Liberal bigots justify their prejudice against a group of people on the grounds of their own supposed bigotry. The racialization of working-class people as 'white' has convinced some that they can hate chavs and remain progressive-minded. They justify their hatred of white working-class people by focusing on their supposed racism and failure to assimilate into multicultural society. 'It's one of the ways people have made their snobbery socially acceptable,' says journalist Johann Hari: 'by acting as though they are defending immigrants from the "ignorant" white working class.'

By defining the white working class in terms of ethnicity rather than social class, liberal chav-haters ascribe their problems to cultural rather than economic factors. It is the way they live that is the problem, not the unjust way society is structured. If white working-class people are oppressed, it is the result of their own fecklessness. While a liberal chav-hater will accept that massive discrimination against ethnic minority groups explains issues like unemployment and poverty and even violence, they do not believe white working-class people have such excuses.

'The "real" working class is supposed to be white, badly educated, "aspirational for wealth", bigoted and easily persuaded,' says prominent trade union leader Billy Hayes, who was born on a council estate in Liverpool. Many of these caricatures appeared in the BBC's *White* season, a supposedly sympathetic series of programmes dedicated to the white working class that aired in 2007. In reality, it simply boosted the image of white working-class people as a race-obsessed, BNP-voting rump. Their problems were not portrayed as economic—things like housing and jobs that affect working-class people of all colours did not get a look-in. They were simply portrayed as a minority culture under threat from mass immigration. 'The *White* season examines why some feel increasingly marginalised and explores possible reasons behind the rise in popularity of far-right politics in some sections of this community,' the BBC announced.[16]

But the trailer for the series said it all: a white man's face being scribbled over by dark-skinned hands with a black marker pen until he disappeared into the background. Accompanying the trailer was the question: 'Is the white working class becoming invisible?' Here it was—all their problems being reduced to the issue of race. Among those angered by this bias was the BBC reporter Sarah Mukherjee, a woman of Asian origin who grew up on a largely white council estate in Essex. The series left a 'nasty taste in the mouth', she said. 'Listening to the patronizing conversations in some newsrooms you'd think white, working-class Britain is one step away from anarchy, drinking themselves senseless and pausing only to draw benefits and beat up a few Asian and black people.'

As an example of how chav-bashing can be justified on anti-racist grounds, take a column written by journalist Yasmin Alibhai-Brown. 'Tax-paying immigrants past and present keep indolent British scroungers on their couches drinking beer and watching TV,' she claimed. 'We [immigrants] are despised because we seize opportunities these slobs don't want.'[17] In another column entitled 'Spare me the tears over the white working class', she slams those who resist calling them racist.

> Working-class white men provoked race riots through the Fifties and Sixties; they kept 'darkies' out of pubs and clubs and work canteens. Who were the supporters of Oswald Mosley and Enoch Powell? The disempowered have used us to vent their natural-born hatred against the powerful.[18]

Alibhai-Brown regards herself as a writer of the left—and yet she happily uses a perversion of anti-racism to slam white working-class people. This is chav-bashing as liberal bigotry in full swing. A BBC series presented by Evan Davis tapped into similar sentiments. *The Day the Immigrants Left* had the worthy aim of proving that immigrant workers were not, in fact, 'coming over here and taking all our jobs'. But, after making eleven long-term unemployed people sign up to do jobs (often badly, or failing to turn up at all) favoured by immigrant labourers, the programme portrayed this as a case study of how unemployed working-class people in Britain are slovenly and feckless. The hour-long programme with its selective examples ultimately seemed to show that, actually, people in Britain did not have jobs because of their own abject laziness.

Columnist Janet Daley is among those who have perversely justified chav-bashing as a defence of ethnic minority people. Recounting a run-in with what she described as an 'English working-class sociopath' (their cars clipped each other and he shouted a bit before driving off), she launched into a tirade against 'working-class violence'. British working-class people were, she said, a 'self-loathing, self-destructive tranche of the population' who lacked 'civic culture'. In contrast, she celebrated the 'religion, cultural dignity and a sense of family' brought by ethnic minorities. The only thing holding them back, she claimed, was 'the mindless hatred of the indigenous working classes, who loathe them precisely for their cultural integrity ... I fear long after Britain has become a successful multi-racial society, it will be plagued by this diminishing (but increasingly alienated) detritus of the Industrial Revolution.'[19] It is certainly a creative way of justifying hatred of working-class people. But then again, Janet Daley is not simply a snob: she is a class warrior.

Another myth used to sustain chav-hate is the idea that the old, decent working class has died away, leaving a rump with no moral compass. In one *Daily Mail* column, Amanda Platell, a former speech-writer for the present Coalition foreign secretary, William Hague, blamed the 'shabby values' of this rump for their situation. 'When it comes to looking for the real cause why so many of the working class do worse at school, earn less and die younger, the blame must be placed elsewhere—on the countless number of feckless parents.' She even called the mothers of working-class children 'slum mums'. As part of her argument that they were personally responsible for their situation, she argued: 'The working class of the past had enormous self-respect. Men, however poor, wore suits and ties. Women scrubbed front steps. Mothers wouldn't have been seen dead wearing pyjamas in their own kitchen, let alone in public.'[20]

As Rachel Johnson (editor of the *Lady* and sister of Boris Johnson) puts it: 'What we're having is a media which is run by the middle classes, for the middle classes, of the middle classes, aren't we?' She is spot on. The journalists who have stirred up chav-hate are from a narrow, privileged background. Even papers with overwhelmingly working-class reader-ships join in the sport. Kevin Maguire told me of a *Sun* away day in which all the journalists dressed up as chavs. Chuckle at their venom-ous columns by all means, but be aware that you are revelling in the contempt of the privileged for the less fortunate. In the current climate of chav-hate the class warriors of Fleet Street can finally get away with it, openly and flagrantly: caricaturing working-class people as stupid, idle, racist, sexually promiscuous, dirty, and fond of vulgar clothes. Nothing of worth is seen to emanate from working-class Britain.

This chav-hate has even become a fad among privileged youth. At universities like Oxford, middle-class students hold 'chav bops' where they dress up as this working-class caricature. Among those mocking the look was Prince William, one of the most privileged young men in the country. At a chav-themed fancy dress party to mark the end of his first term at Sandhurst, he dressed in a loose-fitting top and 'bling jewellery', along with the must-have 'angled baseball cap'. But when the other cadets demanded he 'put on a chavvy accent and stop speaking like a Royal,' he couldn't do it. 'William's not actually the poshest-sounding cadet, despite his family heritage, but he struggled to pull off a working-class accent,' one cadet told the *Sun*.[21] Welcome to twenty-first-century Britain, where royals dress up as their working-class subjects for a laugh.

To get a more detailed sense of what the 'chav' phenomenon means to young people from privileged backgrounds, I had a chat with Oliver Harvey, an Old Etonian and president of the Oxford Conservative Association. 'In the middle classes' attitudes toward what you would have called the working-class, so-called chav culture, you've still got to see class as an important part of British life,' he says. 'Chav' is a word Harvey often hears bandied around beneath the dreaming spires of Oxford. 'You'd think people would be educated here, but it's still something people find funny.' Unlike other students, he dislikes the term because of its class meaning. 'I think it shows a patronizing attitude and is rather offensive. It's a word used by more fortunate people towards less fortunate people ... Unfortunately it's now a popular term that has been transplanted into people's everyday consciousness.'

A place like Oxford is fertile ground for chav-hate. Nearly half of its students were privately educated, and there are very, very few working-class people attending the university at all. It helps unlock the truth behind the phenomenon: here are privileged people with little contact with those lower down the scale. It is easy to caricature people you do not understand. And indeed, many of these students owe their place at Oxford to the privileged circumstances that bought them a superior education. How comforting to pretend that they landed in Oxford because of their own talents, and that those at the bottom of society are there because they are thick, feckless or worse.

And yet such open mockery is a recent development, not least because until quite recently, many students felt embarrassed about privilege. 'To be a middle-class student just twenty years ago carried such a social stigma that many graduates in their forties recall faking a proletarian accent for their entire university education,' says *Guardian* journalist Decca Aitkenhead. 'Nowadays, however, a popular student party theme is dressing up as "chavs"—working-class types with a taste for Burberry, but not the budget, whose ideas above their station provide material for half the jokes on campus today.'[22]

Scouring the internet reveals the disturbing levels anti-chav hatred has reached in society at large. A YouTube video with around half a million hits proposes sending chavs to the moon. 'But who'd care anyway if every chav goes to where there's no KFC, no McDonald's, no high street,' the singer croons cheerfully. Before it was finally removed, a Facebook page with nearly three-quarters of a million members was entitled '4000 chavs a year die from tesco cheap booze. Every little helps :).' Type in 'kill chavs' into Google and you get hundreds of thousands of results: like '5 Ways to Kill a Chav' and 'The Anti Chav—Kill Chav Scum Now'. There is even a game called 'Chav Hunter' where you can shoot chavs. 'Chav Hunter is about killing those pikey fucks who dress like 80's rappers. In a sniper fashion, aim for the head,' it recommends.

But the chav phenomenon has sinister implications beyond revealing the growing hatred within the British class system. In early 2009, Ralph Surman, a teacher from Nottingham, launched into a tirade against what he called 'a class of uber-chavs. They are not doing anything productive and are costing taxpayers a fortune.' He knew exactly who to blame: 'The offspring of the first big generation of single mothers were children in the 1980s. Now they are adults with their own children and the problems are leading to higher crime rates and low participation in the labour force.'[23] This dismissal of large swathes of young people may well have dire results. 'The birth of "chavs", as parodied by comedians such as Catherine Tate, can leave working-class people feeling patronized and laughed at,' writes journalist Hannah Frankel in a thoughtful piece on the education system's approach to working-class people.[24]

Catherine Tate's comic character, a lazy teenage girl with an attitude problem and an annoying catchphrase ('Am I bovvered?'), was just one example of how chav-bashing has become national entertainment. Reality TV shows, sketch shows, talk shows, even films have emerged dedicated to ridiculing working-class Britain. 'Chavtainment' has reinforced the mainstream view of working-class individuals as bigoted, slothful, aggressive people who cannot look after themselves, let alone their children. 'On the one hand they're served up as entertainment, you know, *Wife Swap*, whatever,' says Labour MP Jon Cruddas. 'And simultaneously they're something to be feared through this notion of a lawless ASBO nation which is at the gate.' The bigots of privileged Britain have truly put an entire class in the stocks.

The world of reality television must have been a bewildering experience for the late Jade Goody, a twenty-one-year-old dental nurse from Bermondsey. Before she entered the *Big Brother* house, her life had been one of gut-wrenching hardship. When she was one, her mum threw out her junkie father for hiding guns underneath her cot. When she first saw the film *Trainspotting* at the cinema, she threw up when Ewan McGregor's character injected himself with heroin. 'Those faces that he pulls are the same faces I've seen my dad pull, you see,' she recalled. She remembered the first time she rolled a joint for her mother —when she was just four years old. When her mother was disabled by a motorcycle accident, Jade was forced to look after her. 'Losing the use of her arm was infuriating for my mum, and as a result she often beat me.'

Because she was born to a mixed-race father—'which is why I've got such big lips'—she suffered racist abuse both at school and in her local community. 'My mum got into fights with a lot of women who lived in our block because she thought they were prejudiced,' she said, and her mum took her out of school for similar reasons. She worked in various shops before getting the job as a dental assistant. But, with £3,000 of unpaid rent, she faced eviction from her council flat and possible imprisonment for unpaid tax. That was until 2002, when she sent a promotional video of herself to the new Channel 4 reality TV show, *Big Brother*.[25]

There can be few more shameful episodes in the British media's recent history than the hounding of Jade Goody. The youngest contestant, she reacted badly to the claustrophobic pressure of the TV programme. She ate and drank to cope with the stress; she fooled around with one of the contestants; and she was bullied into getting naked on national television (which the producers made sure to feature in the edited highlights). The media despised her. Labelled a 'pig', she was mercilessly ridiculed for not knowing what asparagus was (the horror!) and for asking if 'East Angular' was abroad. 'Vote the pig out!' demanded the *Sun*, which also referred to her as an 'oinker'. Others taunted her as a 'vile fishwife' and 'The Elephant Woman'. As the campaign became a hysterical witch-hunt (indeed, one of the headlines was: 'Ditch the Witch!'), members of the public stood outside the studios with placards reading: 'Burn the Pig!'

It is remarkable that anyone could have turned this avalanche of hatred around. But she did. Her disarming, almost boundless honesty, her disregard for the social graces of 'respectable' society and her tortured background gradually endeared her to millions. When she returned to the world of reality TV, it was in the celebrity version of *Big Brother*. Then came the next wave of anti-Jade spite.

Appearing alongside Jade Goody was Shilpa Shetty, an Indian Bollywood actress from a wealthy background. Jade took an evident dislike to her, and there was open war between the two. It was a much misunderstood dispute. Shilpa suggested that Jade needed 'elocution lessons'. When Jade infamously told the Indian actress to 'go back to the slums'—a phrase wrongly taken to be racist in intent—she was attacking her for being what Jade described as 'a posh, up-herself princess' who should see what real life was like. 'Ultimately, we were fighting because we were from different classes,' she would later claim. 'Who the fuck are you? You aren't some Princess in Neverland,' she screamed at Shilpa when she tried to flush a cooked chicken down the toilet. Other celebrities on the show, such as model Danielle Lloyd, suffered less media opprobrium despite calling Shetty a 'dog' and telling her to 'fuck off home'. But Goody's undoubtedly stupid and racially tinged references to the actress as 'Shilpa Poppadom' helped unleash a vitriolic media campaign.

'CLASS V TRASH' bellowed the *Daily Express*. The paper slammed 'the porcine Jade Goody' and mourned the fact that 'Miss Shetty, a huge star in India, has been forced to endure the kind of bullying usually heard around sink estates ... We are being disgraced around the world by the likes of semi-literate Jade and her unpleasant associates.' The *Express* was outraged because it felt that a thick, ugly girl from a poor background was attacking a beautiful rich woman. 'Jade and her allies clearly feel threatened by the presence of a woman from a very different strata [*sic*] of society from their own,' it claimed.[26] Simon Heffer assailed Goody for indulging 'in the only form of bigotry the law now permits to go unpunished: that of hating your social superiors.' He questioned why Channel 4 had to use *Big Brother* to broadcast the 'repulsive aspects' of society 'when we can see them so easily for ourselves, if we wish, by wandering on to the nearest council estate for half an hour.'[27] Even Stuart Jeffries in the liberal *Guardian* could not resist portraying the clash as 'between ugly, thick white Britain and one imperturbably dignified Indian woman'. He even attacked Jade's garbled English, suggesting she use her fortune for 'remedial education'.[28] But then Stuart Jeffries was being educated at Oxford University while Jade Goody's heroin-addicted father was hiding guns underneath her cot.

On the BBC, Andrew Neil suggested she was just one of 'a bunch of Vicky Pollards' and 'thick bitches' cluttering TV screens. Richard

Littlejohn described her as 'the High Priestess of the Slagocracy', and others offered her as 'proof of Britain's underclass'. In one BBC phone-in, she was described as 'just another chav, the estates are full of them'. The host laughed and suggested 'hosing them down'.[29] Meanwhile, Hamant Verma, the former editor of *Eastern Eye* magazine, attributed 'the open display of racism' to 'Channel 4's decision to give near-illiterate chavs such as Jade Goody so much airtime'.[30] One writer in the *Nottingham Evening Post* described Shetty's tormentors as resembling 'nothing more than a pack of slavering chav estate mongrels spoiling for a scrap'.[31] It was not just Jade Goody under attack in these contributions: it was everybody who shared her background. Those at the bottom of the pile in British society were being presented as little more than animals. 'They smell, they're dirty', was how literary critic John Carey described attitudes towards the poor in interwar Britain. How much have things changed?

As the journalist Fiona Sturges was to later put it: 'Goody once again found herself vilified by the red-tops and held up as a terrible archetype of the white working class.'[32] But when Jade Goody was diagnosed with terminal cancer in 2008, there was genuine and widespread sympathy for her. It was as if the media were trying to atone for their guilt. Well, parts of the media, anyway. When she was initially diagnosed, *Spectator* columnist Rod Liddle penned a column entitled: 'After Jade's cancer, what next? "I'm a tumour, get me out of here"?' Referring to Jade as 'the coarse, thick, Bermondsey chav', he suggested that the cancer had been invented by her publicist, Max Clifford.

Or again, it is not inconceivable, I suppose, that written into Goody's contract was a demand that at some point she be seen to be suffering from a potentially fatal illness, given that without one she isn't very interesting any more. A stroke would have made for more dramatic television, but cancer, you have to say, has a certain cachet.[33]

Just days before Jade Goody's death, some journalists continued to take a pop at her as a proxy for those on the bottom rungs of society. 'A vulgar loudmouth, she initially appeared on the show as a kind of token Hogarthian lowlife,' wrote Jan Moir, a *Daily Mail* columnist. 'First we have this godforsaken wedding, then the christening of her children, then an ungainly, lickety-split spring to death and the ultimate chav state funeral.'[34] Moir was not alone in attacking Jade's decision to allow television cameras to film her last weeks. When a figure such as celebrated journalist John Diamond recorded his own death from cancer through newspaper columns in *The Times*, he was applauded: but then again, he was a middle-class man writing for a middle-class newspaper.

What does the case of Jade Goody show us, other than the capacity of the British media for crassness and cruelty? Above all it demonstrated that it is possible to say practically anything about people from Jade's background. They are fair game.

Big Brother was not the only reality TV show to lift the lid off class hatred. *Wife Swap* is a long-running Channel 4 programme where two wives with different backgrounds swap families for a couple of weeks. As Polly Toynbee has remarked, it should really be called 'Class Swap'. Invariably, one of the parties is portrayed as a 'dysfunctional' working-class family: feckless, unable to look after kids, bigoted, fag-smoking, beer-swilling and so on. One former fan complained in an internet review that it was guilty of 'soon deteriorating into fat uncouth working-class people slagging each other off between cigarettes and swigging canned lager, inviting a more sneering viewer to tune in.' The journalist Toby Young felt sorry for Becky Fairhurst, a twenty-nine-year-old mother of three whose marriage fell apart following the programme. 'She's an uneducated, white, working-class woman, and the programme's makers left no stone unturned in their efforts to depict her as "council trash",' he wrote. He could not help but conclude that the programme 'is designed to appeal to the snob in us. Here was a prime example of that urban species known as "the chav".'[35]

126

The Jeremy Kyle chatshow has a similar purpose. Week after week, dysfunctional individuals from overwhelmingly working-class backgrounds are served up as daytime entertainment fodder. Vulnerable people with complex personal troubles are thrown in front of baying audiences: a 'human form of bear-baiting', as one British judge was to describe it. Intensely emotional problems like suspicions of infidelity and 'who's the real father?' scenarios are exploited for the viewer's vicarious thrills. Little wonder it was lambasted by the Joseph Rowntree Foundation 'as a rather brutal form of entertainment that is based on derision of the lower-working-class population.' By portraying them as 'undeserving' it undermined support for anti-poverty initiatives, the Foundation claimed.[36]

And then, of course, there are the comedy chav caricatures. None has caught the popular imagination like *Little Britain*'s Vicky Pollard, created by comedians Matt Lucas and David Walliams. Pollard is presented as a grotesque working-class teenage single mother who is sexually promiscuous, unable to string a sentence together, and has a very bad attitude problem. In one sketch she swaps her baby for a Westlife CD. In another, when reminded to take her baby home she replies: 'Oh no it's OK, you can keep it, I've got loads more at home anyway.' Johann Hari points out that we are laughing at two ex-private-school boys dressing up as working-class single mothers. Matt Lucas's old school, Haberdashers' Aske's, charges around £10,000 a year. 'But of course, when Jim Davidson dressed up as a black man to say all black people were thick, we quite rightly said how stupid and outrageous it was,' says Hari.

All of this might be explained away as a bit of harmless fun. But consider the fact that a YouGov poll at the Edinburgh Film Festival in 2006 revealed that most people working in television thought Vicky Pollard was an accurate representation of Britain's white working class.[37] Matt Lucas himself has attacked critics 'who resent the fact that he and David are white, middle-class men, implying that they shouldn't be allowed to create characters that are working-class single mums because they're not from that world.' His defence? 'But if the observation rings true and is funny, then why should it matter who is making the observation and what their background is?'[38] It's OK for a privileged individual like him to mock working-class people—because working-class single mums really are like this.

No wonder Vicky Pollard has caught the imagination of right-wing class warriors. According to Richard Littlejohn, 'Matt Lucas and David Walliams' Burberried chavs captured perfectly the gruesome reality of so much of our modern landscape.'[39] James Delingpole—who farcically argued that he was a member of the most discriminated-against group in society, 'the white, middle-aged, public-school-and-Oxbridge-educated middle-class male'—was satisfied that 'the Vicky Pollards and the Waynes and Waynettas of our world have got it coming to them. If they weren't quite so repellent, we wouldn't need to make jokes about them, would we?' Indeed, *Little Britain* was funny because it was true:

> The reason Vicky Pollard caught the public imagination is that she embodies with such fearful accuracy several of the great scourges of contemporary Britain: aggressive all-female gangs of embittered, hormonal, drunken teenagers; gym-slip mums who choose to get pregnant as a career option; pasty-faced, lard-gutted slappers who'll drop their knickers in the blink of an eye; dismal ineducables who may not know much about English or History, but can damn well argue their rights with a devious fluency that would shame a barrister from Matrix Chambers.

Above all, 'these people do exist and are every bit as ripe and just a target for social satire as were, say, the raddled working-class drunks set up by Hogarth in Gin Lane.'[40] It was all right for privileged people like James Delingpole to stick it to working-class girls, because they really *were* ugly, thick and sluttish.

It is not just right-wing pundits who think working-class Britain is populated by Vicky Pollards: even the Beeb is guilty. An online news feature entitled 'What is working class?' was illustrated with a photo of

Vicky Pollard and some of her friends. Below was the caption: 'Does Vicky Pollard sum up the working class?' The article did not answer the question, leaving the possibility open for the reader.[41] As LSE researcher Deborah Finding says, 'in laughing at Vicky Pollard—a fat, chain-smoking, single mother—we are expressing our fear and hatred of a group by projecting onto her stereotypical body the perceived qualities of all working-class single mothers—feckless, stupid and promiscuous.'[42]

The problem is not always that TV programmes deliberately set out to smear working-class people. Take *Shameless*, the long-running Channel 4 series focusing on the chaotic Gallagher family, which lives on the fictional Chatsworth Estate in Manchester. The dad is a drunken layabout who has fathered eight kids with two women. Their lives revolve around sex, benefits, crime and drugs. And yet the creator of *Shameless* is Paul Abbott. He is not some bigot from a pampered background who thinks it is funny to point and laugh at the 'oiks'. In fact, he bases the series on his own experiences as a working-class boy growing up in Burnley. In the programme, one of the children ends up going to university; another is in the gifted and talented stream at school.

The problem with the series is that it fails to address how the characters ended up in their situation, or what impact the destruction of industry has had on working-class communities in Manchester. Class becomes a lifestyle choice, and poverty becomes a bit of a joke—not something that imprisons people and shatters their life chances. The series gives a middle-class viewer who has had no real contact with people from different backgrounds little opportunity to understand the broader context behind the issues raised. When I asked journalist Rachel Johnson who she thought the 'underclass' were, she immediately suggested *Shameless*. 'But aren't they fun! Doesn't their life look more fun than our life?' But why is it fun? 'They're just always having a great big paaaaarty!' (For the last bit, she puts on a Mancunian accent).

Paul Abbott's original plan for the series was rather different to how it actually panned out. According to George Faber, the co-founder of

Company Pictures which produces *Shameless*, Abbott's original idea 'was substantially autobiographical, and he wanted to write it as a single film for television. He wrote about half of it. The tone was very downbeat and grim and he said, "This isn't right, is it?" ' So Abbott reworked the script so that, instead of being a gritty adaptation of his experiences, its main purpose was to make people laugh. 'He was able to return to that period of his life and view it through a comedic prism,' says Faber. "And in so doing, *Shameless* was born.' The danger with the finished version is that the viewer is encouraged to laugh at, rather than understand, the lives of the characters.

You can see the confusion that arises among its middle-class viewers. 'Do the real working-class people of this country watch *Shameless*?' asks Kate Wreford on Channel 4's *Shameless* website. 'I am sort of middle class, but I wonder what the real working classes think of it?'[43] On a student forum, one contributor asks if the series is 'an accurate representation of British working-class people today?' One of the replies was straight to the point. 'Yes, many wc [working-class] people are scum. Many drink too much, smoke, steal and lack ambition.'[44] Little wonder that when Robin Nelson, a professor of theatre and TV drama, interviewed working-class viewers of the series, they 'declared their discomfort in watching *Shameless* because they feel they are being invited to laugh at their own class.'[45]

But modern entertainment does not encourage us only to laugh at the chavs. It also wants us to be afraid of them. There is no more extreme example of this than the film *Eden Lake*. The plot is fairly simple. An affluent, photogenic couple from London flee to the countryside for a romantic weekend holiday break. When they see that the idyllic Eden Lake is being transformed into gated communities, they make some right-on comments, wondering whom they are trying to keep out. They find out the hard way why the middle classes have every reason to fear the lower orders.

After the couple stand up to some local, semi-feral, aggressive dog-owning kids, they are mercilessly hunted down and tortured. Under the direction of a psychopathic ringleader, the kids use their mobile phones to film the boyfriend being slashed with knives before his body is burned. But perhaps most disturbing is the role of the parents—waitresses, painters and decorators and so on—who routinely swear and slap their kids about. In a shocking finale, it is they who apparently torture the girlfriend to death after she kills a couple of the 'chavs' in revenge.

When I asked the director, James Watkins, for an interview, I was told that he was 'very flattered ... but he doesn't want to impose any authorial interpretations on *Eden Lake*, preferring instead the widely divergent reactions to the film.' But it is difficult to imagine any other interpretation than that of the *Sun*'s movie critic, who condemned Watkins's 'nasty suggestion that all working-class people are thugs'. Or, for that matter, the *Telegraph*'s conclusion that 'this ugly, witless film expresses fear and loathing of ordinary English people.' Here was a film arguing that the middle classes could no longer live alongside the quasi-bestial lower orders. I cannot put it better than Stephen Pound, one of the few Labour MPs with a background in manual work, who told me:

I genuinely think that there are people out there in the middle classes, in the church and the judiciary and politics and the media, who actually fear, physically *fear* the idea of this great, gold bling-dripping, lum-penproletariat that might one day kick their front door in and eat their au pair.

It may not come as a surprise that the *Daily Mail* treated *Eden Lake* as though it was some sort of drama-documentary, quavering that it was 'all too real' and urging every politician to watch it. One reader of *Time Out* commented that the film 'hits too close to home and will only grow and spread the anger that society holds for the lower classes. I myself and many of my friends have felt the violence from ignorant "children" ... I have to say this without an ounce of regret if the death penalty ever came to this country ... I would support it.'[46] If you have a society as segregated along class lines as our own, and you show films portraying the working class as a bunch of psychopaths, do not be surprised if middle-class people start believing it.

When I asked Stephen Frears if he thought there was a lack of accurate working-class portrayals on our screens, he replied: 'No, because isn't that what soap operas do?' But the soaps have travelled a long way from their origins. Rather than realistically showing how most people live their lives—with drama thrown in, of course—they have become sensationalized and caricatural. Already in the early 1990s, former *EastEnders* scriptwriter David Yallop savaged the show, arguing that it was 'created by middle-class people with a middle-class view of the working class which is patronizing, idealistic and untruthful. It is a dreary show run by dreary people.'[47]

Has it really changed since then? What relationship is there between *EastEnders*—or *Coronation Street* for that matter—and the lives of millions of people working in shops, call centres and offices? Indeed, both soaps have a disproportionate number of small business people, like pub landlords, café owners, market stallholders and shopkeepers. The soaps compete with each other over frankly ludicrous plots: take the effective resurrection of Dirty Den in *EastEnders*, for example.

The film director Ken Loach thinks that, although soaps are set in working-class communities,

> there's a patronizing view of it in that here are people who are quaint and a bit raw and a bit rough and a bit funny. But you sense there is—and I don't think this was the original intention of *Coronation Street*—but there's now a kind of implied middle-class norm which views them and their antics and their fallings out and their fallings in love ... as, well, 'characters'. It's like they're the rude mechanicals in *A Midsummer Night's Dream* when there's always an implied other set of characters who look down on them.

The working class might not get a proper look-in on telly, but the wealthy are spoilt for choice. Switch on *Britain's Dream Homes* or *I Own Britain's Best Home* and watch Melissa Porter and Rhodri Owen saunter round rural Britain ogling country mansions; watch grand properties being restored in *Country House Rescue*; zap over to *A Place in the Sun* and let Amanda Lamb give you a guided tour of wealthy Britons fleeing to buy up in Greece or Crete. Indeed, property programmes like *Relocation, Relocation* and *Property Ladder* are two-a-penny. Above all, posh is mostly certainly in. Watch Old Etonian chef Hugh Fearnley-Whittingstall rustle up an organic treat; be dazzled by the public-school charm of other TV chefs like Valentine Warner and Thomasina Miers; then enjoy the aristocratic Kirstie Allsopp encouraging you to gaze starry-eyed at unaffordable homes.

Too much of our television consists of promotional spiel for the lifestyles, desires and exclusive opportunities of the rich and powerful. It is all part of the redefining of aspiration, persuading us that life is about getting up that ladder, buying a bigger house and car and living it up in some private tropical paradise. It is not just that ordinary people watching these shows are made to feel inadequate. Those who do not strive for such dreams are thought of as 'non-aspirational' or, more bluntly, failures. The hopes and fears of working-class people, their surroundings, their communities, how they earn their living—this does not exist as far as TV is concerned. Where working-class people do appear, it is generally as caricatures invented by wealthy producers and comedians that are then, in turn, appropriated by middle-class journalists for political purposes.

Chav-hate has even trickled into the popular music scene. From the Beatles onwards, working-class bands once dominated rock, and indie music in particular: the Stone Roses, the Smiths, Happy Mondays and the Verve, to take a few popular examples. But it is difficult to name any prominent working-class bands since the heyday of Oasis in the mid 1990s: it is middle-class bands like Coldplay or Keane that now rule the roost in music. 'There has been a noticeable drift towards middle-class values in the music business,' says Mark Chadwick, the lead singer of rock band the Levellers. 'Working-class bands seem to be few and far between.' Instead there's an abundance of middle-class impersonations of working-class caricatures, such as the 'mockney' style of artists like Damon Albarn and Lily Allen.

The Kaiser Chiefs made a name for themselves with the sort of repetitive indie anthem that lends itself to drunken chanting in a club. Listen carefully to their lyrics, however, and you discover pure class bile. Take 'I Predict a Riot': 'I tried to get to my taxi / A man in a tracksuit attacked me / He said that he saw it before me / Wants to get things a bit gory / Girls scrabble around with no clothes on / To borrow a pound for a condom / If it wasn't for chip fat, they'd be frozen / They're not very sensible.' The last lines reproduce the caricature of the undignified, 'slapper' chav girl.

Working-class people have become objects of ridicule, disapproval and, yes, hatred. Welcome to the world of British entertainment in the early twenty-first century.

The contempt for working-class people that built up under Thatcherism had reached its terrible zenith in the Hillsborough Disaster. Today, football continues to offer clues to the dramatic change in attitudes over the past three decades. By looking at what has happened to the traditional sporting passion of working-class Britain, we can get a good idea of the cultural impact of chav-hate. The 'beautiful game' has been transformed beyond recognition.

Although major clubs shifted away from their origins long ago— for example, Manchester United was founded by railwaymen—they remained deeply rooted in working-class communities. Footballers were generally boys plucked from the club's local area. Unlike the spoiled plutocrats that some Premier League players have become, for much of the twentieth century 'footballers were often worse off than the crowds watching them from the terraces on a Saturday,' as footballer Stuart Imlach's son has written.[48] Back in the early 1950s, there was a maximum salary for players of just £14 a week during the season—not very much over the average manual wage—and only one in five players were lucky enough to earn that. Players lived in 'tied cottages' —houses owned by clubs from which they could be evicted at any moment. Little wonder one footballer, speaking at the 1955 Trades Union Congress, complained that 'the conditions of the professional footballer's employment are akin to slavery.'

Football has gone from one extreme to another. The cold winds of free-market economics had largely been kept out of the football world during the 1980s. In the 1990s, they hit with a vengeance. In 1992, the twenty-two clubs of the old First Division broke away to establish the Premier League, freeing them from the requirement to share revenues with clubs in the rest of the League. Part of the new commercial ethos was to keep many working-class people out of the stadium. In its *Blueprint for the Future of Football*, the Football Association argued that the game must attract 'more affluent middle-class consumers'.[49]

When the old terraces were abolished after the Hillsborough Disaster, the cheaper standing tickets disappeared. Between 1990 and 2008, the price of the average football ticket rose by 600 per cent, well over seven times the rate of everything else.[50] This was completely unaffordable for many working-class people. But some senior football figures were not only aware of this—they even celebrated it. As former England manager Terry Venables put it:

> Without wishing to sound snobbish or to be disloyal to my own working-class background, the increase in admission prices is likely to exclude the sort of people who were giving English football a bad name. I am talking about the young men, mostly working-class, who terrorized football grounds, railway trains, cross-channel ferries and towns and cities throughout England and Europe.

The demonization of working-class people was being used to justify hiking up ticket prices and, in the process, to keep them out.

At the same time, football became big money—and big business. In the early 1990s, Rupert Murdoch's BSkyB signed an agreement to pay £305 million for exclusive rights to the new FA Carling Premiership. In 1997 they signed another four-year deal, with a £670 million price tag. Not only are huge numbers of working-class people financially barred from stadiums: many cannot even watch their team play unless they splash out on a Sky box. Meanwhile, the huge amount of money sloshing about in the game has severed football teams from their local communities. Huge transfer fees mean that players from hundreds or thousands of miles away dominate the major teams. Clubs have become the playthings of American asset-strippers and Russian oligarchs. And, with players paid up to £160,000 a week, they are completely divorced from their working-class roots. Labour MP Stephen Pound mourns the loss of this working-class icon. 'If you look at the working-class heroes —people like Frank Lampard and David Beckham—what's the first thing they do? They move out of the working-class areas into Cheshire or Surrey. The role models don't have the confidence to stick with it.'

It is the ultimate insult. A game that was at the centre of working-class identity for so long has been transformed into a middle-class consumer good controlled by billionaire carpetbaggers. Caricaturing all working-class fans as aggressive hooligans intent on mindless violence has provided the excuse to keep them out.

Football was identified as a potentially lucrative piece of working-class culture, so it was taken away and repackaged. But in today's Britain, nothing about working-class life is considered worthy or admirable. ' "Working class" is no longer a term that can be qualified with the word "respectable", because it is now almost wholly a subtly loaded insult,' wrote the journalist Deborah Orr. 'The term carries with it implications of the worst sort of conservative, retrogressive values.'[51]

None of the chav-bashing we've explored can be understood in isolation. It is part and parcel of an offensive against everything associated with the working class, started by Thatcherism and cemented by New Labour. 'I think culture reflects politics,' says Ken Loach. 'There was a major shift ... during the Thatcher years. ... It was the era of "loads of money", it was the era of "look after number one", all the jewellery, the City Boys with their red braces—it was a worship of capital.' This vanquishing of working-class Britain had inevitable cultural consequences. 'So, after that, the trade unions were diminished, working-class culture was diminished, celebration of working-class culture was diminished —but it stemmed from that political moment,' Loach says.

> A great hero of working-class culture was [left-wing theatre director] Joan Littlewood. And she put on plays at Stratford East, they were probably some of the best theatre we've ever produced. Original, anarchic, humorous, humane, funny, rumbustious; but a great sense of empowerment for working-class people in politics. It's impossible to imagine something like that in the aftermath of the Thatcher regime.

Everything is to be judged by middle-class standards because, after all, that is what we are expected to aspire to. The working class is therefore portrayed as a useless vestige made up of 'non-aspirational' layabouts, slobs, racists, boozers, thugs—you name it.

It is both tragic and absurd that, as our society has become less equal and as in recent years the poor have actually got poorer, resentment against those at the bottom has positively increased. Chav-hate is a way of justifying an unequal society. What if you have wealth and success because it has been handed to you on a plate? What if people are poorer than you because the odds are stacked against them? To accept this would trigger a crisis of self-confidence among the well-off few. And if you were to accept it, then surely you would have to accept that the government's duty is to do something about it—namely, by curtailing your own privileges. But, if you convince yourself that the less fortunate are smelly, thick, racist and rude by nature, then it is only right they should remain at the bottom. Chav-hate justifies the preservation of the pecking order, based on the fiction that it is actually a fair reflection of people's worth.

To what extent is chav-hate just a new wave of old-style snobbery, rebranded for the twenty-first century? Snobbery certainly comes into it. Just look at the mocking of the tracksuit-and-bling style popular among some working-class people, especially teenagers. It is true that people's backgrounds often define how they dress. Walk into the bar of Oxford University's debating society, the Oxford Union, and you will see a crowd of public-school types wearing bow ties, tweed jackets and pink cords. There is even a chance you will spot the odd one with a pipe in hand. You might think that people in tracksuits or people in tweeds look pretty silly—but who cares? Or, alternatively, why *should* we care?

But the reality is that chav-hate is a lot more than snobbery. It is class war. It is an expression of the belief that everyone should become middle class and embrace middle-class values and lifestyles, leaving those who don't to be ridiculed and hated. It is about refusing to acknowledge anything of worth in working-class Britain, and systematically ripping it to shreds in newspapers, on TV, on Facebook, and in general conversation. This is what the demonization of the working class means.

The caricatures thrown up by chav-hate have other consequences. Coupled with the ludicrous mainstream political view that Britain is now a classless society, the 'chav' phenomenon obscures what it means to be working class today. The myth that British society is divided between an affluent middle-class majority and a declining working-class rump has airbrushed the reality of class in Britain today. An overwhelmingly middle-class political and media establishment has been more than happy to foster this image. That is not to say that the working class has not been changed dramatically by the Thatcherite crusade. It's time to look beyond the Vicky Pollards, chav bops and reality TV shows, and ask: 'What is the working class in twenty-first century Britain?'

5

'We're all middle class now'

To say that class doesn't matter in Britain is like saying wine doesn't matter in France; or whether you're a man or a woman doesn't matter in Saudi Arabia.

—Nick Cohen

Is the working class no more? Tony Blair certainly thinks so. His one-time senior advisor Matthew Taylor recalls the former prime minister proudly announcing that 'we're all middle class' at a think-tank event when he was still Labour leader. Some of our newspapers are inclined to agree. 'We're all middle class now, darling,' echoed the *Daily Telegraph*. Or, as *The Times* put it, 'We're all middle class now as social barriers fall away.' The *Daily Mail* goes into greater detail: 'You might say that there are now three main classes in Britain: a scarily alienated underclass; the new and confident middle class, set free by the Thatcher revolution ... and a tiny, and increasingly powerless, upper class.'[1]

The chav caricature has obscured the reality of the modern working class. We are fed the impression of a more or less comfortable 'Middle England' on the one hand, while on the other the old working class has degenerated into a hopeless chav rump.

It certainly used to be easier to answer the question: 'Who is the working class?' When the historian David Kynaston was writing his book on post-war Britain, *Austerity Britain*, he had no trouble identifying the three emblematic occupations of the 1950s. 'They were, in no particular order, miners, dockers, and car workers.' But, partly because of the ruinous economic policies of successive governments, the mines have closed, the docks are deserted, and most of the car factories are empty husks. As these old pillars of working-class Britain crumble, it has become easier for politicians and pundits to claim that we really are all middle class now.

The long, lingering demise of the industrial working class began but did not end with Thatcher. The *Guardian* economics editor Larry Elliott points to the three major culls of British industry: the early 1980s, the early 1990s, and the current recession. 'All of them have been caused by bubbles bursting and by macro-economic mistakes. We were told after the first cull in the 1980s that British industry was leaner and fitter. Then there was another cull in the early 1990s, and we were told after that that British industry was ready to meet the world—and then there was another cull.'

When New Labour swept to power in 1997, manufacturing made up more than a fifth of the economy. A paltry 12 per cent was all that was left by the time Tony Blair left office in 2007. Back in 1979, there were nearly 7 million people working in factories, but today's number is just over 2.5 million.

The policies of governments besotted with City slickers must take much of the blame. 'Labour bought into the whole myth of the boom in the financial sector and the City,' says Elliott. Like previous Tory governments, New Labour presided over an overvalued exchange rate, rendering our manufacturing goods deeply uncompetitive abroad. 'It paid lip service to its old industrial base, but did absolutely nothing to help it, and in fact actually made things a lot worse for the manufacturing sector.'

With all the talk about the 'information economy' and a country where more people work in pop music than down the mines, it is easy to overstate the point. Nearly four out of every ten men are still manual workers. But there is no denying an obvious trend. Industrial occupations are vanishing with every passing year.

Already embattled sectors suffered yet more crippling blows at the hands of the Great Recession of 2008. The crisis may have been caused by the greed of bankers, but manufacturing paid the price. It lost well over twice the proportion of jobs as finance and business services in the first year of the crisis. The City's share of the economy has actually grown since 2005, leaving us more dependent on the part of the economy that caused the crash in the first place. As former City economist Graham Turner puts it, it is 'a staggering outcome of this credit crunch'.

With industrial jobs steadily drying up, it might seem bizarre that the British public stubbornly continues to self-identify as working class. Matthew Taylor recalls reactions to Blair's 'we're all middle class' speech: 'It was quickly pointed out that, interestingly, more people in Britain call themselves working class now than did in 1950.' Opinion polls show that over half the population consistently describes itself as working class, but one poll in 1949 recorded it as just 43 per cent.[2] That was a time when there were a million miners, most people worked in manual jobs and rationing was still in full swing. In the era of de-industrialization, how can most people honestly regard themselves as working class?

You could be forgiven for thinking that there is an identity crisis going on. Multi-millionaire businessman Mohamed Al Fayed once described himself as working class. I have heard of stockbrokers with telephone number salaries who ask with faux puzzlement: 'I work, don't I? So why aren't I working class?'

If you look at the polling numbers, it is true that some people in the top socio-economic category describe themselves as working class. Equally, some in the bottom category think that they are middle class. This triggered my curiosity. When I asked a childhood friend, whom I considered indisputably working class, if he agreed with that characterization, he was almost affronted. 'Maybe in terms of income, but middle class in terms of things like education.' He felt that being working class meant being *poor*, while being middle class meant being *educated*.

The vilification of all things working class seems to have had a real impact on people's attitudes. In the run-up to the 2010 general election, the *Guardian* journalist Simon Hattenstone asked a former bus driver, who had retired in 1981 on £50 a week, which class he belonged to. 'Middle class,' he said after a bit of thought. Why? 'Well, I'm not down on my uppers. If I was on my uppers I'd call myself working class, and I always worked for a living.' He associated being working class with being broke. As Hattenstone put it: 'It's not just for the politicians that the term working class has become pejorative.'[3]

With so much confusion about class, what *does* it mean to be working class? When I put this question to New Labour ex-Cabinet minister James Purnell, he thought a big part of the answer was 'cultural identity' and 'a sense of history and a sense of place'. He represented the northern working-class constituency of Stalybridge and Hyde where, he said, people lived in '*Coronation Street* rows of houses' and 'where I think people think of themselves as working class because of the community where they grew up, and things they do together and all the shared understandings which come from being from a particular place.'

I grew up in Stockport, a few miles from Purnell's former constituency, and a sense of place, shared community and common values certainly were a major part of many people's working-class identities. People grew up with each other; mixed groups of families and friends would do things together, like watching football in the pub; and people felt rooted in a community that they and their families had lived in all their lives. The younger generation would often move only a few blocks away from where they grew up, and they still went out on the town on a Friday night with friends they had known since they were born.

But the reality is that this sense of rootedness has been breaking down for a long time, partly because of the collapse of industry. Entire working-class communities used to be based around a particular factory, steelworks, or mine. Most of the men would work at the same place. Their fathers and their grandfathers may well have worked there and done similar jobs. When industries disappeared, the communities they sustained became fragmented. As Purnell puts it, the working class is no longer made up of 'a whole bunch of men who left the house at the same time to go to broadly the same factory, and then socialize broadly in the same way'.

It is often tempting to think of class in terms of income. So, you could stick a 'working-class' label on someone earning £14,000 a year, and a 'middle-class' label on someone earning £60,000. Yet there are small businessmen—who, after all, live off their profits—who might only make a few grand. A well-paid skilled worker could be getting twice as much as a shopkeeper brings home.

Another challenge to the existence of the working class came from the almost religious fervour with which Tory and New Labour governments have promoted home ownership. Thatcherism certainly saw it as a means of breaking down class identity. Thatcher's right-hand man, Keith Joseph, described the aim as to resume 'the forward march of *embourgeoisement* [becoming bourgeois] which went so far in Victorian times'. Clearly home ownership has promoted individualism, or even a sense of 'everyone for themselves', including among some working-class homeowners. But the fact that millions of people have had to borrow beyond their means, sooner than pay an affordable rent below extortionate market rates.

Alan Walter, the late chair of Defend Council Housing who never lived in any other kind, spoke of working-class homeowners 'now scared out of their wits about whether they'll be able to keep mortgage payments up. The number of people who go to bed every night and have nightmares about getting repossessed is a major issue.' The living standards of some working-class people are lower than they would have been if they were paying cheap council rents rather than often very expensive mortgages. Indeed, over half the people living in poverty are homeowners. There are actually more homeowners in the bottom 10 per cent (or decile) than there are in each of the two deciles above it. As we know, encouraging so many people to take on unaffordable levels of debt had a detonator role in the credit crunch. In any case, as more and more people have become priced out of home ownership, it has gone into reverse: peaking at 71 per cent in 2002–03 and falling back to 68 per cent six years later.

If it is not community, income or living arrangements that defines the working class, what is it? Neil Kinnock may be the Labour leader who laid the foundations for the party's dramatic swing to the right, but he still feels most comfortable with how Karl Marx put it. 'I'd use the broad definition—I always have: people who have no means of sustenance other than the sale of labour, are working class.' This is very clear: the working class as a catch-all term for people who labour for others. When I asked Birmingham supermarket worker Mary Lynch which class she belonged to, she had no doubt that it was the working class. 'I just feel we're working just to pay our way all the time.' These must be the starting points of understanding what 'working class' means: the class of people who work for others in order to get by in life.

But it's only a start. Is a Cambridge don really in the same category as a supermarket checkout worker? The important qualification to add is not only those who sell their labour, but those who lack autonomy, or control over this labour. Both a university professor and a retail employee must work to survive; but a professor has huge power over their everyday activity, while a shop assistant does not. A professor does have broad parameters within which they must work, but there is ample room for creativity and the ability to set their own tasks. A shop worker has a set of very narrowly defined tasks with little variation, and must carry them out according to specific instructions.

A look at the statistics uncovers the working-class majority. Over eight million of us still have manual jobs, and another eight million are clerks, secretaries, sales assistants and in other personal and customer-service jobs. That adds up to well over half the workforce, and still excludes teachers, health workers such as nurses, and train drivers, who are assigned to categories such as 'professional occupations'.

Although income is not the deciding factor, there is a link between the sort of job you do and the money you get. A median-income household receives just £21,000. This is the exact midpoint, meaning that half the population earns less. Here is the real Middle Britain, not the mythical 'Middle England' invented by media pundits and politicians that really refers to the affluent voter.

Most people work for others, and lack control over their own labour. But many of them are no longer toiling away in factories and mines. The last three decades have seen the dramatic rise of a new service-sector working class. Their jobs are cleaner and less physically arduous, but often of a lower status, insecure, and poorly paid. 'In terms of the world that we now live in,' says Mark Serwotka, leader of the Public and Commercial Services (PCS) union, 'and I look at our members, I think the jobs that working-class people do are changing and quite clearly now there aren't miners, there aren't big steelworks in the way there was when I was growing up. But in the new industries, I think we actually see exploitation of working people on a par if not greater than we've ever seen before.'

Mary Cunningham, a fifty-five-year-old supermarket worker in Newcastle, is a child of the old industrial working class. Her father was a miner until the pits closed. She left school in the middle of O-levels to look after her dying mother, although school wasn't for her in any case. Her first job was working on 'the old, press-down tills' at the now defunct Woolworth's, and she remembers being there when decimalization came to replace the old pounds, shillings and pence in 1971.

Mary is an important part of the puzzle of modern working-class Britain. Supermarket workers like her, derided as 'chavs' by websites like ChavTowns, are one of the chief components of the new working class. Retail is the second biggest employer in the country, with nearly three million people working in British shops: that's more than one in ten workers, and a threefold increase since 1980.

Shop work used to be seen as quite a genteel profession, staffed mostly by middle-class women. It has changed dramatically. In the old industrial heartlands, the supermarket has been hoovering up people who once worked in factories—or would have done if it was still an option. 'I would say that the supermarket now is the biggest employer —it's taken over from factories and industries,' Mary says. As well as men from the steel industry, men 'from the factories are coming now into retail and sitting on the checkouts, because there's nothing much else really … We have people in our stores who are qualified to do better jobs than they're doing, but they're just glad they're in employment.'

Like Mary, the majority of shop workers are women—in fact, nearly two-thirds of them. 'There's a lot of housewives, obviously. There's also young mothers who are tying it in with picking their children up from school, a lot of them single mothers.' Retail has changed as it has expanded. 'I think in the latter few years it has got worse, got harder,' Mary says. 'When I started, you could have a little bit of time with the customer, and get to know your customer, you had your regulars that came to you because you had that little bit of rapport with them. Now it's get on with the job, you have to have targets … you're supposed to get through so many customers an hour.' Retail is becoming increasingly automated, to resemble old-style mass production in a factory.

Supermarket workers like Mary are often at the mercy of autocratic or abusive managers. Mary and some of her colleagues were forced to lodge a complaint against one: 'If you work with her, she'll bang her fist on the counter and say "why isn't that done?" in front of customers, and she has grown women that daren't approach her … She costs the company money because of all the retraining, everyone wants to be off that department, or they leave.'

The bullying doesn't just come from managers. According to the shop workers' union USDAW, up to half a million shop workers endure verbal abuse from customers every day. Little wonder that one survey showed that nearly a fifth of retail staff were prepared to jump ship for the same or slightly less money.[4] According to USDAW, the average staff turnover for shop workers is 62 per cent a year.

And then there's the pay. If you work on a checkout in Mary's supermarket, you can expect to make just £6.12 an hour. Lunch is unpaid.

This is pretty standard: indeed, fully half of retail workers earn less than £7 an hour. Shop workers face arbitrary attacks on these already poor wages and conditions. Less than two years into the economic crisis that began in 2007, one in four retail and sales workers had their pay slashed. Nearly a third had their hours cut, and over a fifth lost benefits.[5]

If you think shop workers have it bad, consider now the call centre worker. There are now nearly a million people working in call centres, and the number is going up every year. To put that in perspective, there were a million men down the pits at the peak of mining in the 1940s. If the miner was one of the iconic jobs of post-war Britain, then today, surely, the call centre worker is as good a symbol of the working class as any.

'Call centres are a very regimented environment,' says John McInally, a trade unionist leading efforts by the PCS to unionize call centre workers. 'It's rows of desks with people sitting with headphones. There's loads of people in the room, but they're separate units. They're encouraged not to talk, share experiences, and so on ... The minute you get in the door, your movements are regulated by the computer.' Here is the lack of worker's autonomy in the workplace taken to extremes.

In some call centres he has dealt with, a worker in Bristol or Glasgow who wants to leave fifteen minutes early has to go through head office in Sheffield to be cleared. 'We've likened conditions to those you'd have seen in mills or factories at the end of the nineteenth century.' Think that's an exaggeration? Then consider the fact that, in some call centres, workers have to put their hands up to go to the toilet. Computers dictate the time and duration of breaks, with no flexibility whatsoever. Employees are under constant monitoring and surveillance, driving up stress levels.

Many call centre workers have told McInally that the whole experience is 'very dehumanizing. People talk about being treated like robots. Everything is regulated by machines.' The working lives of many operators consist of reading through the same script over and over again.

According to the Royal College of Speech and Language Therapists, increasing numbers of call centre workers are being referred to speech therapists because they are losing their voices. The cause? Working long hours with little opportunity to even have a drink of water.

That's one reason why the sickness rate in call centres is nearly twice the national average. The other is deep alienation from the work. In one call centre McInally dealt with in Northern England, sickness rates had reached nearly 30 per cent. 'That's a sign of low morale,' he says—as is the fact that annual staff turnover is around a quarter of the workforce. And, like so much of the new working class, the salaries of call centre workers are poor. A trainee can expect £12,500, while the higher-grade operators are on an average of just £16,000.

Twenty-eight-year-old Carl Leishman has been a call centre worker in County Durham for eight years. For seven of those, he worked in a bank's call centre; today he is with a phone company. He works bruising twelve-hour shifts, three days on and three days off. 'I would probably have started off life as middle class,' he says of his upbringing. 'But the way I am now—and obviously the wage I get paid—I would say that I'm down to working class. That sounds awful, but …!'

At his previous job, stiff targets had to be met. Four per cent of his working hours were set aside for needs like going to the toilet or getting a drink. 'You'd get ratings at the end of each month, and if you'd gone above those percentages, then your rating would drop, affecting in the end what bonuses and pay rises you were getting.' Carl didn't need to go to the toilet too often—'whereas some other people, like pregnant women, could really struggle to stick to that.'

He describes the training at his current job as 'woefully inadequate', particularly when it comes to dealing with abusive customers who, he says, are a daily occurrence. His employers have a no-hang-up policy, even if the customer is swearing or being aggressive. 'You'll see quite often on the floor people in tears at the way people have spoken to them,' he says. It is a job that can have consequences for your health, too. 'Your throat gets incredibly dry. There are people I've known

148

whose throats have gone from doing it. A lady I used to work with had to actually leave because her voice was just completely shot.'

At the core of his experience at work is the lack of control over what he does. 'We're set in rows, which I hate, to be honest. It can sometimes feel very much like a chicken factory, as though you don't have too much control over what you're doing: "This is the way you're doing things, and that's it, deal with it, because that's the way it is, don't think outside the box" ... You don't need to think for yourself too much.' Little wonder that Carl says that 'one of the most fulfilling things is when you do get a bit of time off the phone. But trying to balance that with obviously getting the customer serviced is nigh on impossible sometimes.' His current employer does offer things like a television in the break room, and free teas and coffees: but these do not offset the basic alienation Carl feels from his job.

Carl's salary is just £14,400 a year. When the Conservative-led government announced that it would hike up VAT, it was the last straw and he decided he had no choice but to move back in with his parents. Does he think he is paid too little? 'For the grief you get, definitely! It's one of those jobs that you've got to put up with the abuse of customers and long hours as well, which can be hard work. But I think, definitely, the wages aren't representative of the amount of work you put in.'

Both Mary and Carl work with a number of part-time and temporary staff. Their numbers have soared over the last thirty years as successive governments have striven to create a 'flexible' workforce. In part, they have made it far easier and cheaper for bosses to hire and fire workers at will. But we have also been witnessing the slow death of the secure, full-time job. There are up to 1.5 million temporary workers in Britain. A 'temp' can be hired and fired at an hour's notice, be paid less for doing the same job, and lacks rights such as paid holidays and redundancy pay.

Agency work is thriving in the service sector, but an incident at a car plant near Oxford in early 2009 illustrates where the rise of the temp has brought us. Eight hundred and fifty temps—many of whom had worked in the factory for years—were sacked by BMW with just one hour's notice. Sacking agency workers was, of course, the cheapest option because the company did not have to give them any redundancy pay. The workers, with no means of defending themselves from this calamity, resorted to pelting managers with apples and oranges. 'It's a disgrace, I feel as though I've been used,' said one.[6]

It is not just agency and temporary workers who suffer because of job insecurity and outrageous terms and conditions. Fellow workers are forced to compete with people who can be hired far more cheaply. Everyone's wages are pushed down as a result. This is the 'race to the bottom' of pay and conditions.

It might sound like a throwback to the Victorian era, but this could be the future for millions of workers as businesses exploit economic crisis for their own ends. In a document entitled *The Shape of Business—The Next Ten Years*, the Confederation of British Industry (CBI)—which represents major employers—claimed that the crash was the catalyst for a new era in business. The document called for the creation of an even more 'flexible' workforce, which would mean firms employing a smaller core of permanent workers and a larger, fluctuating 'flexiforce'. This means even more temporary workers deprived of basic rights and conditions, who can be hired and fired at a moment's notice. Indeed, one survey in 2010 found that nearly nine out of ten businesses would either be maintaining or increasing their use of temporary workers.

The other striking feature of the new working class is the rise of the part-time worker. Over a quarter of Britain's workforce now works part-time, one of the highest levels in Europe. The number has soared during the recession as sacked full-time workers are forced to take up part-time work to make ends meet, helping to keep unemployment figures down. For example, figures released in December 2009 showed that the number of people in work had started to rise despite the recession. But, of the 50,000 new jobs, the majority were part-time—'confirming the gradual trend towards "casualised" working', as the *Independent* reported. 'Full-time work is still falling, driven by continued job losses in manufacturing and construction,' according to Ian Brinkley, associate director at The Work Foundation.[7]

When I discussed the rise of the hire-and-fire service sector with leading Tory MP David Davis, he was soothingly sceptical. 'There's no real reason to believe that, let's say, Sainsbury's would have any less job security than somebody working in Ford. It's the reverse in many ways, because they're growing. So I think the hire-and-fire idea— you've just run past me a piece of Old Labour mythology, frankly. The idea that the only good jobs are ones where you have to lift a half-ton weight every day is unmitigated crap.' But the evidence contradicts him: every passing day sees the further consolidation of a hire-and-fire workforce in Britain.

Many of the new jobs are not only more insecure than the ones they've replaced; the pay is often worse. According to 2008 figures, half of all service sector workers were on less than £20,000 a year. But the median in manufacturing was £24,343, or nearly a quarter more. A recent example illustrates how well-paid manufacturing jobs are being replaced by a stingier service sector. When Longbridge carmaker MG Rover went bust in 2005, 6,300 jobs went to the wall. The median annual income of the workers in their new jobs was just £18,728, a fifth less than the £24,000 they were earning back at Rover. For the third or so lucky enough to stay in the manufacturing sector, wages had stayed more or less the same. But, for the 60 per cent now in the service sector, earnings were considerably less.[8]

It is the same story in other areas hit by the destruction of industry— old mining regions, for example. 'Obviously the new jobs are cleaner than working down a mine,' says former Nottinghamshire miner Adrian Gilfoyle. 'But the money is worse. We used to be on bonuses and all sorts for cutting coal, and you used to earn really good money. Now you're lucky if you bring in £200 a week. And with the cost of living nowadays, it's not a lot of money.'

As Eilís Lawlor of the New Economics Foundation expressed it to me, the disappearance of skilled jobs is creating a 'missing middle'.

'We've seen a polarization of the labour market, as relatively well-paid manufacturing jobs are replaced by less well-paid jobs in the service sector,' she says. Others call it the 'hourglass' economy: highly paid jobs at one end, and swelling numbers of low-paid, unskilled jobs at the other. The middle-level occupations, on the other hand, are shrinking.

Hairdressing is an example of a booming low-paid service sector job. It's one of the worst-paid jobs in Britain: the median salary for a female stylist is less than £12,000.[9] There are over 170,000 hairdressers in Britain today.[10] Other rapidly expanding low-paid jobs include data input, security guards, receptionists, care assistants and cleaners. These low-paid jobs are the only ones on offer for growing numbers of workers who, in a different time, would have taken up a middle-level job with relatively good pay.

'It wasn't just that manufacturing was wiped out. I mean, in London we used to have a million and a quarter manufacturing jobs, now it's just over 200,000—that's mainly high-end printing,' says former London mayor Ken Livingstone. 'But there's a whole layer of really well-paid jobs in the utilities which, as they were privatized, were all wiped out. And so, for a working-class person, the jobs have been dramatically narrowed.'

One of the things that distinguished the old industrial working class was a strong trade union movement to fight its corner. Back in the late 1970s, over half of all workers were union members. Today unions remain the biggest civil society organizations in the country, but their membership has steeply declined from thirteen million in 1979 to just over seven million today. The decline becomes even starker when you consider that, while over half of public sector workers are union members, the same is true of only 15 per cent in the private sector. The new service sector jobs are more or less a union-free zone.

Thatcher's pummelling of the unions certainly goes a long way toward explaining this weakness. As former Labour Cabinet minister Tony Benn points out, the laws 'are more restrictive on trade union rights than they were a hundred years ago'. Their presence on the statute books puts Britain in violation of its obligations as a signatory to International Labour Organization conventions. Not only do they make it difficult for unions to organize in the workplace, the laws also prevent them from fighting on behalf of their members. Unite was taken to court by British Airways in 2010, over a long-running dispute with cabin crew. Despite eight out of ten workers voting for strike action on the back of a 78 per cent turnout, the judge banned the strike. Why? Because the union had failed to give notice by text message that eleven out of 9,282 votes had been spoilt.

Industrial relations specialist Professor Gregor Gall is right to point out that unions were stronger in manufacturing because of 'the time in which unionization occurred. This was an era of greater union and worker rights, far more progressive public policy and law and less powerful employers.' The dog-eat-dog individualism unleashed by Thatcherism also undermined the collective spirit at the heart of trade unionism. And it is more difficult for unions to put down roots in the transient service sector. Factories with hundreds of workers who were there for the long haul were simply easier to organize.

'There are huge challenges,' says Jennie Formby, the national officer for Unite's food, drink and hospitality sector:

> It is very difficult to organize in hotels and restaurants and pubs because there are thousands of them. How do you actually have a concentrated campaign to cover every site? There's a very high turnover of labour and large numbers of migrant workers without English as their first language, particularly in hotels, so it is harder to deliver a sustainable organizing campaign. It is much easier for us to organize factory workers, for example in meat and poultry processing factories—where we've been extremely successful over recent years in organizing thousands of predominantly migrant workers—than it is to organize the often almost invisible workforce who work in their thousands in Britain's hotel sector.

She recalls the very successful Unite-led campaign to stop employers counting tips as part of their workers' wages. Among the obstacles that the union was up against were the very real threats many workers faced from their employers if they engaged in any kind of union activity, or spoke out about the exploitation they were suffering. Some were threatened with disciplinary action, including outright dismissal. 'Our members were basically being robbed of their earnings that customers had chosen to give to them to reflect the good service they had received, but companies saw it as a huge threat to their income if the legislation was changed, as they were making millions out of short-changing these hard-working and low-paid restaurant workers,' Formby says. 'However, successful as the tips campaign has been in winning for our members, it was actually more about lobbying government and getting changes in the law than it was about organizing workers.'

Mary Cunningham's supermarket boasts a good union presence. When she took over as union rep there were only fifty-one members, but now it has reached 400. This is a testament to her organizational drive. But as she says herself, this is rare. Since 1996, the percentage of union members in retail has never reached 12 per cent. Not a lot, it would seem—but pretty high by service sector standards. Because of the turnover, Mary says, 'you're recruiting just to stand still. You might recruit thirty people in a matter of months, but by that time people have left—you're losing them all the time ... Obviously when you get successes, it's easier to recruit, so when people can say, "Mary did this, and a worker got their job back"—that's a positive thing, and people say, "Oh, I think I'll join." '

Again, Mary does not lack stories of management clamping down on unions. 'At one big company that's been around for years, I had a hundred people wanting to join the union. I had a meeting off the premises with two ladies, and they took a hundred forms back and most of them were filled in, until the company found out about it and said anybody that filled a form in on the premises, or caught with a form, would be disciplined.'

After three decades of persecution, unions are no longer part of workplace culture—and that is particularly true in the service sector. 'A lot of people these days don't even know what a union is about,' says Mary. 'Which is sad, really.'

John McInally has been leading valiant attempts by the PCS union to organize call centre workers. He believes that there are real grounds for optimism, because of one key similarity between call centres and old-style factories: large numbers of workers concentrated in one place. But he has no illusions about the obstacles that are in the way, not least because of how regimented the work is. 'You could have four hundred people in a room, or a couple of rooms, who may see each other every day but never speak to each other,' he says. Just as factory workers were stuck at their looms in Victorian times, call centre workers are stuck at their desks. There is one major difference, though: unlike Victorian workers who could shout to each other over their looms, call centre workers have earphones plugged in all day and so are prevented from communicating. 'People are treated like units of production, unlike factories where there is a more organic interaction between people.'

Some unions that have been prepared to take action to defend their members have grown, like the transport workers' union the National Union of Rail, Maritime and Transport Workers, and a handful of others. But the reality is that unions continue to shrink in number and barely exist in the service sector. What is particularly scandalous is that those who most need unions are the least represented. According to the 2008 Labour Force Survey, less than 15 per cent of workers earning less than £7 an hour are union members. For those on between £15 and £20 an hour, the proportion is well over four in ten.

It is not the unpopularity of trade unionism that is to blame for its crippled state. According to a poll conducted by union group Unions 21, around half of non-unionized workers think that unions have a future, compared to 31 per cent who think they do not. While women were most likely not to join because of the cost, for men the biggest turn-off was a sense that unions did not achieve anything. According to Trades Union Congress organizing officer Carl Roper, unions had not done enough to recruit in the private sector: 'There doesn't seem to be a union approach to how we look at those workers.'[11]

It is not just that the failure of unions to recruit low-paid and moderately paid service sector workers condemns them to poor wages and conditions. It undermines the collective identity of working-class people. It deprives them of a voice, leaving millions of people virtually invisible and without a means to articulate their concerns and aspirations, which can be easily ignored by politicians and journalists alike. Furthermore, it helps to consolidate the idea that you can only improve your lot through your own individual efforts and that, accordingly, those in poorly paid jobs deserve their lot.

The weakening of trade unions goes a long way to explaining why workers' pay stagnated even during the boom years. The huge sums being made benefited mostly the bosses, because of the lack of an organized force to win a share of the spoils for the millions working some of the longest hours in Europe. Similarly, this lack of pressure from below explains how workers' rights have been chipped away, one by one.

Even before the recession hit, the wages of working-class Britain were going nowhere fast. In 2005, for example, company profits were the highest since records began, but workers suffered a hit to their weekly earnings of nearly half a percent. The income of the bottom half flatlined after 2004; for the bottom third, it actually went into reverse.[12] Following the crash in 2008, wage freezes became the norm as workers were left to pick up the tab for a crisis caused by the greed of wealthy bankers. The 9.4 million people in low-income households had nothing to fall back on in hard times. The decline in their income is all the more shocking because it happened under a Labour government. Compare and contrast with the much-maligned Labour administrations of the 1960s, when the poorest 10 per cent saw their real income go up by 29 per cent, compared to the 16 per cent increase enjoyed by everyone else.

New Labour loyalist and former Cabinet minister Hazel Blears admits that life got harder for working-class people. She argues that the government was trying to 'square a circle', fearing that intervening too much to help struggling workers would make Britain 'uncompetitive' and throw people out of work. 'As ever in politics it's about striking the balance, and sometimes you get that balance right, and sometimes you get it wrong.' But she concedes that, in New Labour's later years,

> just getting on day-to-day for a lot of working-class people became increasingly difficult. You're either on short-time, your wages were depressed, things that you had enjoyed—like taking your family out to eat once a week, going to the pictures, going on holiday—began to be very difficult. And the quality of life, I think, in some families just became work and sleep, work and sleep, with no fun at all.

What makes all of this so spectacularly unfair is that workers' wages have stagnated even as their productivity has steadily gone up. In the past, growing productivity has translated into rising wages. But the annual increase in productivity has been twice that of wages in twenty-first-century Britain. Overall, wages represent a much smaller slice of the economy following the ravages of Thatcherism. Nearly two-thirds of the nation's wealth went on wages back in 1973. Today, it's only a little over half.

It's not just the legacy of Thatcherism that workers have to thank for their stagnating pay packets: globalization has played a role, too. When China, India and the former Soviet bloc entered the global market economy, Western companies suddenly had access to hundreds of millions of new workers. Not only did this make labour plentiful, it also made it cheap because corporations could get away with paying far lower wages in the developing world, not least because of international deregulation pushed by the likes of the World Trade Organization. This has dealt a crippling blow to workers' bargaining power. After all, companies can simply relocate to the third world if their Western workforces refuse to stomach low wages and poor conditions.

Stagnating wages and low-paid service sector jobs played their part in the economic crisis. To maintain their spending power, workers began to borrow. In 1980 the ratio between debt and income was 45. By 1997 it had doubled, before reaching an astonishing 157.4 on the eve of the credit crunch in 2007. As people's purchasing power slowed, more and more credit was splashed out on consumer goods. Between 2000 and 2007, consumers spent £55 billion more than their pay packets, courtesy of the plastic in their wallet or hefty bank loans. This huge increase in household debt is just one reason Britain experienced a credit-fuelled boom before the bubble inevitably burst.

'If you're in a situation where your income is not increasing in real terms, and if you actually find yourself in a situation where your income is declining, then one way to meet that gap and "keep up with the Joneses" is to borrow more money to do so,' says debt expert Chris Tapp, director of Credit Action. And that is exactly what millions of people did, borrowing way beyond their means to supplement the gap left by stagnating real wages. Reckless consumerism played its part, too, as credit allowed consumers to splash out on expensive holidays, televisions, iPhones and so on because, as Tapp puts it: 'Society screams at us: "This is what you need, this is what you need to be accepted, this is what you need to be valued." And credit, easy credit, allows you to do that.'

As well as being poorly paid, many of the service sector jobs have a markedly lower status than the manufacturing jobs they replaced. Miners and factory workers had a real pride in the work they were doing. Miners were supplying the country's energy needs; factory workers had the satisfaction of investing skill and energy into making things that people needed. The jobs were well regarded in the local community. Of course, there are many conscientious supermarket and call centre workers who put real effort into their jobs and into providing good customer service. But there is no doubt that there is not the same pride and prestige attached to their jobs.

'Despite the problems of manufacturing industry in the 1970s the workers were very well skilled,' says political historian Ross McKibbin.

'They were very well paid. They were nearly all unionized. And they had very high levels of pride in work. And I think that has declined. In what one might call the industrial working class, the pride in work is less than it used to be, and the effort to have pride in work has declined.'

Little wonder that, in one survey, four out of ten middle-income workers felt that their occupation had a lower status than their father's, compared to only 29 per cent who felt that it had a higher status. Those who are now classified by statisticians as 'lower middle class'—like clerical and admin workers and supervisors, for example—are now mostly lower down the income scale than they would have been as members of the skilled working class a generation earlier.[13]

That said, the low status accorded to many non-industrial jobs can be grossly unfair. Part of the problem is that we have developed a distaste for socially useful but poorly paid jobs. This is a spin-off from the new religion of meritocracy, where one's rank in the social hierarchy is supposedly determined on merit. The problem lies in how to define 'merit'. The New Economics Foundation (NEF) think-tank published a report in 2009 comparing the social value of different occupations. Hospital cleaners are generally on the minimum wage. However, NEF calculated that—taking into account the fact they maintain standards of hygiene and contribute to wider health outcomes—they generated over £10 in social value for every £1 they were paid.

Waste recycling workers are another example. They fulfil all sorts of functions, like preventing waste and promoting recycling, as well as re-using goods and keeping down carbon emissions. The NEF model estimated that, for every £1 spent on their wages, another £12 was generated. But when the think-tank applied the same model to City bankers—taking into account the damaging effects of the City's financial activities—they estimated that for every £1 they were paid, £7 of social value was destroyed. For advertising executives it was even more: £11 destroyed for every £1 popped into their bank account.[14] In modern Britain, you may end up having a low-paid, low-status job even though the contribution you are making to society is enormous.

This decline in occupational status is just one way the death of manufacturing has undermined the quality of workers' lives and their sense of worth. Another is that the new service sector jobs simply do not foster the same sense of community as industry once did. 'This kind of strong, community-based working-class culture has certainly been reduced very markedly,' says sociologist John Goldthorpe, something he has noticed from visiting the former pit village where he grew up. 'There used to be the occupational culture of mining, too. Everybody knew about mining. There was talk about mining in the pubs and clubs, there was this kind of shared occupational culture as well as the community.' The service sector has simply not replicated the sense of belonging and community that manufacturing could foster.

'Society has become increasingly atomized,' is former Labour Cabinet minister Clare Short's verdict. 'In the street I grew up in, all the kids played together, they went in and out of the adults' houses, everyone knew roughly who each other were, what they did, and helped each other ... There were always people in the houses because not so many women worked. It was culturally completely different. And there's been a lot of loss, in my view, in the changes. They're not all for the better, and the sense of community and belonging is massively reduced.'

The balance between work and life has also suffered. Four in ten of us put in hours on a Saturday, for example, more than in any other EU country. Another bleary-eyed 13 per cent work night shifts, again higher than most European countries. As well as working irregular hours, we spend more time holed up in our workplaces than elsewhere in Europe. The downward trend in working hours skidded to a halt in the 1980s—and has gone the other way. By 2007, full-time workers were putting in an average of 41.4 hours every week, up from 40.7 hours a year earlier. In the EU, only Romanian and Bulgarian workers put in longer hours.[15]

Shamefully, Britain negotiated an opt-out from the European Working Time Directive that caps the working week at 48 hours. In theory, workers can only work longer than this if they agree to. But, according to a survey conducted by the Trades Union Congress (TUC), one in three workers do not know the option even exists, and another two in three who regularly work more than 48 hours were never given a choice. We have ended up in the shocking situation in which around one in five of us regularly work more than the 48 hours enshrined in the Directive.[16]

But there is even more damning evidence of exploitation. In 2009, over five million workers did more than seven hours of unpaid overtime on average each week—and the trend is up. Having so many people working for free is worth a huge amount to bosses. According to the TUC, business made a stunning £27.4 billion out of it—that's £5,402 per worker.[17] It is a figure worth recalling the next time you hear businesses complaining about the cost of sick leave: according to the CBI, the resulting losses are less than half the amount.

We are not even compensated with time away to unwind. British workers get an average of 24.6 leave days a year, below the EU average and well below Sweden's thirty-three days. No wonder stress has become endemic. A fifth of workers surveyed by the mental health charity Mind had phoned in sick on some occasion because of 'unmanageable' stress levels.

We have seen how service sector workers in particular have had an increasingly rough ride over recent years. But what about the one in five who work in public services? After all, both right-wing journalists and politicians have encouraged the idea that public sector workers are overpaid, underworked and living it up at the expense of the taxpayer. When the government bailed out the banking system and suffered a collapse in tax revenues from the City, a political consensus developed around 'savage' cuts to public services. The reality of Britain's six million public sector workers is nowhere to be seen in all of this.

'Going back many, many years, people may have seen this image of white-collar workers who perhaps thought they were doing alright, had quite an easy job, good conditions and were fairly well paid,' says union leader Mark Serwotka. 'I think that caricature has been deliberately put out there by all political parties in order to, firstly, justify attacking them and, secondly, trying to spread a very divisive image: that "Well, they're bureaucrats who don't really do anything, we can cut them, they're not real people who offer stuff to society." '

Serwotka believes this 'demonization of the public sector ... was a deliberate political strategy to try and see off any opposition to the massive cuts they announced.' He bitterly recalls then-Chancellor of the Exchequer Gordon Brown sacking 100,000 civil servants on live TV in 2004. The union was not even consulted beforehand. 'We saw [former Tory leader] Michael Howard at the 2005 election with his 500 cardboard cut-outs of bowler-hatted, pin-striped mandarins, and it's the same story.' When the Tories came to power after the 2010 election, they immediately set to work cultivating this image, harping on the 172 civil servants who were paid more than the prime minister as if they were in any way representative of the public sector.

Like the service sector, the public sector has filled part of the vacuum left by the collapse of industry in many working-class communities. Nearly 850,000 new public sector jobs were created in the New Labour era. There were around six million public sector workers before the Conservative-led coalition unveiled its programme of cuts in May 2010. Again, as in services, women dominate. According to economics expert Professor Prem Sikka, eight out of every ten new jobs taken by women since the late 1990s were in public services. In a former industrial heartland like the North East, around one in two women work in the public sector.

Yet the idea that these employees are in any way 'pampered' is a myth. Nearly a quarter of workers earning less than £7 an hour can be found in the public sector. 'We have 100,000 members in the civil service earning £15,000 a year or less,' says Mark Serwotka. 'We have 80,000 people on less than the average wage in the country in the civil service. We're told that they have "gold-plated" pensions yet the average pension of all civil servants is £6,200 a year. If you strip out the top mandarins, it's £4,000 a year.'

Consider, too, the fact that public sector workers do the equivalent of 120 million hours of unpaid overtime a year. According to researchers at Bristol University's Centre for Market and Public Organisation, that's the equivalent of employing an extra 60,000 people. One in four public sector workers put in unpaid overtime worth almost £9 billion a year—compared to one in six in the private sector. Pampered? On the contrary. Public sector workers rank among some of the most exploited, low-paid people in the country.

It is these workers who face the brunt of the cuts programme, because a crisis of private greed has been cynically transformed into a crisis of public spending. But as politicians sharpen the knives, it will not just be those workers directly employed by the state who will suffer. If you are in the bottom fifth of the population, over half of your income comes from state support. In the fifth just above that, it is still over a third. Even in the middle fifth, 17 per cent of people's income comes from the government. Huge numbers of working-class people depend on having their income topped up by the state to make ends meet—through tax credits and housing and child benefits, for instance, many of which face real-term cuts.[18]

The great, continuing legacy of Thatcherism is that the working class is, for the time being, on the losing side of the class war. 'There's class warfare, all right,' as multi-billionaire US investor Warren Buffett put it a few years ago, 'but it's my class, the rich class, that's making war, and we're winning.'

Over recent years we have witnessed an astonishing wealth grab by Britain's businesses at the expense of their workforces. At the turn of the millennium, top bosses took home forty-seven times the average worker's wage. By 2008, they were earning ninety-four times more.[19] In some companies, this gap has become mind-bendingly wide. Take Bart Becht, chief executive of Reckitt Benckiser, which makes everything from the painkiller Nurofen to the household cleaning product Cillit Bang. Lucky old Mr Becht makes do with the equivalent income of 1,374 of his workers put together. Or behold Tesco boss Terry Leahy, pocketing 900 times more than his checkout workers and shelf-stackers.[20]

You might think that the greatest economic crisis since the 1930s would have given major businessmen pause for thought. Not for long, though. In October 2008 it was revealed that boardroom pay had soared by 55 per cent in just a year, leaving the average FTSE 100 chief executive with a wage packet 200 times that of the average worker. This bonanza did not stop them pressing ahead with pay freezes and mass redundancies. And when the *Sunday Times* published their annual Rich List in 2010, it revealed that the collective wealth of the 1,000 richest people in Britain had increased by 30 per cent. This was the biggest rise in the history of the Rich List.

Call centre worker Carl Leishman recalls being made redundant by his former employer at the height of the financial crisis. 'I was in the interesting position of working for a bank when it all kicked off. The whole thing is the reason I got made redundant. I think the day after I officially finished with the bank they announced £8.3bn profits. Yeah, that stung a little. "Yeah, by the way, you've got no job now, but we've made £8.3bn profits this year." Well, that's it: everyone suffering for what a few idiots did, and they're still getting paid millions for it.'

Such is the extreme distribution of wealth that the top 1 per cent scoffs a hefty 23 per cent slice of the national pie. The bottom half, on the other hand, has to make do with a meagre 6 per cent between them. Even this is misleading, because much of the 'wealth' of the bottom half is borrowed, through mortgages and credit. The top 1 per cent owns its wealth outright.

This 'trickle-up' model of economics has not come about because the people at the top have become more talented or more profitable. It has been driven by the smashing of the trade unions, a hire-and-fire labour force, and a taxation system rigged to benefit the wealthy. Even Jeremy Warner, a right-winger and deputy editor at the conservative newspaper the *Daily Telegraph*, finds something amiss: 'It is as if a small elite has captured—and kept for itself—all the spectacular benefits that capitalism is capable of producing.'[21]

'There's no doubt that the current tax system is regressive,' says chartered accountant Richard Murphy. After all, we live in a country where the top decile pay less tax as a proportion of income than the bottom decile. Murphy identifies a number of reasons, including the fact that poorer people spend more of their income on indirect taxes like VAT; that National Insurance is capped at around £40,000; and that those earning between £70,000 and £100,000 a year can claim £5,000 of tax relief a year over and above their personal allowance.

'We are intensely relaxed about people becoming filthy rich,' New Labour's high priest, Peter Mandelson, once said, 'as long as they pay their taxes.' In practice, wealthy businessmen and corporations go to great lengths to avoid paying tax at all. Murphy calculates that tax evasion costs the Treasury around £70 billion a year—that's seventy times more than the estimates of benefit fraud. With armies of lawyers and tax experts, the economic elite has become skilled at exploiting loopholes and shuffling money about to avoid paying a penny.

'There's some quite blatant activity, particularly within the middle classes and the wealthy, where there's a lot of income splitting going on,' he says. 'Tax shifting by moving income from one part within the relationship to another has become an extremely common way of avoiding significant amounts of tax. The self-employed are also past masters at this, through limited companies.' What better example than Philip Green, a British billionaire businessman appointed by the Conservative government to advise on its spending review. Sir Philip gets away with paying no tax in Britain because he has given his Monaco-based wife legal ownership of key companies such as Topshop.

Looking beyond the statistics for a moment, clearly we are dealing with two groups of people with irreconcilable differences. On the one hand those who scrimp and save, relying on often poor and stagnating wages to pay the rent or the mortgage. Their long hours and growing productivity have gone unrewarded. They send their kids to local schools and when they get ill, they depend on the local GP and hospital. They pay their taxes. With the death of industrial Britain, many of them depend on relatively low-paid, insecure service sector jobs. Their needs and concerns are ignored by the middle-class worlds of politics and the media.

On the other hand we have a wealthy elite whose bank accounts have exploded in value, even in the midst of economic meltdown. They live global, jet-setting lifestyles, with mansions, villas and penthouse suites scattered around the globe. They may work hard and for long hours, but can be paid as much in a day as other hard-working people earn in a month. Many of them pay little or no tax, they send their kids to expensive private schools and use costly private health-care schemes. They have opted out of society. Not that this has dented their power and influence. After all, the tentacles of big business reach far into each of the main political parties. As well as their huge political power, it is this rich elite who run our major newspapers and broadcasters.

The idea that the working class has withered away, with just a 'chav' rump left, is a politically convenient myth. But there is no denying that it has changed profoundly over the last three decades. The old working class tended to thrive in communities based around the workplace. Most were men who had the same job for life, which was very likely to be the same as their father and grandfather before them. Many of these jobs had genuine prestige, and were well paid. People were more likely than not to be members of unions, and enjoyed genuine power in the workplace.

The modern working class resembles the old in one respect: it is made up of those who work for others and lack power over their own labour. But the jobs they do are generally cleaner and require less brawn: how fast you type is more important than how much you can lift. They work in offices, shops and call centres, often for relatively less pay and with greater job insecurity. Even before the Great Recession, wages were stagnating or, in many cases, declining. Millions of workers hop from job to job with an ever-growing frequency. A sense of community, belonging and pride in work has been stripped away. Terms and conditions are often poor, particularly for the army of temps who enjoy virtually no rights whatsoever. Entire swathes of the workforce are non-unionized, and labour's bargaining power is weaker than ever.

A blue-uniformed male factory worker with a union card in his pocket might have been an appropriate symbol for the working class of the 1950s. A low-paid, part-time, female shelf-stacker would certainly not be unrepresentative of the same class today. But this contemporary working class is almost absent from our TV screens, the speeches of our politicians and the comments pages of our newspapers. Tory leader David Cameron spoke of the 'Great Ignored' during the 2010 general election. Who has better qualifications for this label than the British working class?

There is an insidious side to the pretence that class no longer exists in modern Britain. Rarely a day goes by without some politician or commentator paying homage to 'meritocracy', or the idea that anyone with talent and drive can make it big in modern Britain. The tragic irony is that the myth of the classless society gained ground just as society became more rigged in favour of the middle class. Britain remains as divided by class as it ever was.

6

A Rigged Society

The Britain of the elite is over. The new Britain is a meritocracy.
—Tony Blair, 1997

'I'm definitely middle class, but I'm married to a man who's upper class,' Rachel Johnson said to me in the same cut-glass accent as her brother Boris. There seemed no more appropriate place to talk about class than in the rather quaint Covent Garden offices of Britain's poshest weekly, the *Lady*. Johnson has been the magazine's editor since 2009, but even a woman with her privileged background feels as though she lives in a different world from its blue-blooded readership. 'I'm sort of on the tectonic plates, at the grinding plate of two class systems, class divides … It's like the San Andreas Fault in British society, which is between the aspirant middle class and the downwardly mobile aristocracy. That's what we're seeing at the moment which I think is an interesting area for me to talk about, rather than the working class or the lower middle class.'

Perhaps surprisingly, I discovered that the sister of London's Old Etonian mayor felt like an outsider. 'I come from a very odd background and I'm completely unrepresented in British society because all my … How many great-grandparents do we have? Eight?' She goes through the nationalities of each, one by one. French, Swiss, Turkish … 'So I've never felt remotely within the bloodstream of the class system.'

Rachel Johnson may not seem the most likely person to offer a searing indictment of the class system. But that is what she does. What we have seen, she argues, 'are the middle classes sort of sailing into the jobs, taking all the glittering prizes as a result of their contacts and peer group. And the working-class or the lower-middle-class children struggling to get their first foot even on the ladder.'

At the root of the problem, she says, is the 'nepotistic way that British society operates'. Is that really still a big factor, I ask?

It's a *massive* factor! All middle-class parents do is go around sorting out jobs and work experience for their offspring with their mates ... The one thing that the middle classes are really good at is survival. They never lose out. If you look at how they work systems ... the NHS, the state education system, they're the ones who are going to win, because they're prepared to put in *everything*.

Johnson's fear is that cuts—which she knows 'are going to be brutal'— will make this imbalance a whole lot worse.

This is going to inevitably, in a sense, entrench the middle classes and the upper middle classes in their positions of power and influence, because they have the money to have their children living at home with them, they have the money to support children through unpaid work experience, which can go on for years. To support them through university without saddling them with student loans, which means when they approach employment they can pick and choose a bit more than those who come into adulthood or the post-training period with huge debts. I mean, the playing field has not levelled, it has become ... I don't know what the opposite of levelled is. It has become much less fair, less of a straight playing field.

She lists a few of the myriad ways in which middle-class people grab a head start. What she calls 'add-ons', for instance. 'Like work experi-ence, you know: "I trained as a tennis inspector in my long vac", sort of thing ... The sort of things that middle-class graduates can display are now the things that differentiate them to employers.' If more people are achieving the same high grades, she argues, then the middle-class hand is even stronger. 'This is going to mean that the middle classes are going to have 12 A*s *and* grade 8 violin, *and* they're a judo blue ... But of course, that's why the middle classes are always going to succeed. Because they can build on the extras that employers are going to want.'

When I asked her how class divisions could be overcome, her solution was rather surprising for a woman of her background.

> You know what I'm going to say. Education! You probably have to abolish private schools, and introduce a French lycée system where everybody—whether you're in the sixteenth arrondissement, or whether you come from an Algerian *banlieue* [suburb], goes to the same school. It's easy! No one's going to do it. We can't do it in a free society. We *should* do it, though, for the sake of everybody, actually. Even for the sake of David Cameron's Tory Party they should do it!

Rachel Johnson can hardly be accused of having an axe to grind. She is no left-wing hammer of the middle classes: she finds Margaret Thatcher 'inspirational'. She is simply being honest about the class she was born into. But her analysis puts her at odds with politicians and commentators who believe that inequalities are explained by a 'lack of aspiration' among working-class people. The reality is that we live in a society rigged in favour of the middle class at every level.

As Johnson underlines, private schools are one of the most obvious ways the wealthy can buy their offspring a guaranteed place at the top table. They are the training grounds of the British ruling class. Only seven out of every hundred Britons is educated privately, but they are—to say the least—disproportionately represented in every major profession. Nearly half of top civil servants were privately educated, as were 70 per cent of finance directors, over half the top journalists and close to seven out of ten top barristers.[1] The same goes for top universities. According to the Sutton Trust, one hundred elite schools—out of 3,700 total schools in the UK—accounted for a third of admissions to Oxbridge over the last few years. Overall, over half of Oxbridge students went to fee-paying schools.

But class can dictate people's life chances in rather more subtle ways than effectively buying your kids better grades. Only 15 per cent of poor white boys and 20 per cent of poor white girls leave state schools with basic skills in reading, writing and arithmetic.[2] This is way behind middle-class kids. Why is the link between education and class so strong? If you believe the former chief inspector of schools, Chris Woodhead, it is because middle-class children have 'better genes'. This perverse Social Darwinism led him to criticize ministers for thinking that they could make children 'brighter than God made [them] … Life isn't fair. We're never going to make it fair.'[3]

Of course, this theory is as ludicrous as it is offensive. It is the cards stacked against working-class kids that are to blame, not their genetic make-up. 'It's largely because the gap opens up so early on and then it never gets closed again,' says leading educational campaigner Fiona Millar. Having the luck to be born into a comfortable background has a huge impact. A 2005 study showed that a five-year-old whose parents earn more than £67,500 has reading skills four months more advanced than those of her peers in families with combined incomes of between £15,000 and £30,000. For those in households getting between £2,500 and £15,000, the difference is more than five months.[4] Once established, this disparity follows children all the way through school. A fifth of all boys eligible for free school meals do not obtain five or more GCSEs, compared to around 8 per cent for everybody else.

Why is there such a disparity, from infancy on? A lot of it is down to what Fiona Millar calls a 'horrible phrase': 'cultural capital'. This means having parents who, thanks to their own middle-class background, themselves enjoyed a better education, probably to degree level; being exposed to their wider vocabulary, being surrounded by books when you are growing up, in an environment where going to university is the 'done thing' and the logical first step to a seemingly inevitable professional career—those sorts of things.

As former Labour Cabinet minister Clare Short puts it, there 'used to be many more routes to a dignified life with a decent income for children who were not particularly academic in school.' Or, in the words of a report published by the National Union of Teachers: 'Thirty years ago a fourteen- or fifteen-year-old working-class young person could walk out of school and into a decent working-class job. That is no longer the case.' The demise of the old manufacturing industries means that having good educational qualifications is more important than ever, even in getting a modestly paid job. And, of course, middle-class people, with their abundance of cultural capital, are in a much better position to achieve that.

For insight into how class impacts on a child's education, I spoke to Helena Button. Miss Button—as I knew her—was one of my teachers at Cale Green Primary School in Stockport, in the early 1990s. As an Ofsted report noted a few years after I left, the school 'is located in an area of high economic deprivation in Stockport ... The percentage of pupils who are eligible for free school meals is well above the national average.' Cale Green was in the bottom 5 per cent for national test results.[5]

'Most of the parents tended to have some kind of work, but it was very low paid—like shops, local industry, or whatever was about,' Helena recalls. 'I remember that a lot of these kids, they had no aspiration ... But you'd have to be pretty amazing, to come from a working-class background like Daniel [one of my former classmates] and aspire to something different. I don't know if I ever reached those kinds of people.' Try as they might, she feels, many of the parents of working-class kids with learning difficulties struggled to help them. 'The fathers often had learning difficulties themselves, so they weren't able to help their kids. People from educated, middle-class backgrounds have parents who can help and encourage them with their homework.'

Helena was, in fact, an extremely good and inspiring teacher, despite the difficulties she faced in what she described as an under-resourced, 'rough school'. But in the end, I was the only boy in the class to go to a sixth-form college, let alone a university. Why? Because I was born into a middle-class family—my mother was a lecturer at Salford University, my father an economic regeneration officer for Sheffield Council. I grew up in an educated milieu and was simply following in the footsteps of well-paid, professional people who went to university. I did not suffer from the instability and stresses that scraping by in life can cause a family. I lived in a decent house. These are things denied to huge numbers of working-class people.

Contrast the opportunities that I had to those of Liam Cranley, who grew up in Urmston, on the edges of Greater Manchester, in the 1980s and 1990s. His dad worked in a factory that once employed hundreds of workers in Trafford Park but, along with several others in the area, has since closed; his mother went through various low-paid jobs. 'All of my friends were pretty similar to me, they had pretty similar backgrounds,' he says. 'Everybody else was in the same position, in that the parents said: "Get a trade behind you! Maybe do an apprenticeship—but make sure you get a trade behind you." If we had aspirations, it would be to get an apprenticeship, if you were smart.'

The trouble was that these trades were vanishing fast, as large swathes of British industry collapsed. His nieces, for example, ended up working in shops at the Trafford Centre complex—as he says: 'There's nothing else on offer! Most of us didn't have a plan at all: it was just a case of, you were at school because you had to be, then you finished.'

For parents who had grown up in hardship, the priority was making sure that their children could stand on their own two feet. 'Our parents' biggest aspiration for us was that we had a job, that we could provide, because that really was something to aspire to. When my dad grew up, they had nothing.'

The idea of going to university was not even within the realms of imagination. 'I'm not exaggerating here: I literally didn't know what university was, aged sixteen,' Liam recalls. 'University, to be honest, was kind of where posh people go! It wasn't a case of aspiration; it was almost, "you know your place". That's what posh people do; it's just not an option. It's just not what we do, it's just not on the radar. The aspiration thing is bullshit, it really is. You can only ever really aspire to something if you know it and understand it.'

With the exception of photography, Liam failed all of his GCSEs. 'I didn't even go back to school to get my results,' he says. For six years, he worked as a printer in a factory. 'It was horrible. I hated it, every minute of it, because it was just monotonous and soul-destroying and boring. I came very close to having a breakdown. Eventually I just walked out.'

But Liam is an exceptional case. Aged twenty-three, he started an Access course specially designed for mature students with ambitions to go to university. 'It was a confidence-building exercise,' he explains, recalling how he initially struggled with basic spelling and grammar. Yet his ability was such that he ended up studying at the University of Sheffield, one of the best in the country. Surrounded by middle-class students for the first time, he suffered from constant 'impostor syndrome': a sense that he did not deserve to be there and would be found out at any moment. It meant sometimes dealing with patronizing or even outright classist sentiments, even if meant in jest: for example, he recalls one friend introducing him as 'my scally friend from Manchester'.

It is difficult not to be impressed by Liam's achievement. But the reality is that very few children with his background ever make it to university, let alone somewhere like Sheffield: indeed, nobody he grew up with took that path.

Politicians and media commentators who focus on an alleged lack of aspiration among working-class kids often miss the point. Aspire to what? The disappearance of so many good, well-paid working-class jobs in communities across the country means it is difficult to see what lies at the end of school—other than supermarkets or call centres.

What has struck Fiona Millar in her interviews with schoolchildren from more disadvantaged backgrounds is that they often 'don't know why they're there, because they don't see the benefit from it. The parents don't really understand if there's a benefit from it, or they can't convey it to them necessarily ... their expectations are dampened down.' This is particularly true for communities that were badly hit by the collapse of industry. 'The areas that have the biggest problems and the most demoralized schools are very often the areas where a lot of people were thrown out of work in the 1980s. Whether it was steel, coal ... There are no male role models, men haven't worked, kids don't see any future for themselves, they don't see the point in education, because you can't see a job at the end of it. Why would you bother with it?'

To huge numbers of working-class kids, education simply does not seem relevant. No wonder they are far more likely to truant. There are 300 schools in Britain in which one in ten pupils skip school for at least one day a week. In some schools, the figure is as high as one in four.[6] One estimate has around half a million young people on unauthorized absence from school each week.[7] Working-class students are far more likely to truant than their better-off peers. It represents a tragic lack of confidence on their part in the ability of education to be even remotely relevant to their lives.

The problem is that parents and children who are cynical about education have something of a point. More and more university graduates are forced to take relatively humble jobs—never mind those teenagers who stay on to do A-levels and leave it at that. Newcastle supermarket worker Mary Cunningham told me about the growing numbers of graduates working on the checkout. 'There's people who've gone to university, got their degrees, and can't find anything else,' she says. Government advice published in 2009 recommended graduates look at 'entry-level positions in retail or hospitality', or call centres.[8]

'You could have more and more people with higher-level qualifications in relatively low-level jobs, and with relatively low-level earnings,' says sociologist John Goldthorpe. One senior Tory politician has spoken to him about his fears of 'a kind of underemployed intelligentsia who could get very radicalized'. Things are looking even bleaker as the axe falls on the public sector. For years, it has been the most popular choice for students fresh from graduation ceremonies. The fundamental issue is: if you are unlikely to obtain a secure, well-paid job even after years of studying, why bother at all? If you are going to end up working in a shop regardless, it is understandable that slaving away at school for years seems like a waste of time. If we want kids with 'aspiration', we need to give them something to aspire to.

Separating children by class also has an impact on their learning. Fiona Millar points out that there is a highly segregated education system in large swathes of the country, particularly by the time pupils finish primary school. Many better-off children go on to attend grammar or private schools. 'If you go to the independent sector they get totally different experiences, like small class sizes and more resources,' she says. 'In fact, they're the ones who need it least in a way.' Millar points out that this is damaging because having a balanced intake is crucial when it comes to educational attainment and successful schools. 'The real double whammy is if you come from a disadvantaged background and you live in a very disadvantaged community, where there is no social mix at all. I think that can be a very negative and downward spiral.' And the problem then is that schools that cater exclusively for poor, working-class kids end up being—as she puts it—'demonized'.

Middle-class parents have all sorts of tricks up their sleeves to get their kids into the best schools. I have an acquaintance whose landlord pretended to live at the address, so that their child would be in the catchment area of a good local comprehensive. Other parents pretend to find God as a blandishment to a high-performing faith school. And the privileged can pay to top up their children's education by hiring private tutors. As Rachel Johnson says, when it comes to looking after their own, there are no lengths the sharp-elbowed middle classes will not go to.

Millar believes that segregation at such a young age facilitates the development of hostility to working-class individuals and communities.

It sounds so trite that whenever I say it publicly people start booing and hissing from the audience, because they think it's a sort of hearts and flowers point and it isn't a point about hard educational qualifications. But if you've been to a school with lots of different kids, and you've got your friends from a huge circle, then all that demonization of poor children, or children from different races, is broken down.

This segregation is set to get worse. The Conservative government is building on New Labour's introduction of competition and market principles into education. 'There is this stupid assumption by people who think of themselves as New Labour,' says former Labour leader Neil Kinnock, 'that if they put schools in competition with each other, the result will be a better product. Now that might apply to baked beans or even fur coats, certainly cars and telephone design, but bullshit when it's applied to schools! Because no one starts from the same place.' Kinnock, who after all paved the way for New Labour, finds this to be 'worse than idiotic. It's *wrong*, it's fundamentally *bad*.'

The Tories are taking this principle further. One of their flagship policies is to launch 'free schools' set up and managed by parents and private institutions, but funded by the state. Not only will these new independent institutions drain money away from other schools; we already have a good idea where the project will end, because it has been tried in Sweden where it failed with disastrous consequences.

As right-wing Swedish Education Minister Bertil Östberg admitted: 'We have actually seen a fall in the quality of Swedish schools since the free schools were introduced.' All they achieved was more segregation. 'The free schools are generally attended by children of better educated and wealthy families, making things even more difficult for children attending ordinary schools in poor areas ... Most of our free schools have ended up being run by companies for profit.' Instead, he urged politicians to focus on improving teaching quality across the board.[9]

But, as Fiona Millar strongly insists, school is merely one factor. 'The best estimate I have ever seen of the school effect is 20 per cent of the outcome in children.' For her, factors like 'residential geography and housing, peer pressure, educational attainment of the parents, ability of the parents to support their learning' are, taken together, far more important to a child's educational success. Education expert Dr Gillian Evans agrees, arguing that the prospects of a working-class child are dramatically increased by things like safe streets to play in; good schools and housing; supportive families, whatever structure they may take; good local services; and a strong local economy with a wide range of decent working-class jobs.

This is why the calls of some Tory right-wingers for the reintroduction of academic selection are so misguided. The Tory MP David Davis takes 'the view that the demise of the grammar school did massive damage to the levels of social mobility in the country'. The argument is that grammar schools gave bright working-class kids the opportunity to thrive. John Goldthorpe disputes the perception that social mobility has, overall, declined: for men it has stagnated, but for women it has increased. But Davis also argues that 'nearly every education system in the world except ours selects on academic ability one way or another,' overlooking the fact that 164 grammar schools remain, and the Finnish education system—generally ranked the world's best—has no element of selection. In any case, the old British grammar schools (like those remaining today) were overwhelmingly middle class, and huge numbers of working-class children were written off as failures in the old secondary moderns.

The truth is that because of the other important factors that condition a child's educational achievement, the old grammar schools did not even necessarily help the working-class kids who got in. A government report in 1954 showed that, of around 16,000 grammar school pupils from semi-skilled and unskilled families, around 9,000 failed to get three passes at O-level. Out of these children, around 5,000 left school before the end of their fifth year. Only one in twenty got two A-levels.[10] Conversely, recent research has shown that middle-class kids who attend struggling inner-city comprehensives do much, much better

179

than their fellow students.[11] This is because in a class-divided society, the school you attend is one factor among many. The decisive issue is class.

All of us end up paying for an education system segregated by class. According to a report by a world-leading management consultancy, the whole of society foots the bill for 'Britain's rigid class system', due to the 'loss of economic potential caused by children born into poorly educated, low-income families ...' The price they put on it was more than £50 billion a year.[12]

With so many advantages from birth, it is no wonder that the middle classes go on to dominate top universities. According to a report by the Office for Fair Access, intelligent children from England's richest fifth are seven times more likely to go to university than intelligent children from the poorest 40 per cent. This is up from six times as likely in the mid 1990s. As you move up the rankings toward Oxbridge at the summit, the imbalance grows. In 2002–03, 5.4 per cent of Cambridge and 5.8 per cent of Oxford students came from 'low participation neighbourhoods'. By 2008–09, it had fallen back to 3.7 and 2.7 per cent respectively.[13] Or consider the fact that, in the academic year 2006–07, only forty-five children claiming free school meals made it to Oxbridge—out of around 6,000 successful applicants.[14]

The middle-class domination of education is just one way the privileged protect their own interests. Kids from privileged backgrounds also disproportionately benefit from their parents' networks and contacts. Many get into desirable jobs as much through recommendations and friends of friends as through their qualifications. Could a working-class kid from Liverpool or Glasgow even dream of this kind of leg-up?

But nothing has done more to turn major professions into a closed shop for the middle classes as the rise of the intern. Unpaid internships are thriving, particularly in professions like politics, law, the media and fashion. According to a recent survey of 1,500 students and graduates, two-thirds of young people feel obliged to work for free because of the recession. For many, internship can follow internship, with paid jobs dangled like carrots but never offered.

This is not just exploitation. It means that only well-heeled youngsters living off mum and dad can take this first step in the hunt for a paid job. MPs might speak passionately about 'social mobility' from the podium, but they are among the worst offenders. Parliamentary interns provide 18,000 hours of free labour a week, saving MPs £5 million a year in labour costs. According to the parliamentary researchers' union Unite, less than one in every hundred interns receives the minimum wage, and almost half do not even get expenses. I know of one former Labour minister who has made many speeches defending the minimum wage and the importance of being paid for a day's work—at the same time as employing a whole army of unpaid interns.

The rise of unpaid work is why, if you are a working-class kid with dreams of becoming a lawyer, you may as well forget it. A report by Young Legal Aid Lawyers published in 2010 revealed that, because of requirements for unpaid work experience and subsidized training opportunities, much of the law was a no-go area for working-class people. What makes this so perverse is that legal aid exists to help people who cannot afford to pay for legal advice. 'It's already quite unusual to find legal aid lawyers who come from unprivileged backgrounds,' said Laura Janes, the chair of Young Legal Aid Lawyers. 'There is a danger that legal aid will become a "ladies who lunch"-type occupation. Legal aid lawyers are often representing the most underprivileged people in society. A lot of the young people I work with don't understand what their lawyers are saying to them because they come from completely different backgrounds.'[15]

In sum, it is scarcely surprising that many major professions are out of bounds to the working class. Today's professional born in 1970 would have grown up enjoying a family income that was 27 per cent above the average. For professionals born in 1958, the figure is only 17 per cent. But the story with some individual professions is even more disturbing. Take the media. Journalists and broadcasters born in 1958 typically grew up in families with an income of around 5.5 per cent above the average. But, for the next generation born in 1970, the gap has widened to a stunning 42.4 per cent.[16]

This is not to say that social mobility would be the answer to all the problems of working-class Britain. After all, even if there were a few thousand more lawyers who hailed from places like inner-city Liverpool, the vast majority of people would remain in working-class jobs. But, as well as being manifestly unfair, the unrepresentative social composition of the professions ensures that Britain remains dominated by an Establishment from the narrowest of backgrounds. The result is a society run by the middle class, for the middle class.

We have seen some of the subtler ways in which the class system is propped up. But underpinning all of these factors, of course, is wealth. A study by the Organisation for Economic Co-operation and Development in 2010 revealed that in Britain, a father's income has a bigger role in determining how much his son will earn than in any other developed country. Indeed, the link between a father's background and his son's future is three times greater here than in social-democratic countries such as Norway or Denmark.[17] Thus, in Britain, half of the economic advantage that a high-earning father has over a low-earning father is passed on to their offspring. If you take Canada or a Nordic country, the figure is just 20 per cent.[18]

Being born into a prosperous middle-class family typically endows you with a safety net for life. If you are not naturally very bright, you are still likely to go far and, at the very least, will never experience poverty as an adult. A good education compounded by your parents' 'cultural capital', financial support and networks will always see you through. If you are a bright child born into a working-class family, you do not have any of these things. The odds are that you will not be better off than your parents. Britain's class system is like an invisible prison.

The demonization of working-class people is a grimly rational way to justify an irrational system. Demonize them, ignore their concerns —and rationalize a grossly unequal distribution of wealth and power as a fair reflection of people's worth and abilities. But this demonization has an even more pernicious agenda. A doctrine of personal responsibility is applied to a whole range of social problems affecting certain working-class communities—whether it be poverty, unemployment or crime. In Broken Britain, the victims have only themselves to blame.

7

Broken Britain

Has anyone noticed ... that what we used to call the working class has shrunk? Not merely because, as surveys tell us, so many now think of themselves as 'middle class', but because something called the respectable working class has almost died out. What sociologists used to call the working class does not now usually work at all, but is sustained by the welfare state.

—Simon Heffer[1]

Mrs Parry is a woman battered by events that were outside her control. I met her in the centre of Ashington, a 27,000-strong community about seventeen miles north of Newcastle. It was the world's biggest mining village until the local pit closed in 1986, just a year after the defeat of the Miners' Strike. Thousands were thrown out of work; the community has never recovered.

When I asked Mrs Parry what impact the pit's closure had on the community, she interrupted me before I had even finished the question. 'We died!' she responded with a combination of grief and conviction. 'Once all the mines closed, all the community had gone. It's just been a big depression ever since, just struggling to survive, that's all.' Both her father and her then-husband were miners. They split up the year he lost his job. 'We owed not just our livelihoods, but our *lives* to the pits as well. My dad retired, and then he died. My marriage broke up.'

Before the 1840s, Ashington was a tiny hamlet. It became an effectively purpose-built town when coal was discovered. Irish farm workers fleeing the Potato Famine came to the town to work down the pits, as did farm workers from Norfolk, lead miners from Cumberland and tin miners from Cornwall. Six hundred and sixty-five cottages were built in eleven long rows to house them. As the town thrived, working men's clubs sprang up alongside schools, post offices, churches and a police station. Coal had brought the community to life.

Take away the heart of a community and it will wilt and begin to die. 'The community just disintegrated,' says Mrs Parry. 'There was just nothing left for nobody. They tried to fetch various works up to the industrial estate, but every one's just left after two or three years. Loads and loads of men over forty-five never worked again, because they were too old.'

When the jobs disappeared, families began to fall apart. I asked her about the impact on working men's self-esteem when they were thrown out of their jobs. 'It was tremendous! There were a lot of divorces after the pit closed. They'd been together for twenty, thirty years. They just split up because the men weren't useful hanging around the house with nothing to do. Nowhere to go! I mean there was *nothing*. And we're losing all our social clubs now because the money wasn't there, and the older generation that kept it going is dying off.'

I ask her what jobs there are for young people. 'There's nothing! There's *nothing*! My son's twenty-four now and he joined the Army because there was *nothing*. His dream was to be a barman, and he went to the college, and he did silver service and all the training that's around for barmen. And he got jobs, but then they laid him off: "Oh, we haven't got enough work, we haven't got work".'

Before the Army, the only option for her son was to join the ranks of Britain's burgeoning hire-and-fire, temporary workforce with its insecure terms and conditions. 'He tried the factories, but that was no good because a lot of the factories round here—you're put in by somebody else. Agencies! And it meant that he could be working for two weeks solid, and then not work for six weeks. Just had to wait until he got a phone call.'

She has two daughters. One works in Asda, the other is a teenage girl who is expecting her first child. 'It wasn't really a shock,' she said. 'I keep trying to think—it's my first grandson she's having! But I just can't get as excited as I was about the girl [her other daughter's child], and I've been wanting a grandson for years, for *years* ...'

She was in no doubt about who was to blame for trashing her community. 'We've just been totally abandoned. Maggie Thatcher put the knife in and they just left us to bleed to death.'

Her voice started to break. 'Teenagers, I mean young people and teenagers at the time when Tony Blair got in, they were dancing and cheering in the street, and that broke my heart.' Her eyes were now welling up. 'Because they were so disillusioned! I mean we all thought —"Oh, he'll do us the world of good" ... No, no. He didn't do nothing for nobody. I don't think he did anything even in Durham, where he comes from. So it's just been one big lie, one repeated lie after another.'

Further down the road I found Robert, a middle-aged man sitting alone on a bench, staring miserably into the distance. 'I've been on long-term sick for years,' he told me. 'Jobs are bad up here.' For thirteen years he worked in an opencast mine until it closed a couple of decades ago. 'I was on the dole for a long time and, as I say, I come down with long-term sick and I haven't worked since. Even my son— he's a joiner and a kitchen-fitter—he got made redundant a year and a half ago. He can't even get work, and he's got a trade! They're offering him jobs like Asda, you know, just really badly paid jobs. He's got three kids, he can't afford those jobs. It's not worth his while there, to take a low-paid job.'

Those I met who had jobs felt lucky, but anxious and insecure. Rachel is a woman in her twenties: her dad was a builder, her grandfather was a miner. 'It's hard for jobs around here!' she said. 'There's very little going at the minute. I suppose people work up at Main Street. I know lots of people, my friends, work in Newcastle.' Many people she knows are out of work. 'I'm not even saying people who don't have skills or qualifications. People that do have the qualifications and skills, there's just no jobs to put them into.'

Rachel works for Northumberland County Council, the biggest employer in the county. Just weeks before I spoke to her, the council had announced that one in seven workers could face the sack. 'We have been briefed that there's a chance there'll be job cuts in our offices, and I suppose the offices we work with as well. So I know that we're very closely watching what happens with that.' She fears for the future. 'I think that because there's not the jobs at the moment, the fact that they're definitely planning to cut at least one person from our office and possibly more is a worry.'

I asked her if she had noticed things like drugs and crime in her local community. 'I would say that over the years it seems to get a little bit worse here,' she says. 'I don't know what that's to do with, personally. Possibly, possibly, I think that the lack of jobs made people find other ways, I suppose, to spend time doing something or to make money.'

Twenty-four-year-old John Ashburn and nineteen-year-old Anna agreed. I asked if Ashington was a nice place to grow up. 'No, it's full of drugs,' replied John without hesitation. Why did they think drugs were such a problem? 'Because there's nowt to do here, so that's why people just think "Oh, I'll just take some drugs to get high and that", because it's something to do,' said Anna.

Anna lives by herself and is out of work. 'I've always wanted to work in a hospital, but you've got to have loads of skills to work there, and I don't have those skills, so …' John does at least have a job as a factory supervisor, but he has to commute to his workplace in Scotland. 'I drive up every day … Travelling three hours a day each way. And then twelve-hour shifts when you get there … I do my shift then drive back here again. You just have to stay awake constantly—I sleep at the weekend.'

Wandering around Ashington during the day, it was difficult not to notice a number of young mothers. But were they anything like the popular stereotype of the Vicky Pollard-style chav teenage mum? I spoke to nineteen-year-old Emma, out with her ten-month-old child. She had also brought up a four-year-old, from her partner's previous relationship—'in case you thought I had him really young!' Her partner works four nights a week as a milkman in neighbouring Morpeth. Emma was, herself, determined to work as soon as possible. 'I do plan to go back to work. Definitely. I'd go back now but he's too young. My ma says that when he's about eighteen months, she's going to watch him for us and I'll go back to work.' She was particularly keen to get back to work because 'it'll be giving me a break'.

It would be wrong of me to portray Ashington as some sort of post-apocalyptic hellhole or as a society in total meltdown. The town centre is studded with shops like Argos, Curry's, Carphone Warehouse and Gregg's bakery. There's a real community spirit in the air. People are warm towards one another—as they were towards me, a stranger asking them intrusive questions. Communities like Ashington were devastated by the whirlwind of de-industrialization unleashed by Thatcherism, but people do their best to adjust and get on with their lives, even in the toughest of circumstances.

Father Ian Jackson has been the local Catholic priest in Ashington since 2002. 'It's a very warm, caring kind of community. People really look out for each other,' he told me. 'I think it was hit badly with the closure of the mines—there's very little work for people, so it's quite deprived in a lot of ways. But the people, I always find, are very, very caring and very generous.' A number of Filipinos have moved in to the area and, although he says there was hostility towards them to begin with, 'that's all died a death'.

But Father Jackson could not help but notice the terrible impact the lack of jobs has had on Ashington's young. 'For a lot of the younger people, you feel that most of them want to move on and move out, to get out of the town really, because there's nothing for them here! The main industry, I would probably say—you're looking at the big Asda that's just been built, and the hospital ... I think the young people would say: "What is there for me apart from working in a shop?"'

The resulting despair was a major cause of anti-social behaviour.

> I sometimes feel—and I'm not criticizing or knocking young people, I don't mean this as it sounds—that among the younger generations, because maybe they've got no prospects, there's a 'couldn't care less' attitude. Things like litter, and things like that. I see them walking past here, there's bins attached to the lamp posts, but they just throw everything over the wall. And if you say anything, you get a lot of aggression straight away.

A nearby pub that was recently closed because of drugs was a particular source of anti-social behaviour. 'I remember after midnight Mass at Christmas, it was Christmas morning—about half past five—and I was out here, sweeping up the glass and everything before people came to Mass in the morning. Bottles, just smashed—thrown all over the wall, litter everywhere.'

It's not just Britain's former pit villages that have been devastated by the collapse of industry. The Longbridge plant in Birmingham was once the biggest industrial complex in the world. It sustained the local community throughout the twentieth century. But when carmakers MG Rover collapsed in 2005, more than 6,000 workers were thrown on to the dole queue. Although Chinese automobile company Nanjing bought up the remaining assets, fewer than 200 people have jobs.

The collapse of Rover has had a similar impact on the local community as the closure of the mines had on Ashington. At Longbridge (which, according to the ChavTowns website, is home to 'Council Housed Antisocial Vermin ... More chavs hang round here than there are whore chavettes hanging at the dole line'), there are a number of boarded-up houses just next to the train station. Several middle-aged men were out and about on a Wednesday mid-afternoon. In neighbouring Northfield, where many of the Longbridge workers lived (and described by ChavTowns as full of 'the arse drippings of society' and 'toothless tattoed chav mums'), the rather grand-looking Old Mill pub has been abandoned, its windows smashed and its walls covered in graffiti. On the ground surrounding it were discarded scratch cards.

Don is the manager of the Greenlands Select Social Club in Longbridge. He describes a community with its heart ripped out. 'An awful lot of people went to the wall when the plant closed,' he says. The Social Club itself took quite a hit. 'The takings went down about £3,000 a week. Because they used to come in at lunchtime as well as the evenings ... You don't see as many people out. I mean, you used to get sixty to a hundred in the club in the evening. You don't get twenty now.'

Two women in the newsagents vividly described to me what had happened to the local community. 'The young men—you see them at the school. When we had our children, we never saw a man about, you know. But they're at the school picking the kids up,' says one. 'It's because a lot of the women, the wives, can get cleaning jobs and that, so the men are picking up the kids, looking after the kids,' adds the other. 'I don't live round this area, and I was away for seventeen years. But when I came back to work here, I couldn't believe the difference in the area from them years. There seems such a lot of young unemployed and young girls with babies.'

Gaynor works at the nearby pharmacy. Her husband was one of the thousands of Longbridge workers who lost their jobs back in 2005. I asked her how she'd felt when he received his redundancy notice.

Just the shock, really, because they had said that it wasn't closing, and then my other half was one of the ones that got kept on. But he never got called back to work, and apparently on the Friday his manager was just about to ring all the staff up, and Land Rover pulled out of the contract that they'd got. And then we just got up on Saturday morning, and the postman came, and your redundancy notice was on your mat ... When it happened, all the lads were over on Cofton Park, and they just got told: 'Rover's shut, go and get your belongings'—and *finished*. And that was it: it was just fast. There wasn't even any 'you've got two weeks', or 'you've got a month'; it was just: 'We're shut now, get your stuff, get out, lock the gates.'

To begin with, her feeling was 'How am I going to cope?' Five years on, her husband is still out of work.

There's just nothing about. It's desolate round here: nothing at all … I increased my hours slightly, but the worst thing is, because I only do part-time, when he went to the Job Centre, he got told: 'Tell your wife to pack in her job, because you're going to be better off.' Because I refused and increased my hours, and because my money went up that little bit, my tax credits come down to go with it, and he's not entitled to any dole money because of the income that he earned from Rover—so he's never got a penny of dole money—never got a *penny*. We never got one thing. Nothing.

They were told of a funded scheme to help former Rover workers retrain. 'He went in, and because he likes computers, he wanted to do a Microsoft course and was told, "No, it's too expensive". And yet people were doing the gas-fitting course, which cost over £2,000, and the electrical fitting course, which cost over £2,000. His cost £3,000 and he was told "no".' Being without work for so long has had a devastating impact on his self-esteem. 'It's horrible. Because he writes off and half the places don't bother coming back to you, but we'll phone and we'll arrange interviews; he'll phone places up and say: "Oh, I'll come and work for you for a week for free, if you think it's alright then take me on." And it just feels like you're knocking your head against brick walls.'

For some of those who lost their jobs, the desperation has been too much. 'We've lost a few friends, who've committed suicide. Ex-Rover workers. All this crap that they've got the help and whatever. It's a load of rubbish. A load of rubbish! They've had nothing! … All this they're saying—there's all this money in holding. It's not been paid out to them at all.' Payouts of between £5,000 and £6,000 were promised to sacked workers from the Employee Trust Fund but, as legal wrangles continue, workers have not been paid a penny. According to Gemma Cartwright, the chair of the Rover Community Action Trust: 'There have been house repossessions and family break-ups over this.'[2]

One of Gaynor's great fears is for the children growing up in the community, 'because there's nothing round here at the moment. I mean, you've got all the buildings going on, but they're so slow—I'd have thought they'd be a lot quicker going up. You've just got empty land everywhere.'

It's true that there are cranes and men at work in the surrounding areas. Attached to a fence is a sign: 'Longbridge West: Sustainable Community, 10,000 new jobs, new homes, local amenities, public open spaces, design and build opportunities'. Another sign is a bit more vague: 'Up to 10,000 jobs', it claims.

But, in the five years since the Longbridge closure, there has been desperately little work for the men. Many of those lucky enough to find a job have had to accept lower-paid, service sector work. I talked to Mary Lynch who has worked at a local supermarket for eight years. 'We've had a few of the Longbridge workers come and work there and have a career change, so it's been nice getting to know those people and meeting them and that.' It has meant a substantial hit to their pay packet. 'They were disappointed about the level of pay,' she said. 'Obviously the pay wasn't as good as it was at Longbridge, so they've found that a bit disappointing. Because they were on good pay in Longbridge, and supermarket workers don't get the same level of pay. But in the main, they were grateful to have a job.'

There are a lot of similar themes in Ashington and Longbridge. There is the same sense of despair and pessimism about the future. There are the same stories about the shattering effects locally of the collapse of industrial Britain, and its role in issues as disparate as relationship breakdown, anti-social behaviour, drugs and teenage pregnancy. In both communities there is a lack of good, secure jobs and plenty of people out of work through no fault of their own. It would clearly be absurd to blame the local people for the almost inevitable problems caused by the crippling events that have befallen their communities.

But tell that to the politicians. At the centre of the Conservative Party's election campaign in 2010 was the idea of 'Broken Britain': the belief that, as Tory leader David Cameron phrased it, Britain had fallen into a 'social recession'. When two young boys from disturbed backgrounds were indefinitely detained for torturing two younger victims in another mining village, Edlington, Cameron seized on the case as evidence. The case could not be dismissed as an 'isolated incident of evil,' he argued. A whole range of issues were identified as part of the Tory narrative, such as 'family breakdown, welfare dependency, failing schools, crime, and the problems that we see in too many of our communities'.

Cameron did not identify the collapse of industry as having any role in these kinds of social problems. 'Why is our society broken?' he asked rhetorically. His own answer to this would have surprised the people of Ashington and Longbridge: 'Because government got too big, did too much and undermined responsibility.' That the economies of communities like Ashington and Longbridge, right across the country, have been obliterated is apparently irrelevant. The chilly winds of the free market are ignored; it is the overbearing state that has taken away people's sense of responsibility. And now, they are told, people in these communities must start to take individual responsibility for what has happened to them.

The social problems that undoubtedly affect many working-class communities have come to define the 'chav' caricature. Teenagers pushing strollers, yobs, feckless adults: this is what chavs are for many people. The media, popular entertainment and the political establishment have gone out of their way to convince us that these are moral issues, an indiscipline that needs to be rectified. In blaming the victims, the real reasons behind social problems like drugs, crime and anti-social behaviour have been intentionally obscured. Symptoms have been confused with causes. The communities that suffer most are the biggest victims of the class war unleashed by Thatcherism.

When commentators talk in dehumanizing terms about the 'underclass', they are lumping together those sections of the working class that took the brunt of the wrenching social and economic changes of the last three decades. After all, the working class has never been homogeneous. There have always been different groups within it, not all of whom have sat comfortably together: the skilled and the unskilled, those who once lived in slums and those in quality housing, the unemployed and the employed; the poor and the relatively prosperous, the Northern and the Southern, the English, the Welsh and the Scottish. But there's no denying that many of the modern divisions within working-class Britain were forged by the neoliberal economic project of the last thirty years.

Ashington and Longbridge are far from being exceptional. 'The old industrial heartlands have never recovered,' says the *Guardian*'s economics editor, Larry Elliott. 'One way of looking at it, which is entirely spurious, is to look at claimant-count unemployment, which has come down to an extent. But once you unpack that, you find that a lot of those jobs have tended to be part-time, in distribution, and haven't been as well paid as the jobs that were lost.' Claimant count only measures the numbers receiving Jobseeker's Allowance. But that is just a part of the total. According to the government's Labour Force Survey, less than half of those lacking but wanting a job were officially classed as unemployed even before the recession hit.

Conservative Prime Minister David Cameron is among those on the right who have denounced New Labour for 'accepting as a fact of life the eight million who are economically inactive', out of a total of thirty-eight million people of working age. The figure actually includes millions who are 'economically inactive' for good reasons, including students, carers and some retired people. Yet Cameron was right to point out that there are large numbers of people without jobs who don't show up in the official unemployment statistics. But, again, he failed to identify the real culprit: the industrial collapse that was first unleashed by Thatcherism. 'If you go to beyond the M4 corridor then labour market participation will be 80 per cent,' says Larry Elliott. 'If you go to parts of the old industrial heartlands it's 55 per cent, or 60 per cent at most. So you've got far fewer people working in those areas, and the jobs they're working in tend to be much more insecure, much less highly paid.'

Soon after David Cameron came to power in 2010, he started selling the idea that people are out of work due to their personal inadequacies: a sentiment which is, of course, one of the pillars of the chav caricature. The prime minister pledged a crackdown on welfare 'fraud and error', declaring that it cost the taxpayer £5.2 billion. But he had cunningly combined the cost of fraud committed by welfare recipients (just £1 billion a year) with that of errors on the part of officials (amounting to the far more considerable sum of £4.2 billion a year). In doing so, he ensured that a much bigger headline figure associated with benefit fraud was lodged in the popular imagination.

Of course, protesting that benefit fraud is exaggerated does not mean denying its occurrence. But it is often need, rather than dishonesty, that drives it.

For example, a compelling study by the Joseph Rowntree Foundation found that many claimants taking undeclared cash-in-hand jobs did so to pay for food or heating, or pay back debt. 'People in deprived areas are resorting to informal work because they are trying to support, feed and clothe their families,' said report author Aaron Barbour. 'They are hard-working, ordinary people trying to survive day by day.'[3] Indeed, the report revealed widespread fear among unemployed private tenants that if they worked formally they would lose their housing benefit, plunging them yet further into poverty. Above all, those interviewed expressed a strong desire to get formal paid work and leave benefits, or 'go legit', as soon as possible.

Given the poverty levels at which many benefits are set, it's hardly surprising that some 'play the system'. Jobseeker's Allowance, for example, ranks among the lowest of any unemployment benefits in Western Europe. If, as in other European countries, it had been linked with earnings since 1979, people without work would receive £110 per week. Because it is pegged to inflation, it was worth just £65.45 a week in 2010. For those unable to find secure employment, life on benefits is a constant struggle to stay afloat. Can we be surprised if a minority of claimants—particularly those with children—top up the meagre amount they receive from the state with a few hours of paid work on the side?

The 'welfare scrounger' label is not just attached to those claiming benefits while taking on informal work. People claiming incapacity benefits have long been in the firing line of newspaper pundits and politicians of all major parties, who suspected that hundreds of thousands of people were skiving off despite being able-bodied. The numbers of such incapacity benefit claimants explains, in large part, the disparity between the official unemployment statistics and the economic activity levels that Larry Elliott refers to.

Looking at the figures, the critics appear to have a point. Go back to 1963 and there were less than half a million claiming incapacity benefit. Yet by 2009 the figure was around 2.6 million, far higher than the number of people claiming Jobseeker's Allowance even in the midst of recession. It is self-evident that society has become considerably healthier in those forty-six years, thanks to advances in medical sciences and improvements in diet and lifestyle. The number of men with long-standing illnesses that limit their capabilities has decreased significantly, from 17.4 per cent to 15.5 per cent.[4] So how can we possibly explain the jump in incapacity benefit claimants?

The first point is that the number of claimants shot up under the Tory governments of 1979 to 1997. A particularly steep increase took place in the aftermath of the early 1990s recession, adding around 800,000 claimants by the time Prime Minister John Major was voted out of office. It is now generally accepted that incapacity benefit was used to cloak the unemployment figures. 'Over the years IB was, to some degree, used as a way of slightly getting out of the unemployment figures and not being overly honest,' admitted Conservative Secretary of State for Work and Pensions, Iain Duncan-Smith. 'Conservatives and Labour have signed up to that.'[5]

Incapacity benefit recipients are indeed concentrated in the old, industrial areas of the North, Scotland and Wales. In areas of Southern England outside of the capital, on the other hand, the levels are much lower. In a groundbreaking study based on hundreds of interviews, labour market experts Dr Christina Beatty and Professor Steve Fothergill put two contradictory explanations to the test: that claimants did have genuine health problems, and that the concentration of claimants in old industrial areas showed that the main underlying cause was a lack of work. 'The long economic recovery from the mid 1990s onward helped plug the gap, but never completely,' they argued. 'In these circumstances there have never been quite enough jobs—especially reasonably well-paid jobs—to go around. With a continuing imbalance in the local labour market, with the local demand for labour still running behind the potential local labour supply, it was therefore inevitable that some individuals would be squeezed out.'

To begin with, claimants were former industrial workers who had been thrown out of work, like the ex-miner I spoke to in Ashington. Many did have health problems because of their line of work, and could use them to claim incapacity benefits that paid more than unemployment benefits. After all, the collapse of industry wiped out local jobs in these areas, and this was before low-paid service sector and public services jobs started to fill the vacuum to some degree. In the 1990s, between a third and a half of incapacity benefit claimants had been made redundant from their last job. But, as time has passed, some of these have found another job after a while; or they have passed on to the state pension.

So who are today's incapacity benefit claimants? Beatty and Fothergill discovered that they were 'typically the poorly qualified, low-skill manual worker in poor health, whose alternative would at best be unrewarding work or close to the national minimum wage.' That means the type of person claiming incapacity benefit is different than it was even a decade ago, even though the headline figure has remained fairly constant. The researchers looked at the example of Barrow-in-Furness in North West England: a former shipbuilding town hit by industrial collapse. Incapacity benefit claimants in the 1990s were largely laid-off skilled shipyard workers, but now they were low-skill, poorly qualified workers who had dropped out of their last job because of ill-health, and were 'now disenchanted with the idea of ever returning to work'.

In an area with a 'surplus of labour', there was less of an incentive for employers to keep on staff with poor health by, for example, giving them lesser duties. Once they had been made redundant, workers with poor health were at a disadvantage because employers could always hire healthier people. Overwhelmingly, people on incapacity benefit lack any qualifications whatsoever. We know that these days there are far fewer manual job opportunities for these sorts of workers, and if they are physically impaired in some way, there are even less. The researchers' conclusion was that 'the UK's very high incapacity claimant numbers are an issue of jobs *and* of health.'[6]

Glasgow is a particularly striking example of how the de-industrialization of Britain has left continuing—but disguised—mass unemployment in its wake. The city houses more incapacity benefit claimants than any other local authority. The number of people claiming some form of disability benefits peaked in 1995 at one in five of the working population, or almost three times the UK level. A group of Glasgow University and Glasgow City Council experts looked at how the number of recipients increased during the 1980s, and concluded: 'The main reason for the huge growth in sickness benefit claims was the city's rapid de-industrialization.' The number of manufacturing jobs in 1991 had collapsed to just a third of the 1971 figure. Staggeringly, Glasgow rose from 208th to tenth place among local authorities for economic inactivity levels in the decade following 1981.

The situation improved in the noughties as the number of disability benefit claimants dropped from three times to double the national rate.

The key finding was that this decline was, above all, down to a 'strengthening labour market'. No wonder the study dismissed government claims that: 'The problem is not a lack of jobs.'[7] The fact that a considerable number of incapacity benefit claimants are those without work in post-industrial Britain does not mean we should disregard the health issues involved. As both New Labour and, following the 2010 general election, the Conservative-led government began clamping down on claimants even as the recession stripped jobs out of the economy, the Citizens Advice Bureau exposed the scandal of clearly unwell people having their benefits taken away. Over 20,000 benefit claimants got in touch with them after a new, stringent test found them 'able to work'. Terminally ill patients, people with advanced forms of Parkinson's disease or multiple sclerosis, suffering from mental illness or awaiting open heart surgery, were registered as capable of returning to work. One woman had her benefits cut after she missed an assessment appointment—because she was in hospital having chemotherapy for stomach cancer.[8]

Of course there are people who play the system and falsely claim benefits. Right-wing tabloids relish hunting down the most outrageous examples of such fraud. But this small minority is in no way representative of the majority of people out of work. The latest figures available (for 2006/07) reveal that just 6,756 people were successfully prosecuted for benefit fraud. Professor Robert MacDonald has spent years investigating the impact of wrenching economic changes on working-class communities, along with research partner Jane Marsh. I asked him if he thought there was such a thing as an underclass. 'Short answer—no! ... Better, more accurate and truthful terms and theories than "the underclass" can and should be used to describe the situations of those typically called this. "Processes of economic marginalization" is the best we came up with instead.' MacDonald is convinced that the notion of 'welfare dependency' is an overblown issue … Or it is a big problem, in the sense that this is a very powerful and popular idea that obscures the fuller story. No doubt there are households that have 'given up' and resigned themselves to and found ways to get by with a life on benefits. I haven't, however, been able to locate any such households yet, in all the tramping round the estates we've done over the past years, despite being told the neighbourhoods we research are awash with such cultures of welfare dependency.

Like other experts in the field, MacDonald links unemployment to a lack of jobs—something that might sound obvious, but in the current political climate is anything but. His research focused on 'how relatively well-paid, relatively secure, relatively well-skilled working-class jobs have declined in this economic restructuring and been replaced by low-skilled, low-paid and insecure non-manual (and manual) jobs.' He lives in Teesside, now among the poorest areas in the country. This process was 'exactly matched in time and explained by this process of de-industrialization', he says.

What this has meant for poorer working-class people is an insecure working life, 'made up out of scraps of "poor work" interspersed with time on benefits. This was the reality for those in our studies, across genders and age groups. One doesn't hear much about this—just about "benefit dependency" and so on.' A common misconception is that the number of people on benefits is a static figure. In reality, many claimants are moving in and out of poorly paid insecure work. Take unemployed people claiming Jobseeker's Allowance, which, having not kept pace with the rise in earnings, is worth just £65.45 a week. According to the Office for National Statistics, for example, since 1999 around half of the men and a third of the women making a new claim last did so less than six months previously. This makes the idea of a benefit-addicted underclass even more of a nonsense: an unemployed person is more likely to have moved in and out of work.

The reality is that there are simply not enough jobs to go around. In late 2010, there were nearly 2.5 million people officially without work —and that doesn't include the hundreds of thousands of people the government wants to drive off incapacity benefits. Yet there were less than half a million vacancies in the entire country, according to the government's own figures. That did not stop Iain Duncan Smith making an example out of Merthyr, a Welsh town particularly badly hit by de-industrialization and suffering from high levels of unemployment. The local population had become 'static', he suggested, and they should get 'on a bus' to Cardiff to look for work. His argument was torpedoed when it was revealed that there were nine jobseekers for every job in the Welsh capital.[9]

From an employer's perspective, stripping benefits from hundreds of thousands of people living in 'disguised' unemployment would be profitable, to say the least. It would mean even more people competing for low-paid jobs, allowing employers to push down wages even further. Unless the number of jobs miraculously increased at the same time, it would mean driving other workers out of employment. Business might prosper, but for benefit claimant and low-paid worker alike, benefits crackdowns risk forcing them further into poverty.

Above all, unemployment is a class issue. It is a fate you are far more likely to face if you are working class than if you are middle class. In May 2009—about a year into the recession—the unemployment rate for people in professional occupations was just 1.3 per cent, and was not much higher for managers and senior officials. But for skilled workers, it was 8.1 per cent; for sales and customer service workers, it was 10.5; and for workers in unskilled, 'elementary' occupations, it was 13.7 per cent, or over ten times higher than for professionals.[10]

Government cuts are inevitably going to drive hundreds of thousands more working-class people into the nightmare of unemployment. The old industrial areas were hammered by the recessions of the early 1980s and early 1990s: it is they, again, who will suffer the most. As the factories and mines closed, it was the public sector that, in large part, moved to fill the vacuum. As the Conservative-led government's ideological war on the state gathers pace, rising numbers of unemployed ex-public sector workers will inevitably push demand down, hitting the private sector too. On top of that, significant swathes of the private sector depend on state contracts that are now being ripped up. At the end of 2010, the Chartered Institute of Personnel and Development estimated that the government's cuts programme would force 1.6 million people into unemployment—and most job losses would be in the private sector.

You don't need to be jobless to be poor in modern Britain. Poverty is generally defined as households with less than 60 per cent of the nation's median income after housing costs are deducted. Less than five million people lived in poverty on the eve of the Thatcher counter-revolution, or less than one in ten of the population. Today, poverty affects 13.5 million people, or more than one in five. If you are a single adult without children, that means living on less than £115 a week after housing costs are deducted. For a couple with two young children, it is less than £279 a week. There are only four EU countries with higher rates of poverty.

Politicians and media commentators argue for work as the route out of poverty, but in low-pay Britain, having a job is no guarantee of living comfortably. The majority of people living in poverty actually have a job. While there are three million families in which no one works living in poverty, there are another 3.5 million working families below the poverty line. Poverty affects huge numbers of people because, like unemployment, it is not a static figure: there is a broader group of people who move in and out of it over the course of their lifetimes.

When New Labour was in office, it introduced reforms that attempted to tackle the scandal of working poverty. But it did so within the framework of neoliberal economics—that is, allowing the market to run amok. A leading union-backed Labour MP, John McDonnell, sums up the government's approach thus: 'We will introduce tax credits, and we will redistribute wealth, but we'll make sure what we'll do is force you into work where it's low paid, with the lowest minimum wage you could possibly think of. In that way, you then become the guilty person if you can't afford to dig yourself out of poverty. There's a Victorian, patronizing attitude towards working people.'

The minimum wage is a case in point. When it was introduced in 1999—in the teeth of Tory and business opposition—it made a genuine difference to hundreds of thousands of low-paid workers. After all, it was perfectly legal, not so long ago, to pay a worker £1.50 an hour. But the rate was set at the lowest possible level. In 2010, it was just £5.80 an hour if you were aged twenty-two or above. Even worse, it was discriminatory against the young. Workers aged between eighteen and twenty-one were stuck on £4.83, up from £3.57 for the under-eighteens.

Clearly, these are not wages that anyone could live on comfortably. According to the Joseph Rowntree Foundation, a salary of £14,400 is the minimum a single person needs for an acceptable standard of living (never mind if you have kids). If you work a thirty-five-hour week, that works out as £7.93 an hour, or over £2 an hour more than the minimum wage. Yet as the recession hit, the already low minimum wage was held back to below-inflation rises.

Tax credits were the second pillar of New Labour's approach to low pay. Workers on low incomes were given the right to have their pay packet topped up with the Working Tax Credit and, if applicable, the Child Tax Credit. But as a means-tested system, it is bureaucratic and many eligible people do not claim for money they are entitled to. According to Citizens Advice, around £6.2 billion of tax credits go unpaid every year—with up to £10.5 billion of means-tested benefits in total unclaimed. This includes four out of every five low-paid workers without children, who are missing out on tax credits worth at least £38 a week. This 'benefit evasion' dwarfs the amount lost through benefit fraud—a fact that is completely absent in the debate around cracking down on so-called welfare scroungers.

Another major flaw with the tax credits system is that it is prone to overpaying people. That might not sound too bad: after all, so what if the state puts a bit too much into the bank accounts of low-paid workers? The problem is that the state catches up and demands the money back. 'The income goes up and down, and tax credits are annualized so people can have very big lumps of money, and then suddenly they get a letter saying they owe £7,000,' says Labour's Clare Short. Fiona Weir, chief executive of single parent charity Gingerbread, says that the fear of debt among the people she represents can be so strong that 'we come across people who won't apply for a Working Tax Credit, which could give them a lot more money, because they are so scared of an overpayment and then not being able to pay the debt once they get into it.'

Tax credits are a lifeline for many low-paid workers. But, perversely, they make low pay economically viable and create disincentives for employers to do anything about it. After all, why pay your workers more if the state will top up their wages? As the *Guardian*'s Larry Elliott puts it, tax credits are 'essentially the state subsidizing poverty wages'.

'Of course it's all about making work pay, even rotten work, low-paid work,' argues Clare Short, 'but that was their instrument of redistribution, and it's totally defective if you're trying in the long term to build a more equal society, because it props up inequality.' Inequality did not grow under New Labour as fast as it did under Thatcher: but the huge gap between rich and poor that had opened in the 1980s was not reduced. After thirteen years of New Labour government, Britain remained one of the most unequal societies in the Western world—and tax credits and the minimum wage did not change this. Indeed, two-thirds of all the increase in income in the noughties went into the bank accounts of the top 10 per cent of the population.

One of many snide accusations against the poor is that they ruin themselves by spending their money on frivolous and luxury items. The reality could not be further from the truth. Chris Tapp, debt expert and director of Credit Action, reveals that his organization rarely has to educate low-paid people when it comes to budgeting. 'People at the bottom end of the income spectrum are better at managing their money day-to-day than people at the top end, because they absolutely need to be,' he explains. 'If you've got only a very limited amount of money coming in every week, and you've got to pay your bills, buy the food and feed the kids off that, then you have to be darn good at managing that.' Poorer people are much more concerned with spending wisely than wealthy ones are, he says.

We have seen how prejudices about poverty and unemployment converge in the image of the council estate. After all, not for nothing is it often suggested that 'chav' is an acronym for 'Council Housed And Violent'. 'Play word association with the term "council estate",' wrote Lynsey Hanley, who grew up on one in Birmingham, in her ground-breaking book *Estates*. 'Estates mean alcoholism, drug addiction, relentless petty stupidity, a kind of stir-craziness induced by chronic poverty and the human mind caged by the rigid bars of class and learned incuriosity.'[11]

That is not to say that after three decades of social engineering, only one social type lives in council estates. 'I think it's quite difficult to generalize about social tenants, or indeed council housing, because there is a big variety,' says housing charity Shelter's Mark Thomas.

> What you see in one area of the country is not the same as what you see in another area, and I think a lot of the media debate tends to be around quite crude stereotypes of council estates. Someone goes off and they find a photo of a council estate, normally it looks fairly grotty, and people conjure up a mental image in their minds. Actually, partly because of the right-to-buy, often a lot of what people might call 'council estates' are quite mixed in terms of tenure, in any case.

In other words, what were once solid council estates may today include homeowners, private renters as well as council tenants. Thomas is keen to emphasize the different groups of people that can be found in council estates.

You've got people who are retired, you've got people who are disabled, you've got people who are absolutely working, and doing their level best to support themselves, you've got people living in some very affluent areas, in places that you probably wouldn't call estates at all. Let's remember that some council housing is in fact street properties, it doesn't all consist of the archetypal estate. You've got other people who actually are living in not such nice areas. But the public debate is often conducted in quite a crude way.

It is fashionable among Conservative politicians and right-wing commentators to talk of council housing promoting 'dependency' among its tenants, but Thomas fiercely rejects this. 'It's sometimes suggested that social housing is somehow a cause of deprivation, it's actually pushing people into poverty and reinforcing dependency. We wouldn't see it like that. We would see it as a vital safety net that actually provides people with an affordable, stable base from which they can actually go on and prosper, and build up other aspects of their life, without which it's going to be very, very difficult for them to do so.'

On the face of it, the failure of recent governments to build affordable housing looks inexplicable to the point of madness. The number of houses built in 2010 was the lowest since 1922—with the obvious exception of World War II. Before Thatcher came to power, there were never fewer than 75,000 council dwellings built in any year; in 1999, the number was a disgracefully inadequate eighty-four.

For the last thirty years, the dominant mantra has been that 'the market knows best', but the state's retreat from meeting the nation's housing needs in favour of market forces has shown how absurd this quasi-religious belief can be. Aside from the millions who are spending years of their lives on waiting lists, the number of people in temporary accommodation soared by a stunning 135 per cent between 2001 and 2008. And the government might not be spending much on social housing, but instead it spends £21 billion a year on housing benefit, much of which ends up subsidizing private landlords.

With the housing crisis worsening year by year, and with accommodation so central to people's lives, why did a Labour government leave the whole policy to go to rot? I asked Hazel Blears, whose former department when in the Cabinet included responsibility for housing. She accepted that New Labour had failed to build sufficient capacity—but with caveats. 'I think that there needed to be a housing programme. I've never been entirely convinced that it should be a *council* house building programme. I think we brought into Government quite big prejudices against local authorities across the field of policy. And in some ways, quite rightly. Because some of them were rubbish. And you wouldn't have trusted them to wash the pots, let alone run a community.'

Blears argues that local authorities did improve, but the fundamental distrust that New Labour had towards them meant they did everything possible to bypass them.

> I think what the Labour government did was, in its early days, create a series of parallel tracks almost to get around local authorities—whether that was in further education, or housing, or the NHS Foundation Trusts—all that kind of thing was kind of like, not quite trusting the local authorities. Not in a political way: but actually the capacity to deliver. So we had housing associations, we had Arms Length Management Organizations [semi-independent housing bodies], we had stock transfers—we did anything to get control out of the local authorities ...

The union-backed Labour MP John McDonnell contested this reasoning. 'Local authorities couldn't "be trusted to wash the pots" because for twenty years they were undermined in terms of the powers that they had and the resources that they had. So who in their right mind would become a councillor when all you were there for was rationing services and saying "no" to everyone?' He argues that Labour could have returned the powers to local government that Thatcher took away. If it was felt that the process would take too long, then the government could have channelled its energies into reinvigorating co-operative housing.

Blears suggests another reason: there simply was no one in government with enough interest in housing. 'There wasn't a big housing character,' she says. 'Maybe our government needed a kind of housing person whose passion it was to do housing. I don't think that we did, if I think back, in terms of characters.' Blears herself can measure the effects of New Labour's neglect of housing in her own Salford constituency. 'In terms of increasing stock and supply of affordable housing: yes, we should have done a lot, lot more, because it had really quite damaging social effects. I've got 16,000 on the waiting list.'

Under the Conservative-led government, this crisis will get more severe. Just months after coming to power, David Cameron called for the scrapping of lifetime council tenancy agreements. Instead, only the most needy would be eligible for five-year or, at most, ten-year agreements. If it was decided that their conditions had improved sufficiently, they could be turfed out of their homes and made to rent privately. Council estates would become nothing more than transit camps for the deprived. A government whose signature policy was building a 'Big Society' was unveiling plans that would further undermine the cohesion of working-class communities across the country.

As well as leading to social 'cleansing' and unprecedented segregation, some policies will end up throwing people on to the streets. In the first Budget following the 2010 general election, the government announced plans to slash housing benefits. They were right to complain that the amount spent on these benefits had rocketed over the years, but refrained from pointing out that this was because of the ever-growing crisis of affordable social housing. Cutting the level of rent eligible for housing benefits has the effect of reducing the number of properties poorer people can afford to live in, forcing them either to find somewhere cheaper or face homelessness.

Combined with plans to cap benefits to workless families at a maximum of £500 per week, low-income people face eviction from relatively richer areas, forcing them into effective ghettos. According to estimates by London councils, as many as 82,000 households—or a quarter of a million people—were at risk of losing their homes or being forced to move. This would be the biggest population movement in Britain since World War II. 'I have been in housing for thirty years and I have never seen anything like this in terms of projected population movements,' said one senior London housing official. 'London is going to be a bit like Paris, with the poor living on the periphery. In many boroughs in inner London in three or four years there will be no poor people living in the private rented sector ... it is like something from the nineteenth century.'[12]

But it wasn't just the government's opponents who saw social cleansing at the heart of these plans. One unnamed Conservative minister compared the policy to the Highland Clearances—the late eighteenth- and early nineteenth-century evictions of small farmers from the Scottish Highlands—claiming that it would lead to an exodus of Labour voters from London. Indeed, Shaun Bailey, a former Conservative candidate who was defeated in Hammersmith at the 2010 general election, had argued that the Tories would struggle to win inner-city seats 'because Labour has filled them with poor people'. Such was the outrage over the government's all-too-clear agenda that even London's mayor, the Conservative Boris Johnson, came out publicly to say that he would not accept 'Kosovo-style social cleansing' of the capital.[13]

Taken together, this is a toxic brew. Large numbers of people without secure work; low-paid work that fails to give people a comfortable existence; some of the highest levels of poverty in Western Europe; and millions left without affordable housing. In some of the poorest working-class communities in Britain, each of these crises is felt still more acutely. With all the misery, frustration and hopelessness that accompany them, is it any wonder if other social problems arise?

Imagine being a poor working-class youth in Britain today. Like one in three children, you will have grown up in poverty, lacking many of the things others take for granted: toys, days out, holidays, good food. You spent your childhood in a shabby, overcrowded house or flat, with little if any space to do your own thing. Your parents—or parent—may have done their best, but they have had to deal with the stress of lacking enough money to get by, either working in a monotonous low-paid job or having no job whatsoever.

There are few, if any, decent local jobs for you to look forward to. Indeed, one in four young people are 'Neets' at some stage: that is, sixteen- to eighteen-year-olds who are 'not in education, employment or training'. And, of course, the disappearance of industrial apprentice-ships has left few options for many young working-class men. 'It is well established that industrial restructuring has played a significant part in the restructuring of working-class youth transitions to adulthood,' says Professor Robert MacDonald. With so little hope for so many young people, how can anyone be surprised at the prevalence of anti-social behaviour in many deprived, working-class communities?

Of course this a problem that can easily be exaggerated. 'You hear, "Oh, they're all hoodies"—but they're not!' a retired Birmingham pattern-maker told me. 'I used to hang around with a gang of lads. I used to wear a three-quarter-length coat. Winklepickers and jeans you could hardly get into. I was called a ruffian. We survived! And I'm sure this genera-tion will grow up and the next generation will have something different that people will be moaning about. No, I don't think they're a bad lot really. You might get one or two, but then again you always did!'

MacDonald agrees that it is 'an age-old theme'. As he sees it, 'swathes of ordinary, working-class young people get branded, corralled, herded, moved on, labelled as "trouble" simply for passing their evening leisure time in unremarkable, un-troublesome friendship groups on the streets. This street-corner society was the dominant form of leisure for ordi-nary working-class young people in our studies. Wasn't it ever thus? Was for me!'

And yet the approach of politicians and the media has been to encourage fear and loathing of working-class youth, making no attempt to understand the root causes of anti-social behaviour where it occurs. Of course, that does not stop the bad behaviour of a small minority being a nuisance—or worse—for other members of the community. But, as Ashington showed, all too often it can be a cry of despair: of anguish at the lack of a future, and a feeling that there is nothing to lose.

Boredom is undoubtedly another factor. Unfettered free markets have been allowed to dismantle our local communities, bit by bit. Places where young people—and the rest of that community, for that matter—could congregate have been disappearing. According to the government's Valuation Office Agency, the number of sports and social clubs fell by 55 per cent in the thirteen years of New Labour rule. Post offices were down by 39 per cent; swimming pools by 21 per cent; pubs by 7 per cent; and public libraries by 6 per cent. The sorts of things that have flourished in their place hardly foster a sense of community, or give young people something to do. Betting shops and casinos went up by 39 per cent and 27 per cent respectively, for example. Little wonder young people have been forced to create their own entertainment—or that a minority have resorted to anti-social behaviour out of boredom, despair, or both.

Nothing sums up the blight of anti-social behaviour in the minds of many than teenage gangs wearing hoodies and loitering menacingly on street corners. But, as the Joseph Rowntree Foundation has found, gangs can be about teenagers grouping together for protection, looking out for each other, and even avoiding trouble. Looking at gang culture in six areas, researchers discovered a strong link between territorial behaviour and poorer communities. Getting involved with a gang provided some young people with fun, excitement and support they otherwise lacked. Furthermore, the charity revealed 'connections between poor housing conditions and often difficult family backgrounds, and territoriality. Territorial behaviour appeared for some to be a product of deprivation, a lack of opportunities and attractive activities, limited aspirations and an expression of identity.' Additionally, gangs 'could be understood as a coping mechanism for young people living in poverty'.[14]

It is common to hear right-wing commentators and politicians blame bad parenting for anti-social behaviour among working-class youth. Simon Heffer, one of the country's leading right-wing columnists, put it to me that we need to be 'punishing—and I mean punishing quite severely—bad parenting. I mean, you've got cases of children growing up engaging in criminality who are below the age of criminal responsibility. Lock up their parents! Put the children into care, and have them make sure the children are properly brought up and educated in care.'

Contrary to this view, successive reports by the Joseph Rowntree Foundation have found that in reality, parents often play a hugely positive role in tough working-class areas. 'There is a widespread view that anti-social behaviour by young people can simply be blamed on bad parenting,' observed Peter Seaman, the co-author of one report. 'Yet the parents we interviewed described sophisticated strategies to minimize their children's exposure to danger and to guard them against temptations to go off the rails.'[15]

Gangs can provide a form of the solidarity that has leaked out of increasingly fragmented working-class communities. To soaring numbers of young people with bleak prospects, gangs can give life meaning, structure, and reward. No wonder they have appealed to some working-class children who have grown up in poverty and have a lack of faith in their future. Indeed, as one investigation put it, they provide an opportunity for 'career advancement' through risk-taking and criminal activity —very often the only kind of success young people believe is available to them. Because of 'the current heavy emphasis in schools on academic success', some young people looked 'elsewhere for validation'.[16]

Yet the New Labour era saw a crackdown on the symptoms, rather than the causes, of anti-social behaviour. The former government's approach—such as issuing thousands of Anti-Social Behaviour Orders, or ASBOs—served to magnify the problem in people's minds and criminalized the young people responsible, without helping in any way to turn their lives around. And to our shame, there are more young people behind bars in England and Wales than anywhere else in

Western Europe. The numbers of young people aged between ten and seventeen with a custodial sentence trebled between 1991 and 2006. But prison most certainly does not rehabilitate: some three-quarters of young people re-offend after release.

New Labour's approach to crime as a whole was authoritarian, disregarding the main root cause: poverty. Before he became Labour leader, the rising star that was Tony Blair won plaudits by committing to a policy of 'tough on crime, tough on the causes of crime'. But, as Blair's political secretary John McTernan has admitted, New Labour's strategy ended up as 'tough on crime, tough on criminals'.[17] Between 1993 and 2010, England and Wales's prison population nearly doubled, from 44,500 to around 85,000.

What is startling about these figures is that the prison population was spiralling out of control even as crime itself was falling. During the 2010 general election, the Tories put allegedly soaring crime rates at the forefront of their 'Broken Britain' narrative. Their figures were a myth. According to the British Crime Survey, crime fell from 18.5 million offences in 1993 to 10.7 million by 2009. This success was not achieved because more people were thrown into prison, as many New Labour politicians would have us believe. Indeed, a secret government memo leaked when Labour was in power in 2006 suggested that '80 per cent of [the] recent decrease in crime [is] due to economic factors ...'[18] Or, consider a 2005 study by the Crime and Society Foundation which argued that escalating murder rates in the 1980s were the legacy of recession and mass unemployment. Indeed, as the economic boom that began in the early 1990s took off, crime rates fell right across the Western world. Even the Conservative-led coalition that took power after the 2010 general election accepted a link between crime and underlying economic factors.

People have got more scared of crime even as the actual levels have gone down, but this has everything to do with sensationalist journalism and inflammatory rhetoric on the part of politicians. Nonetheless, it is important to bear in mind that your risk of becoming a victim of crime depends a great deal on your class. The British Crime Survey shows that working-class people are significantly more likely to suffer from crime than middle-class people. Working-class people are often reproached for being authoritarian when it comes to law-and-order issues—but of course you are more likely to worry if the risk of crime looms larger in your community.

There is little doubt that at the root of much crime in Britain is the illegal drugs industry. When many people think of council estates, they imagine a dirty stairwell littered with hypodermic needles. The truth is that people of all classes have experimented with drugs at some stage in their lives. Millions of teenagers, working class and middle class, have smoked a joint; and a very considerable percentage of young people have swallowed an ecstasy tablet on a night out. 'Looking at the available evidence, in terms of teenagers and young people, there is not an obvious link amongst that group between socio-economic status and levels of drug and alcohol misuse,' says Martin Barnes, chief executive of drugs charity DrugScope. Indeed, cocaine has a long-established reputation as the middle-class drug of choice. A House of Commons Select Committee report recently denounced the fact that 'it seems to have become more socially acceptable and seen as a "safe", middle-class drug'.[19]

But when it comes to problematic drug use, the differences are striking. 'The government Advisory Panel on the Misuse of Drugs published a report a couple of years ago, and it concluded that when you look at levels of drug misuse with older age groups, there was a very clear link with areas of deprivation and unemployment,' says Martin Barnes. This was particularly striking when you looked at working-class communities devastated by economic crisis. 'The experience in some communities in the 1990s was that in those areas that were hit quite hard by unemployment, particularly young people's unemployment, we did see levels of drug misuse increase, not just heroin.'

Barnes is careful to say that, of course, other factors come into play, not least the rise of rampant consumerism in the 1980s and the greater availability of drugs. But he was in no doubt that people often made the leap from being a bit experimental with drugs to full-blown, problematic drug use, either through despair or as a coping mechanism.

You can see why drugs have strengthened their grip over some of the communities that never recovered from the battering they got under Thatcherism. The tragedy of hard drugs is most visible in Britain's crippled mining villages. 'I honestly think that there wouldn't have been half the drug addicts and stuff like that if the mines hadn't closed,' former Nottinghamshire miner Adrian Gilfoyle told me.

A few years ago, Labour MP John Mann launched an inquiry into heroin use in the former mining community of Bassetlaw. It concluded that a health crisis comparable to a smallpox epidemic was raging in the heart of some of Britain's former coalfields. 'People growing up in the coalfields lack the sense of identity afforded to their parents and grandparents who were part of a stable and prosperous mining industry,' the report said. 'The strongest substance used in these communities was beer, and stable employment allowed most a good standard of living.' With the collapse of the mining industry, 'there is a need to escape', and heroin in these areas was associated with a need to 'get away from it all'. 'Mining villages are *Trainspotting* without the glamour,' was its dismal conclusion.[20]

Modern Conservatives blame many of these social problems on the excessive growth of the state. But they also favour another explanation: the breakdown of the traditional family. Single-parent families in particular have found themselves in the firing line. The working-class single mum is, after all, one of the most reviled 'chav' icons. Fiona Weir, of single parents' charity Gingerbread, enumerates some of the notions associated with the people she represents: ' "scroungers", "spongers", "lazy", "doesn't want to work", "happy on benefits"— that group of adjectives. It's very pervasive and it's very directly relevant to a lot of the welfare reform debates that are playing out.'

To get to the heart of these stereotypes, Gingerbread conducted a wide-ranging study into the lives of single parents in modern Britain.

'What we found bore no relationship to the stereotype in the majority of the cases,' she says. 'And what came through is an extraordinary, palpable sense of anger about the stereotyping.' You would not think it from the way they are popularly portrayed, but 57 per cent of single parents actually have a job.

Rebecca is a young, confident single mother with two kids who lives on a Birmingham estate. She is lucky because she has a job she can juggle with being the sole carer of her children. She points to her eight-year-old daughter. 'The job I chose is a teaching assistant, which fits in around them. We're at the same school, so all the holidays we have together. I chose my job purposefully to fit around the children, and then my other one's at senior school, and her holidays are obviously the same, so work is fantastic for me. But I know that other single mums struggle because when you have the six-week summer holiday and Easter, and whatever else, and you have to find someone to look after your kids.'

Despite the difficulties involved, most single parents want to work. According to the 2010 British Social Attitudes survey, 84 per cent of unemployed single parents want to either get a job or to study. But single parents face attack whatever they do. 'We get a phrase used a lot by single parents, which is "damned if I do, damned if I don't",' says Weir. 'Because if you're on benefits you're somehow seen as a lazy scrounger, but if you go out to work, you're somehow seen as neglecting your kids and not knowing where they are while they run around wild.' It is not shiftlessness keeping many single parents from working, but a number of barriers that are difficult to overcome: like having a job compatible with single-handedly raising a kid, and affordable, accessible childcare. As Weir argues, stigmatizing single parents undermines their self-confidence and does nothing to help them get a job.

The Tories often argue that family structure is one of the major deciding factors in whether a child does well at school and in later life. They are on a factual collision course with a recent study by the Children's Society, which showed that conflict in the family has ten times more of an impact on a child's upbringing. 'The evidence base shows that most children from single-parent families turn out fine,' says Fiona Weir. 'There are poorer outcomes for a significant minority, but when you analyse them, they correlate very, very clearly with things like poverty and conflict. And you get similarly poor outcomes in children from couple families that have similar levels of poverty and conflict.'

When people think of single mothers, it is often teenage girls that spring to mind. But in reality, only one in fifty single mothers are under eighteen. The average age for a single parent is thirty-six, and over half had the children while married. Even so, there is no denying that Britain has the highest rate of teenage pregnancies in Western Europe. It is also impossible to deny the class dimension of this issue. Although the numbers overall are low, teenagers from manual backgrounds are eight times more likely to become mothers than those from a professional background. The regions that top the teenage pregnancy tables are those areas where industry was destroyed and low-paid service sector jobs have filled the vacuum. Why?

If doctor-turned-author Max Pemberton, writing in the *Daily Telegraph*, is to be believed, it is because for 'children from working-class families, where aspiration is considered middle class, choices in life consist of becoming a celebrity, working in a shop or becoming a mum. The Holy Grail is ready access to a council flat and state benefits, which is precisely what having a baby gives you.'[21] As Fiona Weir points out, this unpleasant populist caricature of the crafty, benefit-seeking teenage mum is a myth. 'We come into contact with thousands of single parents but somehow we just don't meet ones who fit this stereotype. How we are managing to avoid them, I don't know. As for sixteen- and seventeen-year-olds, they can't get the keys to a council house at that age. They either live at home or they go into supported accommodation.'

Middle-class teenagers are certainly less likely to fall pregnant in the first place, but they are also significantly more likely to have an abortion.[22] I chatted to a few middle-class young women, some of whom had had a termination as teenagers. Their reason for not wanting a child now was the same: fear of the impact it would have on their career at such an early stage. But if you live in an area of high unemployment and with only unappealing, low-paid jobs on offer, why wait for motherhood? 'In some cases there will be an element of people who don't see a lot of routes for themselves in terms of what they can do with their life,' says Fiona Weir. 'They might be looking for a sense of role, and purpose, and meaning, and wanting to be useful and to matter.'

One recent, detailed study showed that teenage pregnancy can bring with it many positives, particularly for young people from poorer backgrounds. 'Our research makes it clear that young parenthood can make sense and be valued and even provide an impetus for teenage mothers and fathers to strive to provide a better life for their children,' said Dr Claire Alexander, one of the report's authors.[23] Indeed, having a child can actually be empowering. As another study put it: 'Particularly amongst those who come from disadvantaged groups, for whom there may be little perceived reward for delaying parenthood, early motherhood can provide the opportunity to attain self-respect and adult status.'[24]

We have seen that some of the things people associate with 'chavs' have a basis in reality. There *are* some alienated, angry young people out there who take out some of their frustrations in anti-social ways. Things like crime and drug addiction are more common in working-class areas than in the average middle-class suburb. A working-class teenager is considerably more likely to give birth than her middle-class peer. But the reality is rather different from the vicious generalizations and victim-blaming that accompanies chav-hate. Poverty, unemployment and a housing crisis provide fertile ground for a range of social problems. These are working-class communities that took the brunt of a class war first unleashed by Thatcher three decades ago. Indeed, it would be far more startling if life had gone on, much like before, even as the pillars of the community collapsed one by one.

*   *   *

Proclaiming that people are responsible for their situation makes it easier to oppose the social reforms that would otherwise be necessary to help them. But such demonization does not stand up to scrutiny. People born into poor, working-class communities do not deserve their fate, nor have they contributed to it. As the industries that sustained their lives disappeared, the once-tight bonds holding many working-class communities together unravelled at a breathtaking pace. Those living there could once look forward to respected, relatively well-paid jobs. Their lives had structure. Today, large swathes of communities are haunted by despair, frustration and boredom. Without real economic recovery, the social diseases that accompany hopelessness have flourished.

It would be wrong to lay all the blame at the feet of the Tories. After all, New Labour left manufacturing to wilt, too. At the end of their rule, they toyed with the beginnings of an industrial strategy to encourage a revival, but it was too little and, for them, far, far too late. Britain did not suffer the same ruinous level of unemployment as in the 1980s and 1990s, even as the economy went into free fall following the 2008 financial crash. But all too often it was part-time and low-paid service sector jobs that filled the vacuum, and they could not resuscitate the communities worst hit by the Thatcherite experiment in the 1980s. This is why many of New Labour's policies amounted to sticking plasters in communities ravaged by the Tories under their eighteen-year rule—plasters that are now being torn off, the wounds still bleeding underneath.

It is not surprising that so many working-class people felt alienated from Labour. They felt it was no longer fighting on their side. Some succumbed to apathy—but not all. Deprived of a narrative to explain what was happening to their lives, some began to grope for other logics. It was not the wealthy victors of Thatcher's class war who found themselves on the sharp end. The frustrations and anger of millions of working-class people were channelled into a backlash against immigrants.

8

Backlash

Labour's treacherous lies and cardinal betrayal of the working classes is obvious to all. But the really good news is that the radical left have all but vanished from defending the working classes.

—Jonathan Bowden, BNP activist

It was not an ideal day for knocking on doors. The 2010 general election was only a couple of months away, and I was pounding the streets with a team of activists to get out the vote for a left-wing backbencher. The long, freezing winter of 2010 had finally drawn to a close and it was one of the first sunny Sundays in months. Families were taking advantage of the warm weather, and houses with anyone inside were few and far between.

After fruitlessly knocking on a few doors, a middle-aged woman wearing an apron finally answered. It was obvious she wanted to speak her mind.

'My son can't get a job,' she said angrily. 'But there are all these immigrants coming in and they're getting all the jobs. There are too many immigrants!'

It would be easy to dismiss someone with these views as a knuckle-dragging racist. But it was clear that she was not. I had to listen carefully to what she was saying, because she had a fairly strong accent—a

221

Bengali accent, to be precise. Here was a woman of Indian origin berating immigrants for taking jobs from British workers like her son. What was going on?

That spring, activists of all political stripes found the immigration issue cropping up again and again. It had not come out of nowhere. Throughout the 2000s, a growing backlash against immigration had developed. Polls reflected an increasing hostility to more people entering the country. At the 2005 election, the Tories tried to tap into this groundswell with their infamous 'It's not racist to impose limits on immigration' posters.

But nothing focused people's minds on immigration more than the rise of the British National Party. In the early days of New Labour, back in 1999, the BNP had won just over a hundred thousand votes in the European elections; a decade later, they would poll not far short of a million. Far-right extremists celebrated jubilantly as BNP leader Nick Griffin and his Nazi-sympathizing colleague Andrew Brons became Members of the European Parliament.

The rising BNP tide spilled over into national elections, too. At the 1997 general election, it polled a paltry 35,832 votes, only a handful more than the eccentric National Law Party. Sixteen other parties did better. Eight years later, over 192,000 voted for BNP candidates, making the party the eighth largest in the country. There was huge relief following the 2010 general election that the BNP did not manage to pick up any seats. Yet it had still attracted nearly 564,000 votes. The BNP was now the fifth biggest party in Britain.

Is the BNP's rise a sign that society is becoming more racist? The short answer is 'no'. Back in 1958, a Gallup poll found that 71 per cent of Britons opposed interracial marriage—and yet there was no racist party even fielding candidates. So few people subscribe to such a view these days that pollsters do not bother recording the figure. Today, Britain has the highest levels of mixed-race marriages in Europe, and only 3 per cent admit to being 'very racially prejudiced'. Four out of five people claim to have no prejudice whatsoever. The irony is that

Britain has become less racist at the same time as it is faced with the most electorally successful racist party in British history.

To understand why people vote for the BNP, it is important to understand what the BNP is. Opinion polls are a bit unreliable because, outside of the anonymity of the polling booth, some potential voters are wary of admitting their support for the BNP. But they clearly show that the average BNP voter is likely to be working class: for example, one YouGov poll found that 61 per cent of BNP supporters were in the bottom three social classifications, the C2s, Ds and Es. The BNP has thrived in traditionally white working-class areas with a long history of returning Labour candidates. Little wonder that the rise of the BNP has reinforced one of the popular 'chav' caricatures of the white working class: a beer-bellied skinhead on a council estate, moaning about hordes of immigrants 'coming in and taking our jobs'.

Indeed, it has suited many politicians and journalists to portray the BNP's rise as a matter of white working-class people trying to preserve their identity from a non-white invasion. Frank Field, a right-wing, anti-immigration Labour MP, told me that the BNP are appealing to 'a sense that people are losing their country without ever being asked whether that's what they want'.

But it is not simply racism that has driven hundreds of thousands of working-class people into the waiting arms of the BNP. The rise of the far right is a reaction to the marginalization of working-class people. It is a product of politicians' refusal to address working-class concerns, particularly affordable housing and a supply of decent, secure jobs. It has been fuelled by a popular perception that Labour had abandoned the people it was created to represent. Karl Marx once described religion as 'the sigh of the oppressed creature': something similar could be said about the rise of the far right today.

The BNP is often compared to the European fascist parties of the 1930s. Yet, in reality, it has flourished for completely different reasons. The fascism of the Great Depression era largely owed its support to small property-owners and big businesses who felt threatened by a growing left, whereas today's BNP is a product of the left's weakness. With no powerful left to answer the bread-and-butter concerns of working-class people in the neoliberal era of job insecurity and housing crisis, the BNP has filled the vacuum.

The Asian lady I spoke to was extremely unlikely to have plumped for the BNP come polling day. But she expressed the same anxiety—about the impact of immigration on jobs—as many BNP voters. This shows that the great backlash against immigration is being driven, above all, by material concerns. There was once a popular narrative that social problems were caused by the injustices of capitalism that, at the very least, had to be corrected. With these ideas forced out of the mainstream, it has been easy for the idea that all social problems are caused by outsiders, *immigrants*, to gain a foothold. It is a myth that, fanned by right-wing newspapers and journalists, has resonated in working-class communities across Britain.

That is not to completely dismiss ethnic identity as a factor. The BNP does well in certain overwhelmingly white areas that have seen a recent influx of new, ethnic minority residents. Former London mayor Ken Livingstone recalls:

> I was the candidate in Hackney North and Stoke Newington in 1977 when the National Front got 5 per cent of the vote at the GLC [Greater London Council] election, just like the BNP did in London in 2008. And they were in Hoxton and Haggerston, the two southern wards. On the night of the GLC election, they didn't have a majority, but they were the leading party in those wards ... But two years ago, they virtually got no votes—just a couple of per cent. So I think you tend to get a problem of racism in an area undergoing transition.'

Hackney is one of the most mixed areas in the country, and as a result the far right has died out there. But it flourishes in areas such as Barking and Dagenham, where mass immigration is a new phenomenon and where the BNP has done well; or, conversely, where there is very little immigration but a tremendous fear of it.

The demonization of the working class has also had a real role to play in the BNP's success story. Although ruling elites have made it clear that there is nothing of worth in working-class culture, we have been (rightly) urged to celebrate the identities of minority groups. What's more, liberal multiculturalism has understood inequality purely through the prism of race, disregarding that of class. Taken together, this has encouraged white working-class people to develop similar notions of ethnic pride, and to build an identity based on race so as to gain acceptance in multicultural society. The BNP has made the most of this disastrous redefinition of white working-class people as, effectively, another marginalized ethnic minority. 'Treating the white working class as a new ethnic group only does the BNP a massive favour,' says anthropologist Dr Gillian Evans, 'and so does not talking about a multi-racial working class.'

It is unlikely that the BNP will ever win significant power, not least because of chronic incompetence and infighting, of the kind that crippled the party after the 2010 general election. But its rise is like a warning shot. Unless working-class people are properly represented once again and their concerns taken seriously, Britain faces the prospect of an angry new right-wing populism.

It was ten days before Christmas, and Dagenham Heathway's Mall shopping centre was thronged with bargain-hunters. I was standing thirteen miles east of the House of Commons, but it felt like a world away from the tearooms of Westminster. Dagenham and neighbouring Barking are solidly working-class areas in the borderlands of East London and Essex. Dagenham was once the manufacturing hub of London: during Britain's industrial heyday in the 1950s, the iconic local Ford factory employed tens of thousands of workers. As one anti-racist campaigner put it to me, this was 'the BNP frontline'.

Barking and Dagenham first appeared on the national political radar in 2006, when the BNP stormed on to the local council with an apparent avalanche of support. With eleven seats in the bag, it was now the main opposition to Labour. It had only stood candidates in thirteen out of the fifty-one seats up for grabs. This was a political earthquake whose tremors were felt across the country. Among the BNP's new councillors was Richard Barnbrook, who would go on to be elected to the London Assembly in 2008.

Why was a once solidly Labour area defecting to what was until recently a fringe racist party? Margaret Owen, a retired home carer, was among the shoppers out that afternoon. I asked her if she lived in a tightly knit community. 'No, I wouldn't say so,' she said. 'It's changing.' When I asked her what she felt the number one issue facing the community was, she paused. 'No. I mustn't.' I gently pressed her again, and she looked cautiously from side to side before leaning in and whispering: 'Well, it's all these foreigners coming in. Our borough is just changing. It used to be so nice.' Over what sort of period had this change taken place, I asked? 'It's changed in the last, what, six or seven years? Yes. Very much.'

It did not take long to understand the real reason for her dislike. 'They're getting the houses, and our people, our children can't get the houses. Foreigners come in here and get places ... I never got that. My children never got it. It's just going down the pan. If I can get out of Dagenham, I will.'

Many local residents harbour similar frustrations. Danny, a lanky, thoughtful man in his late thirties, has lived in the area since he was eight years old. A printer by trade until the industry went bust, he found work in a warehouse in nearby Romford and then in a furniture shop. After that he was made redundant, and was out of a job for two years. Legislation introduced by New Labour compelled him to work for his dole money, and he was told that he would either have to work for a company for nothing, or go into voluntary service. He ended up volunteering in a local charity shop, 'because if I work for a company, I'm earning them money, when all I'm getting is my basic giro, which is below the minimum wage.'

Like Margaret Owen, Danny insisted that housing was the main local grievance. 'There's 10,000 people on the housing list who are trying to get a house,' he said. Danny was wary about discussing the BNP's local rise. It was, he said, a 'dodgy subject' because he feared being labelled a racist.

> Which is not good, because you think that, at the end of the day, there has been a lot of influx of foreigners. Whether they're taking the jobs and the houses is debatable, but they're being housed and fed—you know what I mean?—so they've got to be put somewhere, which is obviously taking away from the people who've lived in Dagenham all their lives, putting taxes in, and they're scooped aside, and getting pushed further and further out of Dagenham.

A friend of his is bringing up a child on her own and has been shunted around temporary accommodation for years. But while there is not enough affordable housing to meet the need, a large prison is being built: a source of real exasperation among the locals. 'Why don't they build houses over there, instead of building a prison?'

Unsurprisingly, the issue of jobs weighs heavily on Danny's mind. At its height, the Ford factory employed 40,000 people and was at the heart of the community. Sam Tarry, a leading local anti-racist campaigner who has lived in East London all his life, points out that 'part of Dagenham was actually built to house the workers from that particular factory.' Danny paints a picture of insecure, low-paid work for many local people in the post-Ford era:

> Because obviously Ford was the main thing round here. I mean, I've not worked for Ford, there were other companies, but they're all going bust. That's the problem. You try and get a job, it's either before Christmas, or it's temporary for six months for Christmas, January comes along and you're back in the same boat again, so it's a vicious circle. Or if you do go and get a job, they don't pay you enough to pay all your bills.

Danny is not short of frustrations, but he has no faith in the ability of traditional political parties to alleviate them.

> I think a lot of the politicians have been to public school ... when they come out they just have no concept of real life. They've never scrimped or scraped, they've never had to do fourteen jobs to earn a living or whatever! Because they're on sixty or eighty grand a year, and then there was all this thing with expenses. They're still taking the mick.

I did not actually meet anyone willing to admit voting for the BNP, and Danny says that he does not vote. But he eloquently describes some of the ingredients that, together, have made a toxic brew: massive housing shortages, a lack of secure jobs, and a convenient scapegoat, plus total disillusionment with the political establishment added in for good measure.

Brendan Duffield, a local trade union official who has lived in the area for three decades, is keen to stress that genuine mixing between communities does take place. 'I've run football teams for over twenty years,' he tells me.

> I've had teams from youngsters right up to men's teams, and I've met every different nationality you could imagine: I've had Irish, I've had Scotch, I've had Africans, I've had Asians ... And they've been great, supportive and everything. And everyone seems to get on very well ... so, I'm a bit amazed that people keep saying that this is a racist area, because I've not really seen too many things in this area happening, like racial attacks ... You get idiots in every area that you go in the country, who've got nothing better to do.

But Brendan has seen the impact that housing shortages have had. 'I'm a bit ashamed to say, but I think this authority now has just started building thirteen houses for the first time in over—I think it's over thirty years, since Margaret Thatcher was in.' He is in no doubt that this issue, above all else, has unleashed a political whirlwind in his community. 'I think if Labour would have carried on building houses in this area, you wouldn't have half the trouble with the BNP.'

There was, undoubtedly, a steep rise in the number of foreign immigrants moving to Dagenham during the New Labour era. This has clearly been a disorientating experience for some who have lived there all their lives. 'Empirically it's the fastest-changing borough in Britain. Empirically, that's a fact,' says local Labour MP Jon Cruddas, who has represented Dagenham since 2001. But what has turned disorientation into outright resentment and hostility is what is on every local resident's lips: housing. 'It's the lowest-cost housing market in Greater London, at a time of exponential rise in the value of property, and at the same time, the effect of right-to-buy means that we have more of a private market,' says Cruddas. 'So you've seen the housing market in one small borough disproportionately take the strain in terms of broader patterns of migration into and within the borough.'

Looming over the whole borough is the shadow of right-to-buy, which massively depleted the borough's council-housing stock. 'You've got many people here who took the opportunity to buy their house under the right-to-buy schemes in the eighties and nineties,' says Sam Tarry. 'Many of them have now reached a point where they've got grown-up children who are either having to live at home, or having to move quite far out of the area to get a house, even just to rent a house, let alone to buy one.' Many of the houses bought up by their owners ended up in the hands of private landlords. They have been particularly attractive to what Sam calls

new kinds of migrant communities, particularly the African community in Barking, because if for the same rent you pay, for the price of a house, you can rent somewhere that's got two, three bedrooms, a back garden, a front garden, compared to the sorts of houses in Tower Hamlets, Hackney and Newham—it's a bit of a no-brainer in terms of wanting to have somewhere that's a bit more pleasant to live!

Again, he identifies insecure employment as an issue further feeding the frustrations of local people. 'The difficulty is that actually the generation of people in their late thirties, forties, fifties, is a generation of people who I think weren't employed by the Ford factory, they didn't have a skilled trade, and left school certainly with no further education qualifications, and very little basic, secondary-level qualifications,' he says.

> And often you find people working in a flexible jobs market, the sort of job where you're more likely to be able to be hired and fired at will, where you're not necessarily going to have a pension, you're often on the minimum wage. It creates a further sense of insecurity, which added to the concerns around housing and other local public services provision, starts to create a tense or uncertain atmosphere.

Cruddas agrees, blaming the 'extraordinary de-industrialization' that has taken place. 'This was the centre of manufacturing in London, with its associated predictabilities in terms of pensions and employment. And it's no surprise that the BNP move in.'

In Barking and Dagenham, the BNP has cleverly managed to latch on to the consequences of unfettered neoliberalism. New Labour was ideologically opposed to building council housing, because of its commitment to building a 'property-owning democracy' and its distrust of local authorities. Affordable housing and secure, well-paid jobs became increasingly scarce resources. The response of the BNP was to delegitimize non-native competition, goading people to think: 'We don't have enough homes to go round, so why are we giving them to foreigners?'

Cruddas describes the BNP as hinging their strategy on 'change versus enduring inequalities, and they racialize it'. All issues, whether housing or jobs, are approached in terms of race. 'It allows people to render intelligible the changes around them, in terms of their own insecurities, material insecurities as well as cultural ones.' Yes, it is a narrative based on myths. After all, only one in twenty social houses goes to a foreign national. But, with the government refusing to build homes and large numbers of foreign-looking people arriving in certain communities, the BNP's narrative just seems to make sense to a lot of people.

The BNP's strategy has been obligingly boosted by the right-wing tabloids. '£5m benefits for disabled migrants who flew home', screams one *Daily Express* headline. 'Secret report warns of migration meltdown in Britain', warns the *Daily Mail*. 'Illegal immigrant mum gets four-bedroom house', gasps the *Sun*. If you are a working-class person struggling to scrape by, who cannot get an affordable home or at least knows others in that position, then being bombarded with these stories gives credence to the BNP narrative: that there aren't enough resources to go round, and immigrants are getting the lion's share of them.

Coupled with this strategy is an audacious attempt by the BNP to encroach on Labour's terrain. With New Labour having apparently abdicated the party's traditional role of shielding working-class communities from the worst excesses of market forces, the BNP has wrapped itself in Labour clothes. 'I would say that we're more Labour than Labour are,' says former local BNP councillor Richard Barnbrook. BNP literature describes the organization as 'the Labour party your grandfather voted for'.

Sifting through the BNP's policies exposes this as a nonsense. Their tax policy, for example, includes abolishing income tax and increasing VAT instead—a policy beloved of extreme right-wing libertarian economists that would benefit the rich at the expense of ordinary working people. The party freely adopts Thatcherite rhetoric, committing itself to the 'private-enterprise economy' and arguing 'that private property should be encouraged and spread to as many individual members of our nation as possible'.

And yet, in communities such as Barking and Dagenham, the BNP has cleverly managed to package itself as the champion of the white working class. As well as counterposing the interests of white working-class people to those of ethnic minorities, the BNP has won support by throwing itself into community politics. Party activists organise fêtes, help to clear rubbish, help out in pensioners' gardens—things that give the impression that they are rooted in the local community. 'You see lots of old people saying "the BNP put on a bingo night", or "the BNP wants people to stop gathering on street corners", and it's really classic community politics that masks what they're really about,' says trade union leader Mark Serwotka.

Disturbingly, it is not just former Labour voters that the BNP has managed to attract. 'One interesting factor, which we certainly saw in the 2006 elections, when the BNP got their eleven councillors elected, was the fact it wasn't just disenfranchised Labour voters,' says Sam Tarry. 'They actually turned out great numbers who'd never voted at all before, so-called virgin voters. To actually motivate people who would usually just not bother with the political system, to actually go and take their first political step and doing it hand-in-hand with the BNP is an extremely worrying sign.' The far right has managed to mobilize people who have never voted before because they feel that the traditional political parties simply do not represent their interests.

It is clear that the BNP has thrived by offering reactionary, hateful solutions to the everyday problems of working-class people. But the demonization of working-class Britain has also played a role. For Tarry, it has fuelled a crisis of identity that accelerated the growth of the BNP and the wider anti-immigrant backlash. As well as recent national soul-searching about what constitutes Englishness and British-ness, the question raised in communities like Barking and Dagenham is: 'What does it mean to be working class?'

'We've seen a switch into a sort of English nationalism, and you'll see a lot of the white families deliberately hanging out the English flag from their windows, almost as though they're staking out the territory, in a slightly aggressive, non-inclusive way,' says Tarry.

For me, there is an element there which I can't quite put my finger on about this sense of what it means to be from a working-class background: what it means to be *English*, and where your sense of identity and purpose and direction actually now come from, because of that decline of those traditional kinds of social structures that gave working-class people their sense of purpose and identity, and kinship and brotherhood through the trade union movement. And that still seems to have declined, even though we still have such a strong trade union movement in this area.

Pride in being working class has been ground down over the past three decades. Being working class has become increasingly regarded as an identity to leave behind. The old community bonds that came from industry and social housing have been broken. But working-class identity was something that used to be central to the lives of people living in communities like Barking and Dagenham. It gave a sense of belonging and of self-worth, as well as a feeling of solidarity with other local people. When this pride was stripped away, it left a vacuum that the waking beast of English nationalism has partly filled.

In a similar way, we have seen Scottish and Welsh nationalism gain new roots in the hitherto Labour-voting estates of Glasgow and the Rhondda Valley. But there is a key difference: Plaid Cymru and the Scottish Nationalist Party (SNP) shun ethnic-based nationalism in favour of a progressive-leaning, inclusive nationalism. Indeed, Plaid Cymru boasts of having more ethnic minority councillors than the other Welsh parties put together, while the first Asian elected to the Scottish Parliament was a member of the SNP. Central to the jingoist streak in English nationalism is the long, sordid history of Empire. 'It's not that long ago, certainly when I was growing up, when you had the map with all the red blocks of where the British Empire ruled,' trade union leader Billy Hayes notes. The centuries-old traditions of domination over other peoples have left a very large imprint in the national psyche, which the BNP constantly manipulates.

The far right have switched their targets of choice over the years: Jews, Irish, blacks and Asians were each the villains at various points.

233

Today, above all others, it is Muslims. An ugly wave of Islamophobia has accompanied the so-called war on terror that was launched following the 9/11 attacks. British soldiers are at war with Muslim peoples in Muslim lands. Aided by hysterical media baiting of Muslims, the BNP has made Islamophobia into the very core of its propaganda.

More perversely, the BNP has cynically manipulated mainstream multiculturalism with its focus on inequality as an issue of race. BNP propaganda has tapped into this by recasting white working-class people as an oppressed ethnic minority, allowing it to appropriate anti-racist language. BNP leaflets are full of bogus talk of the 'white minority' and 'anti-white racism'. When the party was taken to court for its 'whites-only' Constitution, it retorted by asking why it should be any different from other ethnic minority organizations, like the National Black Police Association.

Of course, this represents a distortion of mainstream multiculturalism. Irrespective of its flaws, multiculturalism is essentially about defending the rights of ethnic groups, who make up only one in ten of the population in our overwhelmingly white society. But this is one of the consequences of eliminating class from our understanding of inequality—because a group like the BNP can simply argue that it is defending the rights of whites in a multicultural society, just as others might defend the rights of Muslims or black people.

It would be simplistic to maintain that the waves of immigration that took place under New Labour have had no impact in and of themselves. By historical standards immigration has been high, and this alone would have provoked anxiety or hostility among some people. If you have always lived in a homogenously white area, with little or no experience of—or contact with—different cultures, then a sudden change in your community may, to begin with, be a cause of confusion or alarm. Even though history has shown this tension dissipates within a generation or so when genuine mixing has taken place, there may inevitably be tensions in communities undergoing transition.

But economic insecurities have lent added ferocity to the backlash against immigration—and it is this that the BNP has so successfully manipulated. 'The wider issue is that there weren't jobs created for working-class people and there weren't homes for their children to live in,' says Ken Livingstone. 'And it's easy for the BNP to say, well, the blacks are getting it all. In reality no one was getting any, because they weren't building any or making any.'

It would be wrong to caricature communities like Barking and Dagenham as stuffed with angry white working-class people frothing at the mouth about immigrants. There are many who are disgusted with the BNP and have gone out of their way to welcome immigrants hailing from Eastern Europe, Africa and the Indian subcontinent.

When I asked Leslie, a home carer, and her friend Mora, a pensioner, what the main issues in the community were, they came up with the usual answer: 'That same old thing—housing.' But that did not mean they had automatically rushed into the BNP camp. 'They're bad. They're trouble. Very bad,' they both say. 'I mean, I'm quite happy in Barking and Dagenham,' says Leslie, and Mora agrees: 'We were born here. And I would never move out of Dagenham.' They are both deeply scornful of 'the crap that the BNP are coming out with ... At the moment they're frightening people, they're saying old people can get chucked out of their house, and it's given to the "illegals". If they can say where the illegals are, fine. But there are no illegal immigrants in this borough. There's not. I mean, there's good and bad in every-body. But the BNP are very bad.' 'They're very racist, aren't they?' asks Leslie, drawing a quick response from Mora: 'Very, *very* racist, they are.'

Although neither had faith in politicians at the national level, they did trust their local Labour councillors. But their impression of the BNP was of total incompetence. 'They have done *nothing*. You try and get hold of them, you can't get hold of them. And yet they have the cheek to stand and say that Labour's doing nothing ... You can get in touch with the Labour Party, they do listen to you, they sort out your problems, but the BNP—no!' Both are insistent that they mix with people of all backgrounds in their community. Leslie works with black managers and carers, for example. 'We've got an Indian family across the road from us,' adds Mora. 'Every now and then they bring over a meal. Very, very nice.'

These were the sorts of sentiments that anti-racist campaigners built on in the run-up to the 2010 general and local elections. The 'HOPE not hate' campaign built a formidable network of campaigners, developed literature targeted at particular groups in specific localities and exposed the incompetence of BNP councillors. Community organizing was the backbone of the campaign, and trade unions played a central role in funding the effort and spreading the word among local working-class people.

The campaign paid off beyond the wildest expectations of anti-racist activists. The fear was that the BNP would pick up at least one MP in the two local constituencies; the nightmare scenario was that it would take control of the council. In the event the BNP was completely wiped out, losing all twelve of their councillors. Labour may have faced a disastrous rout at the polls in the May general election, but the local Labour Party took every single seat on Barking and Dagenham Council. BNP leader Nick Griffin responded by throwing his toys out of the pram, claiming that the 'English' had been driven out of London.

Yet there are no grounds for complacency. The BNP was defeated above all by vastly increased voter turnout, itself the product of an extremely effective campaign. In the Barking parliamentary constituency, the BNP vote went up from 4,916 votes in 2005 to 6,620 in 2010: but at the same time overall turnout dramatically increased from 28,906 to 44,343, meaning the BNP vote share dropped. BNP council candidates did lose votes, but only around one hundred votes in each ward; indeed, many candidates topped 1,000 votes. Even before the impact of the most sweeping public sector cuts in modern history had been felt, the BNP had retained a solid base within Barking and Dagenham.

The reality is that the grievances that spurred on the BNP upsurge are greater than ever. There is still a critical lack of affordable housing, and well-paid, secure jobs remain thin on the ground. Working-class people in Barking and Dagenham, as elsewhere in the country, will continue to demand answers. The future of our communities depends on who gives them.

The rise of the BNP is just the tip of the iceberg of the great anti-immigrant backlash of the early twenty-first century. There is no avoiding the difficult truth that the vast majority of Britons believe immigration levels are too high. Take one poll for the *Sun* in October 2007: nearly two-thirds of the population wanted immigration laws toughened. But, while only 6 per cent of people in the top three social categories wanted immigration stopped altogether, three times as many in the bottom third wanted the borders completely sealed. These sentiments are not confined to areas that have experienced large influxes from abroad like Barking and Dagenham. Across the country, anti-immigration has become the rallying cry of people who would never dream of voting for the BNP.

It was the sort of thing we were told belonged to the 1970s. In defiance of some of the most stringent anti-union laws in the Western world, workers at the Lindsey oil refinery downed tools in a spontaneous walkout at the end of January 2009. Media commentators were dumbfounded as sympathy strikes spread to towns such as Grangemouth, Sellafield, Wilton, Staythorpe and Didcot, among others. This was not supposed to happen in twenty-first-century Britain.

But there was a twist to this apparent renewed union militancy. The media spin was that these were semi-racist, anti-immigrant strikes in protest at foreign workers. There were close-up shots of placards being waved on picket lines demanding 'British jobs for British workers', repeating a disastrous promise by the then prime minister Gordon Brown at the 2007 Labour Party Conference. Even to some on the left this looked uncomfortably like chauvinism, reminiscent of the dockers who marched to support Enoch Powell's infamous anti-immigration 'rivers of blood' speech in 1968.

Media coverage went out of its way to confirm this interpretation. In one BBC bulletin, a worker was filmed saying: 'These Portuguese and Eyeties—we can't work alongside of them.' But this turned out to be a gross distortion, and the BBC was forced to apologize for missing out the next sentence: 'We're segregated from them.' The worker meant that they *physically* could not work with foreign workers, because they were prevented from doing so.

The real reasons for the strike, carefully obscured by the mainstream media, shed light on some of the complexities underlying the working-class anti-immigration backlash in modern Britain. The Lindsey refinery's employer, IREM, had hired cheap, non-unionized workers from abroad. Not only did this threaten to break the workers' union, it also meant everyone else's wages and conditions would be pushed down in a 'race to the bottom'.

'We've got more in common with people around this world than with the employers who are doing this to us,' said Keith Gibson, one of the leaders of the strike and a member of the Trotskyist Socialist Party. BNP figures who tried to jump on the bandwagon were barred from the picket line. The demands of the strike committee included the unionization of immigrant labour, trade union assistance for immigrant workers and the building of links with construction workers on the continent. This was the opposite of a racist strike.[1]

However, the Lindsey strike was the exception rather than the norm. In an age of weak unions, the resentments behind the working-class backlash against immigration have lacked this sort of commendable leadership. The fear among large numbers of working-class people is that British jobs are being lost and wages are being forced down because of mass immigration.

A glance at the figures might seem to support the conclusion that a majority of jobs are indeed going to immigrants. Between New Labour's victory in 1997 and its defeat in 2010, the number of jobs went up by 2.12 million. While the number of employed UK-born people has increased by 385,000, the number of workers born abroad has risen by

1.72 million. That means that more than four out of every five jobs created in Britain since 1997 have gone to foreign-born workers.

But this fails to take into account the fact that the British population is actually growing very slowly. There are problems with the figures available, not least because some foreign-born workers will now be British citizens, but they do give us a general picture. The British-born population of working age has only gone up by 348,000 since 1997, while the non-British born working-age population has risen by 2.4 million. Nearly a million Britons have left the country since then, and there are a staggering 5.6 million Britons living abroad: it is often forgotten that migration is a two-way process. The bottom line is that the number of jobs going to British-born workers has gone up more than the British-born working population has increased. Less than three quarters of non-Britons have had any luck getting a job—at least, a job that found its way into the official statistics.[2] It is, statistically, not true that immigrants are taking people's jobs.

In any case, many of our essential services depend on foreign workers. The National Health Service would have collapsed long ago were it not for the thousands of doctors and nurses from other countries who have sustained it almost since its creation. Nearly a third of health professionals such as doctors and dentists are immigrants. However unfounded the fear of immigrants taking scarce jobs from natives, it has been allowed to take root in the popular imagination because of the continued decline of traditional, skilled jobs. There has been no mainstream political voice to put this in the context of globalization and a lack of government support for manufacturing. Instead we are bombarded on a daily basis by distorted propaganda from right-wing journalists and politicians. When Gordon Brown made the spectacular misjudgement of pledging 'British jobs for British workers', he only seemed to confirm the view that the jobs had hitherto been going elsewhere.

When it comes to wages, the impact of immigration gets a lot more complicated. It might be expected that because immigrants would be willing to work for less, other workers would be forced to compete with them, thereby pushing everybody's pay down. A 2009 study by a leading Oxford economist and a senior Bank of England economist, Stephen Nickell and Jumana Saleheen, found that wages were, overall, only slightly depressed by immigration. Their key finding was that the impact was not the same for everyone. It was those workers in the semi-skilled and unskilled service sector who suffered most. A 10 per cent rise in the proportion of immigrants would cause a 5 per cent reduction in pay for these groups.[3]

Another paper, for the Equality and Human Rights Commission (EHRC), also found that the overall impact of immigration on wages was small. Ironically, it discovered that those most affected were likely to be former immigrants, because they would be competing for jobs that did not require 'language fluency, cultural knowledge or local experience'. Even so, it found that all workers in manual jobs could see their wages reduced because an employer could easily replace them with a foreign worker willing to accept less. The same was true for workers who were 'marginal to the labour market', those 'most likely to drop out or become discouraged workers', those 'who work in part-time, low-skilled jobs (such as single mothers and young people)', and those who faced barriers to finding work, such as an inability to travel.

Clearly, then, attitudes towards immigration are liable to depend on the class of the person who holds them. Indeed, prospective employers stand to gain from cheaper foreign workers. 'The effect of immigration at the bottom of the labour market is different than it is on the people who are so pleased they can get a nice cheap nanny, or someone cheap to do the plumbing,' observes former Labour secretary of state for international development Clare Short.

When looking at the impact of immigration on jobs and wages, it has been increasingly fashionable among politicians and the media to contrast the hard-working immigrant to the layabout Brit. But it's not, of course, a fair comparison. After all, immigrants will have travelled hundreds or thousands of miles from poorer countries with the express intention of finding work. It is this that endows them with the qualities that employers find so desirable. As the EHRC report put it:

> Immigrants are willing to work hard in jobs with no clear potential for upward mobility (such as most seasonal agricultural work): because they see this 'low-status' work as temporary; because they are gaining non-financial benefits such as learning English; or because their wage does not seem low in comparison with earnings in their home country. To a certain extent, therefore, it is inevitable that immigrants will be more productive than native workers in certain roles.[4]

The impact of immigration has led the prominent Labour backbencher Jon Cruddas to describe it as a 'wages policy'—that is, a device used to control the levels of pay. Crucially, former New Labour Cabinet minister Hazel Blears says: 'There was actually an economic driver to keep the numbers coming because that kept wages down, in a way, and made us more competitive as an economy, and I think what wasn't fully appreciated was the human impact on families of doing that.' Was immigration deliberately used as a 'wages policy', I asked? 'No, I don't think it was a deliberate instrument of social policy. I don't. But I think that some of the effects were of that kind. But I don't think people sat in a room and said: "Ha ha, let's let millions of people in and then we can grind the faces of the poor, of the working class!" I don't think Labour Government is about that.'

When a number of Eastern European countries joined the European Union in 2004, Britain allowed their workers to immediately enter and freely seek work. None of New Labour's immigration policies caused as much controversy, especially when only Ireland followed suit. Critics claimed that the decision led to a wave of cheap labour entering Britain, particularly from Poland. 'It clearly was madness for the government to allow the situation where Britain and Ireland were the only countries that allowed the accession states in before the two-year gap,' says Ken Livingstone. 'So they all came here. Now, it didn't have an impact in

London because we're used to absorbing waves of immigrants. But in a whole range of the country where they never had to absorb immigrants, in rural areas, a load of people turn up from Eastern Europe. The wages are depressed, they work harder, they get the jobs. It was devastating.'

To the extent that immigration does have an impact on wages, the tabloid-driven campaign has aimed at the wrong targets. If employers have used immigration as a means to push down people's pay, then it is they who should face public opprobrium. 'My take on it is that you can't blame workers who've come over here to better their standard of living,' reasons miners' leader Chris Kitchen. 'Blame the employers who prefer to pay them, because they can pay them less—these firms and agencies that specialize in bringing them over. It's not the migrant workers at fault for coming here to better themselves.'

Following Labour's defeat at the 2010 general election and Gordon Brown's resignation as party leader, the candidates to replace him fell over one another to deplore the effects of immigration. As Ed Balls, an erstwhile close ally of Gordon Brown, argued, immigration had had 'a direct impact on the wages, terms and conditions of too many people across our country—in communities ill-prepared to deal with the reality of globalization, including the one I represent.' His stance inspired Tory leader David Cameron to compare him to the racist comic caricature, Alf Garnett. But the reality is that the scrutiny has been directed at immigration, precisely in order to avoid dealing with issues that have a far greater impact on jobs and wages. We have seen that the effect on wages is small—and indeed it can be corrected without clamping down on immigration by, for example, increasing the minimum wage and preventing foreign workers being hired on lower wages or in worse conditions than other workers.

Wages *have* been stagnating or declining for millions of workers, even before the recession hit. Immigration is a long way down the list of reasons why. The huge pool of cheap labour available in the Majority World and the crippled state of British trade unions are far more important factors. After all, company profits are booming: but employers are hoarding these billions, and there is no pressure on them to share. But the 'race to the bottom' at the heart of modern globalization and the lack of trade union rights are not issues that politicians have any interest in addressing. Jobs are being lost because of an economic crisis caused by bankers' greed and the subsequent disastrous policies of the political establishment. Yet today's mainstream politicians do not want to ask any questions that would challenge some of the most basic assumptions of the modern economic system. Instead, they have focused attention on a secondary issue that enjoys the advantage of appealing to people's prejudices, as well as the vociferous backing of the right-wing media.

This backlash against immigration has led many to conclude that the 'white working class' is racist. In reality, the working class is far more ethnically mixed than the rest of the population. This is a point that can be overstated: after all, nine-tenths of Britons are white. Once you leave big urban areas like London, Manchester and Birmingham, you could easily travel for miles without coming across a single non-white face.

Nonetheless, as trade union leader Billy Hayes puts it: 'As ethnic minorities almost invariably suffer more social disadvantage, we can assume that over 10 per cent of the working class are not white.' Ethnic minorities are disproportionately engaged in working-class jobs—and, in many urban areas, they are far more likely to dominate the most low-status, low-paid jobs. Take the retail sector in London. Ethnic minorities make up 35 per cent of its workforce, and yet they represent a far lower 27 per cent of the capital's population.[5] Fourteen per cent of English bus and coach drivers are from an ethnic minority group, and non-whites are also disproportionately represented in catering, security and hotels and restaurants. Half of Bangladeshi and Pakistani workers in the country are in jobs that pay less than £7 an hour, compared to less than 30 per cent of whites.[6]

At the top of the social hierarchy, the contrast could not be greater. Only 3.5 per cent of partners in the UK's top one hundred law firms come from an ethnic minority background.[7] There is just one ethnic minority CEO among Britain's top one hundred companies. In the financial sector, just 5 per cent of men working in insurance pensions are from an ethnic minority.[8] If you are working class, you are far more likely to rub shoulders with people from different backgrounds than those in elite professions or the corporate world.

The same goes for residential patterns. In London, the most diverse communities are overwhelmingly working class, like Tower Hamlets, Newham and Hackney. Middle-class suburbs like Richmond, Kingston and Bromley, on the other hand, have small ethnic minority populations. According to the last census, there were over 100,000 children of mixed Asian and white origin, and 158,000 who were mixed Caribbean and white. Nearly half of British-born black men, a third of British-born black women, and a fifth of Indian and African men, have white partners.[9] Given that ethnic minorities are far more likely to be in working-class jobs and live in working-class communities, it is safe to presume that this mixing is disproportionately happening in the working class.

Clare Short used to represent the poor, working-class constituency of Birmingham Ladywood, where most people hail from minority backgrounds. She agrees that working-class people mix with people from different ethnic backgrounds more than those higher up the social scale. 'You know, by and large in a place like Ladywood, it's fabulous in the richness of the diversity of the people and the relationships they form, and the understanding of each other's religions and histories. There's something very rich that goes on there. The kids in school always say: "We're very lucky because we have the festivals of everybody."' The working class is still largely white; but less white, in reality, than everybody else.

It cannot be said that the privileged elite is always a bastion of tolerance. Middle-class or upper-class racism can often be more pernicious, while lacking the same economic drivers. Let us not forget Prince Harry, who was caught on camera describing an Asian soldier as a 'Paki'. Anti-Semitism has long been the elite's racism of choice. I know of a public schoolboy whose father refused to buy him an expensive gold watch from Harrods, 'because it looked too Jewish'. A lecturer tells me that when he mentioned to a public school-educated student that working-class people were more likely to have a relationship with someone from an ethnic minority, the student paused for a moment before asking: 'Because they can't find anything better?'

We should beware of going along with a superficial reading of the great twenty-first-century backlash against immigration among working-class people. Anti-immigration rhetoric has gained traction for far more complex reasons than mere culture or race. Indeed, many ethnic minority working-class people share the popular hostility to immigration. But at a time of growing insecurity about jobs and wages, immigration has provided a convenient scapegoat as well as an excuse to dodge questions that are far more relevant—but far more threatening to the status quo. Those responsible are playing with fire.

Right-wing populism is on the rise—and it is shamelessly courting working-class people. The BNP is unlikely ever to establish itself as a credible party, but it is an ominous portent of what could come. The populist right can also boast the presence of the United Kingdom Independence Party (UKIP), which came fourth in the 2010 general election with nearly a million votes, and second in the 2009 European elections. Opposition to immigration and its supposed impact on wages and jobs is at the heart of the UKIP programme. More recently, a new far-right formation named the English Defence League has been orchestrating aggressive anti-Muslim demonstrations in cities across England. More mainstream right-wing forces have also jumped on the bandwagon: the Conservative-backing *Daily Telegraph* has described the white working class as 'Britain's betrayed tribe', allegedly marginalized by the advent of multiculturalism and mass immigration.

The danger is of a savvy new populist right emerging, one that is comfortable talking about class and that offers reactionary solutions to working-class problems. It could denounce the demonization of the working class and the trashing of its identity. It could claim that the traditional party of working-class people, the Labour Party, has turned its back on them. Rather than focusing on the deep-seated economic issues that really underpin the grievances of working-class people, it could train its populist guns on immigration and cultural issues. Immigrants could be blamed for economic woes; multiculturalism could be blasted for undermining 'white' working-class identity.

The reason this could happen—and why the populist right has already made inroads into working-class communities—is because the Labour Party ceased providing answers to a whole range of working-class problems, especially housing, low wages and job insecurity. It no longer offers an overarching narrative that working-class people can relate to. To many former natural Labour supporters, it seems to be on the side of the rich and big business. No wonder so many working-class people have concluded that Labour is no longer a party for 'people like us'. To be fair, this phenomenon isn't exclusive to Britain. The dramatic shift to the right of traditional left parties has opened the door to the far right across Western Europe, with groupings like the National Front in France's former 'Red Belt' and the demagogic Northern Alliance in Italy.

The rise of the far right is a symptom of a larger crisis: the lack of representation of working-class people. Purged from politics, their identity trashed, their power in society curtailed and their concerns ignored, it is perhaps surprising that so few working-class people have opted for parties like the BNP. More have sat on their hands and refused to vote; others have voted for Labour with clothes pegs on their noses. A surge of right-wing populism, mass political alienation, cynicism and apathy could have devastating consequences for British democracy. It is not just the future of the working class at stake. It is the future of all of us.

Conclusion: A New Class Politics?

> Rise like Lions after slumber
> In unvanquishable number—
> Shake your chains to earth like dew
> Which in sleep had fallen on you—
> Ye are many—they are few.
>
> Percy Bysshe Shelley, *The Call to Freedom*

The demonization of the working class is the ridiculing of the conquered by the conqueror. Over the last thirty years, the power of working-class people has been driven out of the workplace, the media, the political establishment, and from society as a whole. Ruling elites once quaked at the threat of working-class boots stomping towards Downing Street, of a resolute mass brandishing red flags and dog-eared copies of *The Communist Manifesto*. Back in the 1970s, right-wingers routinely complained that the trade unions were the real power in the land. Surreal as it now seems, it was the *might* of the working class that was once mocked and despised. But, today, with their power smashed into pieces, the working class can be safely insulted as tracksuit-wearing drunken layabouts with a soft spot for Enoch Powell. Feeble, feckless, rude, perhaps—but certainly not dangerous.

When I asked Carl Leishman, the twenty-eight-year-old call centre worker from County Durham, if he felt that working-class people were represented in society, he laughed at the absurdity of the question. 'No. Not at all!' Did he feel that they were ridiculed?

> Well, yeah, because there's nobody who will really stand up to it, because—and this is going to sound very clichéd—but working-class people don't generally have a voice. Do you know what I mean? You can take the mickey out of a working-class person as much as you want, because you know they're not going to get in the papers particularly, they're not going to get on the news, because they're not the people that can influence things, really. So it's kind of pointless listening to them.

It was a theme that I heard again and again in working-class communities: a crushing sense of powerlessness. 'They don't live among us, do they?' said a Birmingham shop-worker about British politicians. 'They live in a different world to us. And they've lost touch with reality.' As far as many working-class people are concerned, they no longer have a voice. No wonder a BBC poll in 2008 revealed that nearly six out of ten white working-class people felt that no one spoke for them.

That is not to say class politics is dead and buried. On the contrary, it is flourishing in some quarters. In other words it has become the preserve of the wealthy and their political apologists. It has been at the heart of the demonization of the working class.

The first tenet of this class politics of the wealthy is simple: class does not exist. Class denial is extraordinarily convenient. After all, what better way to deflect attention from the fact that huge sums of money are being shovelled into the bank accounts of the wealthy, while the wages of the average worker stagnate? The expulsion of 'class' from the nation's vocabulary by Thatcherism and New Labour has ensured minimal scrutiny of the manifestly unjust distribution of wealth and power in modern Britain.

Pretending that the working class is no more—'disappearing' it, if you like—has proved particularly politically useful. We have seen how the chav caricature has obscured the reality of the working-class majority. As elite class warriors are fully aware, the working class has always been the source of political sustenance for the left. That the left is inextricably tied to the aspirations and needs of working-class people is reflected in the very name of the Labour Party. If there is no longer a working class to champion, the left is devoid of a mission. It no longer has a reason to exist.

If anyone dares to raise the issue of class, their arguments are ignored and they are slapped down as dinosaurs clinging to outdated, irrelevant nostrums—even as their right-wing critics shamelessly promote the sorts of economic theories that flourished in the late nineteenth century. When Labour's deputy leader, Harriet Harman, had the temerity to float the controversial suggestion that someone's class background might just have an impact on the rest of their lives, the liberal *Independent* newspaper was outraged. 'Britain is simply no longer the sort of class-divided country that Ms Harman paints,' it retorted.

Another fashionable idea among these class warriors is that people at the bottom deserve their lot in life. It was not for the government to redress inequalities, because the conditions of the poor would only improve if they changed their behaviour. As the *Independent* editorial went on to acknowledge, ethnic minorities and women still faced discrimination, 'but the country's biggest social blight today is an entrenched group of families and individuals at the bottom of the social pile who are failing to participate in the economic opportunities available in modern Britain.'[1] The conclusion was clear. If these people want to get on, they can—but they are *failing* to do so. The brutal truth was that those at the bottom only had themselves to blame.

It is not simply about holding people responsible for where they are in the pecking order. Smearing poorer working-class people as idle, bigoted, uncouth and dirty makes it more and more difficult to empathize with them. The people at the very bottom, in particular, have been effectively dehumanized. And why would anyone want to improve the conditions of people that they hate?

249

We have seen how 'aspiration' is presented as the means of individual salvation: that is, everyone's aim in life should be to become middle class. Both Thatcherism and New Labour have promoted this rugged individualism with almost religious zeal. Rather than the old collective form of aspiration, based on improving the conditions of working-class people as a whole, the new mantra was that able individuals should 'pull themselves up by their bootstraps' and climb the social ladder. Of course, it is based on a myth: after all, if everyone could become middle class, who would man the supermarket checkouts, empty the bins and answer the phones in call centres? But this glorification of the middle class—by making it the standard everyone should aspire for, however unrealistically—is a useful ideological prop for the class system.

At the same time, politicians and journalists have sneakily misrepresented what 'Middle Britain' actually is. 'One of the most successful things that the wealthy have done is to almost persuade the middle class that they're middle class, too,' says maverick journalist Nick Cohen. When politicians and journalists have used the term 'Middle Britain' (or 'Middle England'), they have not been talking about people on median incomes—the median being, after all, only around £21,000 a year; they actually mean affluent voters in 'Upper Britain'. This is how modest tax rises on the wealthy can be presented as attacks on 'Middle Britain', even though nine out of ten of us earn less than £44,000 a year. But politicians will argue that it is electorally impossible to introduce progressive policies that upset supposedly crucial, but completely misconstrued, 'Middle Britain' swing voters.

It even became fashionable among many politicians and commentators to celebrate inequality. Inequality is good because it promotes competition, goes the theory, and it shows that the people at the top are generating wealth. The corollary of this is the idolization of the rich as 'wealth creators' and entrepreneurs, who have achieved success purely through their own hard work and talent.

The class politics of the wealthy has proved extraordinarily effective at demolishing its opponents. It loudly asserts—as Margaret Thatcher famously put it—that 'There Is No Alternative'. Policies that promote the interests of the wealthiest are presented as necessary for the well-being of society as a whole. And, of course, with the media, think-tanks and much of politics funded by the wealthy and powerful, these ideas have easily achieved domination.

When 'class politics' is mentioned, it is normally understood to mean fighting the corner of working-class people, whether with good, bad or naïve intentions. Not any more. Advocates of the class politics of the wealthy largely dominated Tony Blair's New Labour. It was a pretty stunning turnaround for a party specifically founded to represent the working class. How did it happen?

The legacy of Thatcher's smashing of the unions is certainly a major factor. For a century the trade union movement had been Labour's backbone, ensuring that there was always some sort of working-class voice within the party. But the unions' diminished position within society gave successive Labour leaders a free hand to reduce their internal role. Such is the weakness of the unions that they have ended up repeatedly voting to renounce their own powers within party structures.

Four successive defeats at the hands of the Tories between 1979 and 1992 left Labour demoralized, and willing to accept almost anything to get back into power. Clare Short told me of the despair within Labour's ranks because it 'had lost so often, and felt it had let down the very people it existed to represent, and after losing in 1992 when people thought we were going to win—the whole party was *desperate* to win.' Tony Blair was elected Labour leader in 1994 with around half of the vote against leadership candidates who, Short believes, simply were not credible.

> Then, through their [New Labour's] ruthlessness, they brought in lots of reforms weakening the power and democracy of the Conference, the democracy of the party, the way the National Executive Committee was elected—all sorts of things. And people went along with it because they didn't want to make waves early on. And then it was

kind of too late, the structures had changed, and the power to resist had gone ...

Because of this desperation and demoralization, Blair and his followers were able to impose the Thatcherite settlement on the Labour Party. Part and parcel of this settlement was the idea that everyone should aspire to be middle class. Little wonder that, when asked what her greatest achievement was, Margaret Thatcher answered without hesitation: 'Tony Blair and New Labour. We forced our opponents to change their minds.'[2]

International politics played a part in it, too. After the collapse of communism in Eastern Europe, it seemed as though there was simply no alternative to free-market capitalism. I asked former Labour Cabinet minister James Purnell if he thought New Labour adapted to Thatcherism just as, decades ago, the Tories were forced to capitulate to the post-war welfare state settlement left by Clement Attlee's Labour government. 'Yeah, I do. The combination of 1979 [Thatcher's first election victory] and 1989 [the collapse of the Berlin Wall] meant that a little bit of the left's optimism and confidence about itself died ... Somehow, post-1989, a whole bunch of things were defined as, if not insane, then at least as slightly far-fetched, and therefore people on the left had to argue very, very hard to win arguments about overcoming market outcomes or reducing inequality ...'

In such an ideological atmosphere, it is no wonder that New Labour got away with abandoning the party's role as the political voice of working-class people. The calculation of its political strategists was, in the words of New Labour spin-doctor Peter Mandelson, that they 'would have nowhere else to go'.[3] After all, commentators often refer to working-class loyalty to Labour as 'tribalism'. With all of its implications of primitive, unthinking loyalty, this is a word used pejoratively and almost always towards what is patronizingly described as Labour's 'core vote', rather than being applied, say, to the Tory electoral base in the Home Counties.

It is certainly true that, partly out of fear and hatred of the Tories, huge numbers of working-class people thought of Labour as 'their' party, come what may. When campaigning on the doorstep, Labour canvassers often report working-class voters talking about the party as kind of an errant relative who was testing their patience, but, after all, it was family. Yet as the wheels began falling off the New Labour project, growing numbers of disillusioned working-class voters began to disprove the 'nowhere else to go' assumptions of Blair and Brown's strategists.

New Labour's bright young things did not factor in what in Sweden is called the 'sofa option'—working-class people sitting on their hands rather than reluctantly dragging themselves out to vote for their traditional party. In the 2010 general election, over three-quarters of voters in the top, disproportionately Tory-voting social category went out to vote. But only around 58 per cent of working-class voters in the social groups C2 and DE turned out. The turnout gap between professionals and skilled or semi-skilled workers was a whopping 18 per cent.[4] It is almost as though universal suffrage is being pulled down by stealth. More voters overall identified Labour rather than the Conservatives as their natural political home, but the depth of disillusion was such that this was not reflected in votes.

Refusing to come out and vote was one option: putting an 'X' in a different box was another. In Scotland and Wales, huge numbers of working-class voters defected to the welcoming arms of nationalist parties. In the 2008 Glasgow East by-election, Glaswegians turfed Labour out for the first time since the 1920s and voted in the Scottish Nationalist candidate as a protest. In England, as we have seen, the racist BNP picked up the votes of hundreds of thousands of traditionally Labour voters.

The theory that Labour's prospects for remaining in office were tied to keeping the middle classes onside has decisively been proven to be a myth. According to pollsters Ipsos MORI, the decline in support for Labour between 1997 and 2010 in the top social categories (the ABs) was only five percentage points. Among the bottom two social categories (the C2s and DEs), on the other hand, a fifth of all supporters went AWOL. Indeed, while only half a million AB voters abandoned Labour, 1.6 million voters in each of the C2 and DE social groups evaporated.

Even some of New Labour's leading lights are waking up to the party's loss at the hands of working-class disaffection. During his successful campaign for the Labour leadership following the 2010 general election, Ed Miliband described 'a crisis of working-class representation'—a phrase normally confined to left-wing conferences. 'Put it at its starkest, if we had enjoyed a 1997 result in 2010 just among DEs, then on a uniform swing we would have won at least forty more seats and would still be the largest party in Parliament,' he observed.

Maverick Blairite Jon Cruddas calls for a return to what he describes as 'early New Labour': that is, the period between 1997 and 2001. But of all the voters that New Labour ended up losing, half vanished in precisely those four years. Of the five million voters that Labour has lost, four million abandoned ship when Tony Blair was at the helm. These voters did not drift to the right. After all, the Tory vote only went up by a million between 1997 and 2010. The rot had set in early, but it was New Labour's relentless sidelining of working-class Britain that led to its thorough defeat in 2010.

The defeat was not just electoral: it was political on a far more profound level. All the gains New Labour achieved for working-class people—modest as they are compared to previous Labour governments—relied on funding public services and social programmes with the cash flowing from the City. But, following the collapse of financial services and the installation of a Tory prime minister in Downing Street intent on slashing public spending, this model has been swept away forever. In Clare Short's view, New Labour triumphantly believed that: ' "We're a great success because we're market-friendly, we're business-friendly, but we're spending lots of money on poor people, so we've cracked it!" And of course it was a boom, and lots of the projections of the cuts that are going to come suggest that most of the increases in public spending under New Labour will be slashed away.'

The retreat from the politics of class is far from unique to the Labour Party. Across the whole of the left—and by that I mean social democracy, democratic socialism and even the remnants of revolutionary socialism—there has been a shift away from class politics towards identity politics over the last thirty years. The pounding suffered by the labour movement under Thatcherism, particularly following the nadir represented by the defeat of the Miners' Strike, meant that class no longer seemed to be a plausible vehicle of change for many leftists. Identity politics, on the other hand, still felt radical and had achievable aims: history actually seemed to be on the side of those fighting for the emancipation of women, gays and ethnic minorities.

In the 1950s and 1960s, left-wing intellectuals who were both inspired and informed by a powerful labour movement wrote hundreds of books and articles on working-class issues. Such work would help shape the views of politicians at the very top of the Labour Party. Today, progressive intellectuals are far more interested in issues of identity. In his epic *The Intellectual Life of the British Working Classes*, Jonathan Rose published the results of a search he did using an online academic resource, the *MLA International Bibliography*, for the years 1991 to 2000. There were 13,820 results for 'women', 4,539 for 'gender', 1,862 for 'race', 710 for 'postcolonial'—and just 136 for 'working class'.[5]

Of course, the struggles for the emancipation of women, gays and ethnic minorities are exceptionally important causes. New Labour has co-opted them, passing genuinely progressive legislation on gay equality and women's rights, for example. But it is an agenda that has happily co-existed with the sidelining of the working class in politics, allowing New Labour to protect its radical flank while pressing ahead with Thatcherite policies. Take all-women shortlists, promoted by New Labour to increase the number of women candidates standing as Members of Parliament. This is a laudable goal, but it has largely ended up promoting middle-class women with professional backgrounds rather than candidates sharing the backgrounds of millions of working-class women: in low-paid, part-time, service-sector jobs.

The left continues to champion the most marginalized groups in society—as indeed it should—but all too often this has been in search of something to 'replace' the working class with. A classic example is the Respect Party founded by George Galloway as a left-wing, anti-war alternative to Labour. Respect rightly took a stand against the rampant Islamophobia that has gripped Britain in the era of the 'war on terror'. But Respect's electoral base was overwhelmingly in Muslim areas, such as East London and parts of Birmingham. It did not pitch to working-class people as a whole; instead, it substituted them for a Muslim community that was understandably particularly angered by the brutal invasion of Iraq. Class politics was abandoned for communalist politics. 'The left has accepted that it's still class based, but it's gone off on single-issue campaigns and not related them back to the class issue,' says left-wing Labour MP John McDonnell.

One of the 'safe havens' that the left has retreated into is international politics, particularly when it comes to taking a stand against wars in Iraq, Afghanistan and Palestine. Now, it would be unfair to portray this simply as the obsession of sandal-wearing middle-class liberals living in Islington. That was certainly the image conjured up by New Labour minister Kim Howells back in 2006, in response to an anti-war question from Labour MP Paul Flynn: 'It is not enough to assume that if people eat the right kind of muesli, go to first nights of Harold Pinter revivals and read the *Independent* occasionally, the drug barons of Afghanistan will go away. They will not.'

Howells might be surprised to discover that middle-class people are actually more likely to support the Afghan War than working-class people. One typical poll by Ipsos MORI in 2009 revealed that, while 52 per cent of the top social category backed the war and 41 per cent opposed it, just 31 per cent of the bottom social category backed it while 63 per cent were in the anti-war camp. When I asked Mrs Parry in the former mining village of Ashington whether we should bring the troops home, she summed up the stance of many working-class people: 'Yes. Definitely. Definitely! It wasn't our fight in the first place!' Similarly, the movement against the war in Iraq mobilized hundreds of thousands from a range of backgrounds—the author included—in one of the biggest political struggles of recent times. Working-class anti-war sentiment certainly surprised journalist Nick Cohen, who is a staunch backer of the wars in Iraq and Afghanistan. When I put it to him, he was momentarily lost for words, before conceding: 'I'm genuinely surprised by that.'

The problem comes with the *priority* given by the left to international issues. Many working-class people may oppose the war, but that does not mean their opposition trumps concerns like housing or jobs. It is difficult to focus your energies on what is happening thousands of miles away when you are struggling to pay the bills, or your children are desperately searching for secure work or an affordable house. While the BNP are cynically offering hateful solutions to many of these bread-and-butter issues, left-wing activists are more likely to be manning a stall about Gaza outside a university campus. Again, an important issue: but the same energy and commitment that has been shown in opposing unjust foreign wars has not been applied to championing the pressing issues facing working-class people.

Yet as a government of millionaires led by an Old Etonian prepares to further demolish the living standards of millions of working-class people, the time has rarely been so ripe for a new wave of class politics.

After all, the relentless championing of the interests of the wealthy has had disastrous effects for all of us. The destruction of industry that began with Thatcherism left the economy dangerously reliant on the City. The dismantling of council housing helped send house prices soaring, creating a housing bubble that is now imploding, and injecting record levels of debt into the economy. The crushing of the trade unions contributed to the stagnation of wages in the noughties, leading many to top up their income with credit and, in doing so, stoking up a debt-fuelled boom. The credit crunch is, in part, blowback from the class war started by Thatcher over three decades ago.

Disillusionment with the free market has not been stronger or more widespread since the launch of what Tony Benn calls Thatcher's 'counter-revolution' in 1979. Polls consistently show overwhelming support for higher taxes on the wealthy. To add to the brew, Labour is out of office because it lost working-class support, and millions of disenfranchised working-class people have abandoned the ballot box altogether. This is why the biggest issue in British politics today is the crisis of working-class representation: those same people so often caricatured and dismissed as 'chavs'. 'Tony Blair tried to bury it, but class politics looks set to return,' was the headline of one *Guardian* column by Polly Toynbee, in which she observed: 'Over the years denying them-and-us class feeling may have alienated more voters than it won.'[6]

But what would a new class-based politics look like in twenty-first-century Britain? It is clear that only a movement rooted in the left can meet the challenge. The politics of the soggy centre have demonstrably failed to meet the needs and aspirations of working-class people, driving millions either to apathy or into the clutches of the far right. As the left's numerous disastrous experiments in bolting its agenda on to those of other groups has shown, its own future as a political force depends on re-establishing a base in working-class Britain.

At the centre of a political agenda must be a total redefinition of aspiration. 'I think you start from the basic notion of aspiration,' says Jon Cruddas, 'because this was the real cynical element within the worst elements of New Labour post-2001—the way they stripped out from the notion of aspiration any communitarian element. Any sense of duty, obligation, any sense of something that unites people, rather than this dominant atomized, consuming, acquisitive self.' The new aspiration must be about improving people's communities and bettering the conditions of the working class as a whole, rather than simply lifting able individuals up the ladder.

A return to class politics as it was practised and preached in, say, the 1970s, would not be appropriate. After all, the working class on which it was based has changed fundamentally. The old smokestack factory skyline has gone. With it has disappeared (or is rapidly disappearing) the largely male, industrial working class, with jobs-for-life passed on from generation to generation, and whole communities based around the workplace. A new movement has to speak to a more fragmented, largely non-unionized workforce marked by job insecurity and growing numbers of part-time and temporary workers. The jobs they are doing are generally cleaner and involve less physical exertion, but they come without the same sense of pride and fulfilment that many of the old industrial jobs had. Skilled jobs with prestige have, in many cases, given way to shelf-stacking.

Class-based movements of the past looked solely to the workplace. This is still important: after all, it is what defines the working class and, on a day-to-day basis, it is what shapes working-class life. But, with people so much more likely to jump from job to job—which, in some cases, can happen more than once a year—progressive movements today have to establish roots in communities as well. In their own perverse way, that is exactly what the BNP have been doing: throwing themselves into community politics. From local fêtes to dealing with anti-social behaviour, litter picking to campaigning for affordable housing, the BNP has, with varying levels of success, striven to establish a presence.

We have seen how working-class people are increasingly less likely to vote. Barack Obama owed his election as US president in 2008 to the mobilization of hitherto disenchanted, poorer voters, regardless of how this movement was then squandered: in other words, the extension of the electorate was key to victory. One of the priorities in this country must surely be to similarly mobilize those working-class people who, because of the increasing irrelevance of politics to their lives, have become effectively disenfranchised.

It will also mean straddling the internal divisions within the working class that widened under Thatcherism. These should not be overstated.

As John McDonnell puts it, 'There have always been different elements within the working class. The difference between skilled workers and unskilled workers; the difference between temporary workers, and all the rest of it.' But Matthew Taylor, Tony Blair's former head of strategy, argues convincingly that 'the conditions of employed, home-owning working-class people are so different to the conditions of people in social housing', with what he calls 'worklessness' being more concentrated in the latter, for example. I have certainly encountered heartfelt—and understandable—working-class resentment against those who, it is believed, are falsely claiming benefits.

Part of the problem is that unemployment has become depoliticized. The fight against it used to be one of the left's great crusades, as epito-mized by the iconic Jarrow March in 1936. Fewer people were out of work in the 1970s than today, but back then it was seen as the definitive political issue of the day. Margaret Thatcher's Tories savaged James Callaghan's government with the notorious 'Labour Isn't Working' poster, when a million were out of work.

Because successive governments have manipulated unemployment figures using incapacity benefits, the terms of the debate have been changed. Unemployment becomes recast as a public health issue—and specifically about whether a sizeable chunk of claimants are *really* ill enough not to work. The argument used by both New Labour and Tory politicians to drive claimants off benefits is essentially correct: individuals and their families are, generally speaking, better off with work. But they completely neglect to answer the question: 'Where are the jobs to put unemployed people into?' Even where there are jobs available, they are often low-paid, temporary and of poor quality.

Another core demand must surely be for decent, skilled, secure, well-paid jobs. It would not just be for the sake of the unemployed. It would also provide a possible alternative for many low-paid service sector workers. 'The thing we talk about is trying to have an industrial policy,' says Eilís Lawlor from the New Economics Foundation. 'That means actually deciding that you're going to support and promote industries that would fill the "missing middle" of skilled jobs, and you would tilt them spatially towards poor areas and areas that have been affected by recessions, but also policies to target particular industries.' The fag end of the last Labour government began toying with an industrial policy—but after thirteen years of collapsing manufacturing, it was nowhere near bold enough. But now, with even the Tories talking about 'rebalancing the economy' and 'Britain making things again', there is ample political space to make the case for a new industrial strategy.

The campaign for good jobs could be the catalyst for far-reaching social change. Jobs could be created to help solve the deep-seated problems affecting working-class communities. Housing is one of the biggest crises facing many working-class families: a national programme to build socially owned housing would need an army of skilled labour, as well as stimulating the construction industry and in turn creating yet more good jobs. As Defend Council Housing's Alan Walter put it in the dying days of New Labour, now that the market had failed to provide for people's needs it was time to 'invest in building a third generation of first-class council homes that are well built and designed to the highest environmental standards, with good community facilities and transport links, and we can finally get away from housing being something you speculate on and concentrate on providing homes for the twenty-first century.'

A jobs movement could also meet the challenge posed by environmental crisis. A 'Green New Deal' that builds a thriving renewable energy sector and launches a national crusade to insulate homes and businesses could employ hundreds of thousands of people. 'I think there's a role for government there in actually marrying its economic policy with environmental policy,' says *Guardian* economics editor Larry Elliott.

> There are large numbers of people who are not unskilled, but semi-skilled people working in construction or the building trade,

for whom the government can make a very, very big difference. It could do good things like insulating homes, and at the same time creating a new green sector. The products that they'd actually be fitting in the homes could help the manufacturing base. You'd get some kind of multiplier effect through this government action that creates jobs and new industries.

As well as providing an array of new jobs, it would give working-class people a stake in the environment by transforming it into a bread-and-butter issue. This is class politics with a green tinge.

Clearly, these new jobs would not replace the old ones, and nor should they. Get rid of all the cleaners, rubbish collectors, bus drivers, supermarket checkout staff and secretaries, for example, and society will very quickly grind to a halt. On the other hand, if we woke up one morning to find that all the highly paid advertising executives, management consultants and private equity directors had disappeared, society would go on much as it did before: in a lot of cases, probably quite a bit better. So, to begin with, workers need to reclaim a sense of *pride* and social worth. Doing so would be a big step forward in making the case that the wages and conditions of low-paid jobs must be improved in order to reflect the importance they have in all of our lives.

We have seen how work in modern Britain is much more insecure than it used to be. British employers have more freedom to dispose of their workers than practically anywhere else in the Western world. There is an army of temporary agency workers, lacking even basic rights, who can be dismissed at a moment's notice. As well as the feeling of insecurity that hire-and-fire conditions breed, it is thoroughly dehumanizing to be treated like chattel or a mere economic resource that can be thrown away as soon as it is no longer needed. There have been recent cases of workers being sacked by text message or even by megaphone. Job security must be at the heart of a new progressive movement.

But it must be about much more than wages and conditions. A new politics with class at its heart needs to address the deep-seated alienation many workers feel, particularly in the service sector: the sheer tedium and boredom that often accompanies routine, repetitive work. It is not just about skilling up jobs and providing variation in workers' daily tasks, though that is part of it. It is also about giving workers genuine control and power in the workplace.

One of the ideas floated by the Tories before the 2010 general election was to create supposed workers' co-operatives in the public sector, offering a 'power-shift to public sector workers' and 'as big a transfer of power to working people since the sale of council house homes in the 1980s,' as then-Tory Shadow Chancellor George Osborne put it. In reality, he was audaciously raiding traditional Labour language as a ruse to cover up the privatization of large pieces of the public sector. But this rhetoric could be taken at face value, upping the ante with the response: 'Why not apply the same principle to the private sector?'

Such a call would be about bringing genuine democracy to the economy. With so many disillusioned with the ravages of the market, it would surely strike a popular chord. Instead of economic despots ruling over the British economy with nothing to keep them in check, key businesses could be taken into social ownership and democratically managed by workers—and consumers, for that matter. It would be a real alternative to the old-style, top-down, bureaucratic form of nationalization introduced after World War II by Peter Mandelson's grandfather, Herbert Morrison. Working-class people would be given genuine power, instead of being mere cogs in the machine.

Inevitably, solutions must be sought to working-class concerns that hitherto have been cynically manipulated by the right. For example, rather than dismissing the anti-immigration backlash as ignorance and racism, a modern class-based politics has to understand it as the misdirected frustrations of working-class people at unanswered grievances. If anti-immigrant sentiment is to be defused, it means recognizing and tackling the issues that are really to blame and affect working-class people of all colours, like the lack of affordable housing and secure, well-paid jobs.

The tragedy, of course, is that the scapegoating of immigration has meant that the elites who are really responsible have been let off the hook. If working-class frustrations could be redirected towards those really responsible, there would be a genuine opportunity to unite working-class people, regardless of their background. 'Something like £70 billion is stolen from the Exchequer every year through tax evasion. That is never couched as ripping off the white working class,' says journalist Johann Hari. 'But some poor Somali person running for their lives: they're ripping you off, rather than those ripping billions of pounds off. A much healthier and more productive way to think about the divisions in our society is for white working-class people and immigrants to think of themselves as on the same side, against the corporations and very rich people who really are ripping them off.'

Anti-social behaviour is another good example of a working-class concern that could be reclaimed from the right. Although overblown as an issue, it disproportionately affects people in working-class communities and is a genuine blight on some people's lives. On the one hand, a new class politics has to attack the root causes, like youth unemployment, poverty and a lack of facilities for young people; on the other, it has to defend people from being terrorized in their own communities but without falling into New Labour's trap of stigmatizing young working-class kids. 'New Labour's emphasis on anti-social behaviour and attacks on civil liberties was about encouraging people to attack one another and blame one another for what was going in their communities, rather than the system itself,' says John McDonnell. 'And that doesn't absolve individual responsibility or anything like that—but it's trying to get it into context. In every working-class community, you've always had rogues, you've always had people who behaved badly—and what you try and do is overcome that—but people do that by controlling their own communities.'

It should go without saying that a challenge to the grotesque redistribution of wealth and power to the very richest over the last thirty years is long overdue. Some might call this class war; but surely that phrase applies more appropriately to the fact that, while recession was ravaging workers' living standards and throwing thousands out of work, the wealth of the top 1,000 richest people shot up by 30 per cent between 2009 and 2010—the biggest hike ever recorded. Or the fact that, while the Conservative-led government is reducing corporation tax to 24 per cent—one of the lowest rates in the developed world—VAT, a tax that disproportionately hits the poor, was increased to 20 per cent. *This* is class war, and a new class politics must answer it.

While the financial crimes of the poor, such as benefit fraud, are frequently in the crosshairs of politicians and journalists, the far greater financial crimes of the rich are largely ignored. That is why fire must be redirected from welfare fraud to tax evasion which, as we have seen, costs the taxpayer seventy times more. And, of course, the whole tax system has to be rebalanced so that the burden falls properly on the wealthy. After all, during the boom times, the profits of the wealthy increased by unparalleled amounts: there is certainly no lack of money at the top.

The objection is always: 'Won't the rich just flee abroad to escape the taxman?' Chartered accountant and former company director Richard Murphy points out that this was the argument used against the new 50 per cent tax rate that was introduced in the dying days of New Labour for those earning £150,000 and above. 'It was said that they're all going to be fleeing to Switzerland—but the number of applications to work in Swiss finance from the UK in 2009 was 7 per cent down on 2008. And the total number of questions was just over a thousand, and most of them were from the backroom—the technical people, IT and administration—not from the dealing room.' The six major corporations that left were not even paying tax in Britain in the first place. Indeed, despite all the controversy, the tax receipts flowing into Treasury coffers were actually higher than estimated.

It will take a lot more than changing the tax system to stop the nation's wealth being sucked into the bank accounts of the rich elites. There is little real pressure to stop them amassing huge riches while their employees' wages stagnate or even decline. At the heart of this scandal is the destruction of the power of workers as an organized force—that is, the trade unions. 'There are studies that show that one of the features of more equal societies is stronger trade union movements,' says Professor Richard Wilkinson, co-author of seminal book *The Spirit Level*.

> I think the ability of people at the top, the bankers and chief executives and so on, to give themselves these huge bonuses reflects the fact they're in a situation where there are no constraints on them. If there were strong trade unions and perhaps a union or employee representative on the company's board, it would become more embarrassing for CEOs to award themselves huge pay increases and bonuses while holding down wage demands from employees.

The decline of the trade unions lies at the heart of many of the problems of the working class: the fact that they don't have a voice; their stagnating wages; their lack of rights in the workplace, and so on. As Tony Blair once boasted, even with New Labour's changes, the law remains 'the most restrictive on trade unions in the Western world'. Indeed, Britain is actually in violation of its obligations as a signatory to various International Labour Organization conventions. 'Although workers look for representation in the workplace, the anti-trade union laws have undermined the ability of trade unions to represent people,' says John McDonnell. 'The unions do their best in a difficult, very cold climate.'

Despite all the hammering that unions have suffered, they remain by far the biggest democratic civil society organizations in the country, with over seven million members. At the heart of the unions' weakness is the fact that they have more or less been evicted from the private sector. While over half of public sector workers are union members, it is only the case for 15 per cent of their private sector counterparts. The restrictive laws are partly to blame—as Ken Livingstone says, 'the intervention of the state to guarantee fairness in employment could change it overnight'—but the nature of the hire-and-fire, fragmented service sector with its high numbers of temporary and part-time workers makes it difficult to organize. At the turn of the twentieth century, the mission of trade unions was expanding from their relatively privileged skilled base to recruit largely non-unionized unskilled workers. It was called 'New Unionism'. If the trade union movement has a future, it needs a New Unionism that focuses specifically on organizing the new service-sector working class.

In an era of cuts and austerity, it also means that the unions have to reach out far and wide. 'They need to form coalitions with user groups so that powerful enough alliances can be formed to defeat the cuts agenda of the government through extra-parliamentary action,' says industrial relations expert Professor Gregor Gall. 'Unions need to do this as a union movement, not just as individual unions. The rationale here is that defending jobs and pay is synonymous with defending the quality and quantity of public services.' For example, the argument has to be made not just about public sector workers facing the sack, but also about the loss of services for users, and the economic knock-on effects imperilling the jobs of private sector workers too.

Above all, the unions have to adapt to the working class as it is today. 'You have to recognize that the labour movement is different, and it's never going to be what it was thirty years ago,' says trade union leader Billy Hayes. 'It can regain its strength, but it's looking for that next generation of leaders who will come up with ideas and initiatives that people like me aren't capable of developing.'

It will be said that a movement with class at its heart will alienate the middle class. But there is no automatic rule that it has to. One politician put it to me that it was 'the politics of despair' to stand on the most con-servative of programmes, merely 'because you'll never convince those people in Surbiton'. That was Hazel Blears, a stalwart defender of New Labour, and I happen to agree with her.

Most middle-class people cannot afford to go private, and want good, properly funded local schools and hospitals. Polls show that middle-class people support higher taxes on the rich—and indeed there is no reason why they would be any less happy to see the wealthy pay their fair share than a working-class person. It is in the interest of middle-class people to live in a society with less crime, and reducing the social causes is a major way of achieving that. As Richard Wilkinson and Kate Pickett's groundbreaking study of inequality, *The Spirit Level*, has shown, all groups in society benefit from greater equality—including the middle class.

But a new class politics cannot simply be a British phenomenon. As the ultra-rich business elite has globalized, so too must working-class people. With multinational corporations able to hold elected governments to ransom, only the power of a strong, international labour force can meet the challenge. Only by making common cause with the burgeoning workforces of India and China can British workers hope to stem the consequences of a global 'race to the bottom' in pay and conditions.

It would be tempting to make all sorts of doom-laden, apocalyptic predictions about what will happen if such a movement fails to get off the ground, and warn darkly of riots and revolutions. The reality is just downright depressing. The working class will remain weak and voiceless. They will still be the butt of jokes at middle-class dinner parties, detested in angry right-wing newspaper columns, and ridiculed in TV sitcoms. Entire communities will remain without secure, well-paid work, and the people that comprise them will continue to be demonized for it. Living standards will go on stagnating and declining, even while the richest rake it in like never before. Ever fewer working-class people will bother to vote. Right-wing populism will tap into growing disillusionment and fury at the manner in which working-class people have become so despised. Mainstream politicians will continue to focus their energies on satisfying the demands of a small, wealthy elite, while growing ever more indifferent to the needs of an increasingly apathetic working class. Politics will revert to what it was in the nineteenth century: essentially, a family argument between competing wealthy factions.

At its heart, the demonization of the working class is the flagrant triumphalism of the rich who, no longer challenged by those below them, instead point and laugh at them. As this Conservative-led government pushes ahead with a programme of cuts that makes the working class pay for the crimes of the elite, they have much to laugh at.

But it does not have to be this way. The folly of a society organized around the interests of plutocrats has been exposed by an economic crisis sparked by the greed of the bankers. The new class politics would be a start, to at least build a counterweight to the hegemonic, unchallenged class politics of the wealthy. Perhaps then a new society based around people's needs, rather than private profit, would be feasible once again. Working-class people have, in the past, organized to defend their interests; they have demanded to be listened to, and forced concessions from the hands of the rich and the powerful. Ridiculed or ignored though they may be, they will do so again.

Acknowledgements

This book was made possible only by the enthusiasm, advice and experiences of others.

Without the encouragement of Jordan Goldman and Dominic Sandbrook, I would never have put pen to paper in the first place. I could not be luckier to have an agent as committed as Andrew Gordon, who helped kick the original idea into shape, offered invaluable advice from the very beginning, and never wavered in his support. The book would not have happened without his efforts. Tom Penn has been a brilliant, patient editor who improved the book immeasurably, not least by ruthlessly clamping down on some of my clunkier prose. I'm honoured that Tariq Ali was enthusiastic about the project from the very beginning and made sure Verso took it on.

Sarah Shin has been a tireless publicist for the book, and it is partly down to her dedication that the book made the impact it has. Like every Verso author, I owe a huge thanks to Rowan Wilson; he is a major reason why the company punches above its weight. Mark Martin and Lorna Scott Fox mercilessly purged the book of my grammatical cock-ups, misused words and long-winded sentences; *Chavs* is far more readable because of their efforts.

I'd like to add a special tribute to Clara Heyworth, Verso's brilliant Marketing Manager in the United States, who tragically died not long after the book was released. I had the privilege of meeting her in New York and corresponding with her, and was struck by her warmth

271

and intelligence. It wasn't foreseen than *Chavs* would make any headway in the United States; it is down to her efforts that it did. I know she is sorely missed by everybody at Verso and all her loved ones, and my thoughts are with them.

A number of specialists kindly sacrificed their time to offer their expertise, bounce ideas around and clarify some of my own thoughts. They include: Alan Walter (an inspirational campaigner for council tenants who tragically passed away during the writing of this book), Martin Barnes, Phillip Blond, Prof. John Carey, Nick Cohen, Prof. Danny Dorling, Larry Elliott, Dr Gillian Evans, Prof. Gregor Gall, Prof. John Goldthorpe, Lynsey Hanley, Johann Hari, David Kynaston, Eilís Lawlor, Prof. Rob MacDonald, John McDonnell MP, John McInally, Dr Ross McKibbin, Fiona Millar, Richard Murphy, Sam Tarry, Matthew Taylor, Mark Thomas, Graham Turner, Fiona Weir, Peter Whittle and Prof. Richard Wilkinson.

I was very lucky to have had the love and support of my friends throughout the writing process. A number of people read through early drafts and offered crucial suggestions and criticisms. I am eternally grateful to them. They are: Grant Archer, Ruth Aylett, Graham Bash, Alex Beecroft, James Bevan, Liam Cranley, David Easton, Andrew Fisher, Tim Flatman, Lola Frears, Rob Jones, Leah Kreitzman, Eleanor Mae O'Hagan, Sue Lukes, Dorothy Macedo, Sarah Morrison, Mike Phipps, Jamie Rann, David Roberts, Dr Adam Smith, Stefan Smith, Tom Stoate, Wes Streeting, Chris Tapp, Jemima Thomas and Chris Ward. George Taylor went through the struggle of his life not long after the book came out. He did so with courage and dignity, and I am very proud of him.

I am hugely thankful to everyone who gave up time to be interviewed. This is particularly the case with those people in working-class communities across the country who agreed to answer intrusive questions, often with little or no notice. No other interviews in this book are as authoritative, perceptive or revealing as theirs. It is more important to me than anything that I have done justice to their experiences and opinions. I hope that I have.

Notes

Preface

1. Child Poverty Action Group, 'Government must act urgently on devastating child poverty warning', cpag.org.uk, last accessed 30 January 2012.
2. 'FTSE 100 directors' earnings rose by almost half last year', *Guardian*, 28 October 2011.
3. Deborah Mattinson, 'From cloth caps to cafetières: you are what you buy', *Independent*, 20 March 2011.
4. BritainThinks, 'What about the workers?: A new study on the Working Class by BritainThinks', 2011, britainthinks.com, last accessed 30 January 2012.
5. 'Number of job-hunters chasing every post jumps to 23', *Daily Telegraph*, 28 December 2011.
6. 'Stop and search "racial profiling" by police on the increase, claims study', Guardian, 14 January 2012.
7. William Lee Adams and Nick Assinder, 'London riots: Fires spread on third night of violence', *Time*, 9 August 2011.
8. Gareth Morrell et al., 'The August riots in England: Understanding the involvement of young people', National Centre for Social Research, October 2011, p. 13.
9. Randeep Ramesh, 'London's richest people worth 273 times more than the poorest', *Guardian*, 20 April 2010.
10. Morrell, 'The August riots', p. 17.
11. Paul Lewis, Tim Newborn, Matthew Taylor, and James Ball, 'Rioters

say anger with police fuelled summer unrest', *Guardian*, 5 December 2011.

Introduction

1. Michael Kerr, 'A "chav-free" break? No thanks', *Daily Telegraph*, 21 January 2009.
2. http://www.dailymail.co.uk/debate/article-1295459/A-perfect-folk-hero-times-Moat-popularity-reflects-societys-warped-values.html
3. Simon Heffer, 'We pay to have an underclass', *Daily Telegraph*, 29 August 2007.
4. Zoe Williams, 'The chavs and the chav-nots', *Guardian*, 16 July 2008.
5. Christopher Howse, 'Calling people chavs is criminal', *Daily Telegraph*, 17 July 2008.
6. Emily Pykett, 'Working classes are less intelligent, says evolution expert', *Scotsman*, 22 May 2008.

Chapter 1

1. Quoted by Peter Wilby, 'The nursery-tale treatment of a real-life nightmare', *Guardian*, 14 May 2007.
2. Allison Pearson, 'Poor Shannon was already a lost child', *Daily Mail*, 27 February 2008.
3. Allison Pearson, '98 words that broke my heart', *Daily Mail*, 9 May 2007.
4. India Knight, 'Every mother's nightmare', *The Times*, 6 May 2007.
5. Roy Greenslade, 'Why is missing Shannon not getting the same coverage as Madeleine?', *Guardian*, 5 March 2008.
6. Andrew Norfolk, 'Poor little Shannon Matthews. Too poor for us to care that she is lost?', *The Times*, 1 March 2008.
7. Melanie Reid, 'Shannon Matthews is the new face of poverty', *The Times*, 17 March 2008.
8. Cole Moreton, 'Missing: The contrasting searches for Shannon and Madeleine', *Independent on Sunday*, 2 March 2008.
9. Maureen Messent, 'Home's no place for shy Shannon', *Birmingham Evening Mail*, 28 March 2008.

10. Melanie Phillips, 'Why Shannon is one more victim of the folly of "lifestyle choice"', *Daily Mail*, 17 March 2008.

11. Neil Sears, 'Calls for Tory councillor to resign after he suggests parents on benefits should be sterilised after one child', *Daily Mail*, 24 March 2008.

12. MailOnline, 'Calls for Tory councillor to resign', dailymail.co.uk, 24 March 2008.

13. Lucy Thornton, 'Mocked... but we all stick together', *Mirror*, 10 April 2008.

14. N/A, 'A feckless existence', *Huddersfield Examiner*, 5 December 2008.

15. Alastair Taylor, 'Estate is like a nastier Beirut', *Sun*, 9 April 2008.

16. Carole Malone, 'Force low-life to work for a living', *News of the World*, 7 December 2008.

17. N/A, 'Plea for the victims of welfare Britain', *Daily Mail*, 6 December 2008.

18. Joe Mott, 'Shameless attack on our poor', *Daily Star*, 13 April 2008.

19. Melanie McDonagh, 'Shannon Matthews case: Five fathers, one mother and a muddled family saga', *Independent on Sunday*, 13 April 2008.

20. Bruce Anderson, 'The night a grim malaise was hammered home', *Sunday Telegraph*, 16 November 2008.

21. There are numerous examples of the *Daily Mail* glorifying stay-at-home mothers. See for example Steve Doughty, 'Children perform better if mother stays at home', *Daily Mail*, 9 June 2006; Daniel Martin, 'Betrayal of stay-at-home mothers: Millions lose state pensions after Government U-turn', *Daily Mail*, 20 December 2007; Steve Doughty, '"Superwoman is a myth" say modern women because "family life suffers with working mums",' *Daily Mail*, 6 August 2008.

22. Centre for Social Justice, centreforsocialjustice.org.uk, 2 December 2008.

23. Ibid.

24. David Cameron, 'There are 5 million people on benefits in Britain. How do we stop them turning into Karen Matthews?', *Daily Mail*, 8 December 2008.

25. Gaby Hinsliff, 'Tories to probe long-term jobless', *Observer*, 7 December 2008.

26. The Sutton Trust, *The Educational Backgrounds of Leading Journalists*, suttontrust.com, June 2006.

27. Christina Patterson, 'Heaven help the white working class now', *Independent*, 24 January 2009.

28. The Sutton Trust, suttontrust.com, 9 December 2005.

29. Allison Pearson, 'I looked at Ivan and thought, "We're going to get through this. He's lovely" ', *Sunday Telegraph*, 16 October 2005.

30. Vincent Moss, 'Tory leader David Cameron at centre of a political storm', *Sunday Mirror*, 23 March 2008.

31. Dylan Jones, *Cameron on Cameron: Conversations with Dylan Jones*, London 2008, p. 207.

32. Gaby Hinsliff, 'Public wants taxes that hurt the rich', *Observer*, 4 January 2009.

33. Department for Work and Pensions, *Households Below Average Income Report 1994/95–2006/07*, dwp.gov.uk.

34. Julian Glover, 'Riven by class and no social mobility–Britain in 2007', *Guardian*, 20 October 2007.

35. John Harris, 'Bottom of the class', *Guardian*, 11 April 2006.

36. Chris Holmes, *Housing, Equality and Choice*, London 2003, p. 3.

37. John Harris, 'Safe as houses', *Guardian*, 30 September 2008.

38. George Jones, 'More high earners should live on council estates, professor tells Whitehall', *Daily Telegraph*, 21 February 2007.

39. John Hills, *Ends and Means: The Future Roles of Social Housing in England*, London 2007, p. 45.

40. Richard Pendlebury, 'Downfall of a decent clan', *Daily Mail*, 16 April 2008.

41. Alison Park et al, eds, *British Social Attitudes: The 24ᵗʰ Report*, London 2008, p. 242.

42. Whitney Richard David Jones, *The Tree of Commonwealth 1450–1793*, London 2000, p. 136.

Chapter 2

1. C. A. R. Crosland, *The Future of Socialism*, London 1956, p. 61.

2. Hugo Young, *One of Us*, London 1990, p. 127.

3. Margaret Thatcher, 'Don't undo my work', *Newsweek*, 27 April 1992.

4. Conservative Central Office, *The Right Approach: A Statement of Conservative Aims*, October 1976.

5. John Cole, *As It Seemed to Me: Political Memoirs*, London 1995, p. 209.

6. Posted by Andrew Sparrow, *Guardian* politics blog, guardian.co.uk, 9 March 2009.

7. Chris Ogden, *Maggie: An Intimate Portrait of a Woman in Power*, New York 1990, p. 333.

8. Mary Shaw, Daniel Dorling, David Gordon and George Davey Smith, *The Widening Gap: Health Inequalities and Policy in Britain*, Bristol 1999, p. 147.

9. Earl A. Reitan, *The Thatcher Revolution: Margaret Thatcher, John Major, Tony Blair, and the Transformation of Modern Britain, 1979–2001*, Oxford 2003, p. 77.

10. Eric J. Evans, *Thatcher and Thatcherism*, London 2004, p. 139.

11. Shaw et al, *The Widening Gap: Health Inequalities and Policy in Britain*, pp. 144, 145, 147.

12. Stewart Lansley, *Life In The Middle: The Untold Story of Britain's Average Earners*, London 2009, p. 15.

13. Interview with *Catholic Herald*, 22 December 1978, margaretthatcher.org.

14. Nicholas Ridley Memorial Lecture, 22 November 1996, margaretthatcher.org.

15. Interview with *The Times*, 22 November 1989, margaretthatcher.org.

16. Julian Buchanan, 'Understanding Problematic Drug Use: A Medical Matter or a Social Issue?', *British Journal of Community Justice*, 4(2): 387–397.

17. Mark Duguid, *Cracker*, London 2009, pp. 67, 70.

18. Euan Ferguson, 'Best Foot goes ever forward', *Observer*, 4 March 2001.

Chapter 3

1. Polly Toynbee, 'Tony Blair tried to bury it, but class politics looks set to return', *Guardian*, 10 July 2010.

2. Francis Elliott and James Hanning, 'The many faces of Mr Cameron', *Daily Mail*, 17 March 2007.

3. James Hanning and Francis Elliott, 'David Cameron's band of Etonian brothers', *Independent*, 20 May 2007.

4. Daniel Hannan, 'If you pay people to be poor, you'll never run out of poor people', *Daily Telegraph*, 18 April 2009.

5. Allegra Stratton, 'Tories get their sums wrong in attack on teen pregnancy', *Guardian*, 15 February 2010.

6. Amelia Gentleman, 'Teenage pregnancy more opportunity than catastrophe, says study', *Guardian*, 12 February 2010.

7. Randeep Ramesh, 'Talking tough on teenage pregnancy', *Guardian*, 17 March 2009.

8. Melissa Kite, 'Coalition to tell unemployed to "get on your bike" ', *Telegraph*, 26 June 2010.

9. Paul Waugh, 'Plot to rid council estates of poor', *Evening Standard*, 10 July 2009.

10. Charles Murray, *Underclass: The Crisis Deepens*, London 1994, pp. 5, 8, 32.

11. Anushka Asthana, 'George Osborne's budget cuts will hit Britain's poorest families six times harder than the richest,' *Observer*, 27 June 2010.

12. Jason Groves, 'Tory minister under fire for gaffe as he tells MPs: "Those in most need will bear the burden of cuts"', *Daily Mail*, 11 June 2010.

13. Rosalind Ryan and Andrew Sparrow, 'No 10 plays down Flint's social housing plan', *Guardian*, 5 February 2008.

14. James Kirkup, 'James Purnell defends welfare reform after accusations of "stigmatising" benefits claimants', *Daily Telegraph*, 10 December 2008.

15. Martin Bright, 'Interview: James Purnell', *New Statesman*, 18 September 2008.

16. Anthony Horowitz, 'Hoodies and baddies', *The Times*, 23 July 2005.

17. Michael Young, 'Down with meritocracy', *Guardian*, 29 June 2001.

18. Jon Swaine, 'White working class "feels ignored on immigration" ', *Telegraph*, 2 January 2009.

Chapter 4

1. P. J. Keating, *The Working Classes in Victorian Fiction*, London 1971, p. 21.

2. George Orwell, *A Collection of Essays*, New York 1953, p. 57.

3. Andrew Billen, 'Meet the romantic lead in the new Merchant-Ivory film. (Just kidding)', *Observer*, 5 January 1997.

4. Daily Mail reporter, 'Rising toll of Waynettas ...', *Daily Mail*, 14 January 2010.

5. Lee Bok, *The Little Book of Chavs: The Branded Guide to Britain's New Elite*, Bath 2004.
6. Lee Bok, *The Chav Guide to Life*, Bath 2006, pp. 11, 12.
7. Mia Wallace and Clint Spanner, *Chav!: A User's Guide to Britain's New Ruling Class*, London 2004, pp. 14, 51–2, 75, 235.
8. Jemima Lewis, 'In defence of snobbery', *Daily Telegraph*, 1 February 2004.
9. David Thomas, 'A to Z of Chavs', *Daily Mail*, 20 October 2004.
10. David Thomas, 'I'm a Chav, get me out of here', *Daily Mail*, 12 February 2004.
11. Brendan O'Neill, 'Roasting the masses', *Guardian*, 27 August 2008.
12. Johann Hari, 'Jaded contempt for the working class', *Independent*, 22 January 2007.
13. Rachel Williams, 'Affluent teenagers drink more, study shows', *Guardian*, 24 June 2010.
14. Janet Daley, 'The real reason for all those louts on holiday', *Sunday Telegraph*, 9 August 2009.
15. Michael Odell, 'This much I know: John Bird', *Observer*, 27 August 2006.
16. N/A, 'BBC to explore Britain's white working class', *Daily Telegraph*, 21 November 2007.
17. Yasmin Alibhai-Brown, 'God bless the foreigners willing to do our dirty work,' *Independent*, 23 August 2006.
18. Yasmin Alibhai-Brown, *Independent*, 5 January 2009.
19. 'The Janet Daley column', *The Times*, 2 June 1994.
20. Amanda Platell, 'It's shabby values, not class, that are to blame for society's ills', *Daily Mail*, 30 January 2010.
21. Duncan Larcombe, 'Future bling of England', *Sun*, 10 April 2006.
22. Decca Aitkenhead, 'Class rules', *Guardian*, 20 October 2007.
23. Nick Britten, 'Britain has produced unteachable "uber-chavs"', *Daily Telegraph*, 9 February 2009.
24. Hannah Frankel, 'From the other side of the tracks', *Times Education Supplement*, 30 October 2009.
25. Jade Goody, *Jade: My Autobiography*, London 2006, pp. 23, 31, 41, 58.
26. Paul Callan, 'LEADER: How can bosses defend the show that shames us?', *Daily Express*, 19 January 2007.

27. Simon Heffer, 'What we're actually seeing is class hatred,' *Daily Telegraph*, 20 January 2007.

28. Stuart Jeffries, 'Beauty and the beastliness: a tale of declining British values', *Guardian*, 19 January 2007.

29. Johann Hari, 'Jaded contempt for the working class', *Independent*, 22 January 2007.

30. *Evening Standard* letters, 18 January 2007.

31. N/A, *Nottingham Evening Post*, 18 January 2007.

32. Fiona Sturges, 'Jade Goody: Reality TV star and media phenomenon', *Independent*, 23 March 2009.

33. Rod Liddle, 'After Jade's cancer, what next? "I'm a tumour, get me out of here"?', *Spectator*, 23 August 2008.

34. Jan Moir, 'The saddest reality show of all: Are we so desensitized that watching a woman's death is acceptable entertainment?', *Daily Mail*, 21 February 2009.

35. Toby Young, 'Couples on Wife Swap are divorced from reality', *Mail on Sunday*, 7 November 2004.

36. Andrew Sparrow, 'Jeremy Kyle Show "undermines anti-poverty efforts", says thinktank', *Guardian*, 10 September 2008.

37. Lorna Martin, 'Cracker creator blasts "chav" TV', *Observer*, 27 August 2006.

38. Matt Lucas, David Walliams and Boyd Hilton, *Inside Little Britain*, London 2006, p. 245.

39. Richard Littlejohn, 'Welcome to Britain, land of the rising scum', *Daily Mail*, 14 November 2008.

40. James Delingpole, 'A conspiracy against chavs? Count me in', *The Times*, 13 April 2006.

41. N/A, 'What is working class?', news.bbc.co.uk, 25 January 2007.

42. London School of Economics, 'Little Britain filled with "figures of hatred" not figures of fun', lse.ac.uk, October 2008.

43. 'Be a shameless groupie for the day', channel4.com.

44. Posted by 'Objectivism', thestudentroom.co.uk, 12 July 2005.

45. Robin Nelson, *State of Play: Contemporary 'High-end' TV Drama*, Manchester 2007, p. 50.

46. Nigel Floyd, 'Eden Lake', *Time Out*, 11–17 September 2008.

47. N/A, '"EastEnders" writer wins £68,000 from BBC', *Independent*, 17 October 1992.

48. Gary Imlach, *My Father and Other Working-Class Football Heroes*, London 2005.
49. Jason Cowley, *The Last Game: Love, Death and Football*, London 2009, p. 326.
50. Ibid., p. 238.
51. Deborah Orr, 'Your class still counts, whatever you call it', *Independent*, 31 January 2003.

Chapter 5

1. N/A, 'The good news, Dave: We're ALL middle-class now', *Daily Mail*, 6 December 2005.
2. Andrew Adonis and Stephen Pollard, *A Class Act: The Myth of Britain's Classless Society*, London 1998, p. 9.
3. Simon Hattenstone, 'General election highlights Britain's confusion over social class', *Guardian*, 14 April 2010.
4. *Talking Retail*, 15 September 2009.
5. *Retail Week*, 1 June 2009.
6. Simon English, 'Mini workers hurl fruit as 850 sacked', *Evening Standard*, 16 February 2009.
7. Sean O'Grady, 'New part-time jobs boost rise in employment', *Independent*, 17 December 2009.
8. *Regeneration and Renewal*, 20 July 2009.
9. Posted by Simon Rogers, 'What do people get paid?', guardian.co.uk/news/datablog, 12 November 2009.
10. Irene Krechowiecka and Jan Poynter, *A-Z of Careers and Jobs*, London 2004.
11. René Lavanchy, 'Unions have a future, workers tell survey', *Tribune*, 19 March 2010.
12. Department for Work and Pensions, *Households Below Average Income: An Analysis of the Income Distribution 1994/95–2007/08*, London 2009, p. 19.
13. Stewart Lansley, *Life in the Middle: The Untold Story of Britain's Average Earners*, TUC pamphlet 2009, pp. 3, 10, 17.
14. New Economics Foundation, *A Bit Rich: Calculating the Real Value to Society of Different Professions*, 2009, pp. 3–4.

15. David Litterick, 'Britons work almost two hours more per week than average European', *Daily Telegraph*, 3 September 2008.

16. Office for National Statistics, *Social Trends*, No. 39, London 2009, p. 54.

17. Press Association, 'Unpaid overtime soars to "extreme" levels, says TUC', *Guardian*, 26 February 2010.

18. Department for Work and Pensions, *Households Below Average Income*, p. 14.

19. Megan Murphy and Nicholas Timmins, 'Boardroom pay gap doubles in a decade', *Financial Times*, 27 November 2009.

20. Ashley Seager and Julia Finch, 'Pay gap widens between executives and their staff', *Guardian*, 16 September 2009.

21. Jeremy Warner, 'Capitalism has forgotten to share the wealth', *Daily Telegraph*, 29 January 2010.

Chapter 6

1. Alan Milburn, *Unleashing Aspiration: The Final Report of the Panel on Fair Access to the Professions*, London 2009, p. 18.

2. Jessica Shepherd, 'White working-class the worst GCSE students, study finds', *Guardian*, 27 March 2008.

3. Jessica Shepherd and Polly Curtis, 'Middle-class pupils have better genes, says Chris Woodhead', *Guardian*, 11 May 2009.

4. Amelia Hill, 'Children of rich parents are better at reading', *Observer*, 6 February 2005.

5. Ofsted, *Cale Green Primary School: Ofsted Report 2003*, p. 3.

6. Richard Garner, 'Revealed: The schools where 1 in 4 play truant', *Independent*, 13 January 2010.

7. Phil Mizen, *The Changing State of Youth*, Basingstoke 2004, p. 44.

8. Julie Henry, 'Graduates told to work in call centres', *Daily Telegraph*, 23 May 2009.

9. Gary Anderson, 'Flagship Tory free schools scheme condemned by Swedish education minister Bertil Ostberg', *Daily Mirror*, 30 May 2010.

10. Gillian Plummer, *Failing Working-Class Girls*, London 2000, p. 16.

11. Nicola Woolcock, 'Privileged children excel, even at low-performing comprehensives', *The Times*, 21 February 2008.

12. David Turner, 'Class split "will cost Britain £50bn"', *Financial Times*, 15 March 2010.

13. George Monbiot, 'Plan after plan fails to make Oxbridge access fair. There is another way', *Guardian*, 24 May 2010.

14. Alice Tarleton, 'How many go from free school meals to Oxbridge?', blogs.channel4.com, 15 February 2010.

15. Afua Hirsch, 'Cost and class raise barriers to legal aid lawyer careers', *Guardian*, 1 March 2010.

16. Milburn, *Unleashing Aspiration*, p. 22.

17. Randeep Ramesh, 'Britain's class system–and salaries–inherited from fathers', *Guardian*, 11 February 2010.

18. Larry Elliott, 'OECD: UK has worse social mobility record than other developed countries', *Guardian*, 10 March 2010.

Chapter 7

1. Simon Heffer, 'We pay to have an underclass', *Daily Telegraph*, 29 August 2007.

2. N/A, 'Suicide toll on former MG Rover staff in Longbridge', *Birmingham Mail*, 10 July 2010.

3. Joseph Rowntree Foundation, '"Need not greed" motivates people to work informally, according to new research', jrf.org.uk, 16 June 2006.

4. Christina Beatty and Steve Fothergill, *Incapacity Benefits in the UK: An Issue of Health or Jobs?*, Sheffield 2010, p. 4.

5. Nicholas Watt and Patrick Wintour, 'Iain Duncan Smith: I will tackle root causes of poverty', *Guardian*, 26 May 2010.

6. Beatty and Fothergill, *Incapacity Benefits in the UK*, pp. 20–2.

7. David Webster, James Arnott et al., 'Falling Incapacity Benefit Claims In a Former Industrial City: Policy Impacts or Labour Market Improvement?', *Policy Studies* 31 (2010): 2, 164, 165, 167, 176, 181.

8. Amelia Gentleman, 'Response suggests many people wrongly judged fit to work', *Guardian*, Joe Public blog, 29 March 2010.

9. Public and Commercial Services Union, 'Nine jobseekers for every job in Duncan Smith's Cardiff', pcs.org.uk, 23 October 2010.

10. Stewart Lansley, *Unfair to Middling: How Middle Income Britain's Shrinking Wages Fuelled the Crash and Threaten Recovery*, London 2009, p. 20.

11. Lynsey Hanley, *Estates: An Intimate History*, London 2007, p. 7.
12. Patrick Wintour, 'Benefit cuts "will force thousands into suburbs"', *Guardian*, 4 October 2010.
13. Joe Murphy, 'Welfare cuts "will be like the Highland Clearances"', *Evening Standard*, 7 October 2010.
14. Joseph Rowntree Foundation, *Young People and Territoriality in British Cities*, York 2008.
15. Speaking on BBC News (20 February 2006), about Joseph Rowntree Foundation, *Parenting and Children's Resilience in Disadvantaged Communities*, York 2006.
16. Caroline Roberts, 'Gangs', *Times Educational Supplement*, 23 June 2006.
17. John McTernan, 'The Blairite case for Ed Miliband', *New Statesman*, 14 October 2010.
18. David Cracknell, 'Secret memo warns Blair of crime wave', *Sunday Times*, 24 December 2006.
19. Alan Travis, 'Police failing to tackle "middle-class" cocaine abuse, say MPs', *Guardian*, 3 March 2010.
20. John Mann, 'Heroin in Bassetlaw: Report of the inquiry convened by John Mann MP', johnmannmp.com.
21. Max Pemberton, 'Teenage pregnancy: a national talking point', *Daily Telegraph*, 13 July 2009.
22. Posted by Unity, '16, pregnant and middle class—What the papers don't say', liberalconspiracy.org, 18 February 2010.
23. Amelia Gentleman, 'Teenage pregnancy more opportunity than catastrophe, says study', *Guardian*, 12 February 2010.
24. Susan Hallam and Andrea Creech, *A Review of the Literature Relating to the Parental Aspirations of Teenage Mothers: Executive Summary*, CfBT Education Trust, p. 4.

Chapter 8

1. As an aside, it is worth pointing out that the International Workingmen's Association—often known as the 'First International' because it pre-dated the 'Second' Socialist International and the 'Third' Communist International, and which counted Karl Marx amongst its founders—was instituted in 1864 for similar reasons. The International's main original

purpose was to prevent foreign workers being imported to break strikes.

2. Stephanie Flanders, 'Have British jobs gone to British workers?', BBC News, 21 April 2010.

3. Stephen Nickell and Jumana Saleheen, 'The Impact of Immigration on Occupational Wages: Evidence from Britain', *SERC Discussion Paper*, October 2009, p. 20.

4. Will Somerville and Madeleine Sumption, *Immigration and the Labour Market: Theory, Evidence and Policy*, EHRC, 2009, pp. 3, 16–17.

5. Business Link in London, 'Diversity in London's retail sector', businesslink.gov.uk, last accessed 29 November 2010.

6. The Poverty Site, 'Low Pay by Ethnicity', poverty.org.uk, last accessed 29 November 2010.

7. Luke McLeod-Roberts, 'Thompsons Solicitors crowned most diverse in BSN's latest league table', *The Lawyer*, 17 December 2009.

8. Hilary Metcalf and Heather Rolfe, *Employment and Earnings in the Finance Sector: A Gender Analysis*, EHRC, 2009, p. 14.

9. Lucy Bland, 'White Women and Men of Colour: Miscegenation Fears after the Great War,' *Gender & History* 17 (April 2005): 51–2.

Conclusion

1. Leading article, 'The class struggle is over, it's all about social mobility', *Independent*, 11 September 2008.

2. Posted by Conor Burns, 'Margaret Thatcher's greatest achievement: New Labour', conservativehome.blogs.com, 11 April 2008.

3. Mark Seddon, 'Has Labour handed Stoke to the BNP?', *Guardian*, 2 April 2010.

4. Ipsos MORI, 'How Britain voted in 2010', ipsos-mori.com, 21 May 2010.

5. Jonathan Rose, *The Intellectual Life of the British Working Classes*, Yale 2001, p. 464.

6. Polly Toynbee, 'Tony Blair tried to bury it, but class politics looks set to return', *Guardian*, 10 July 2010.

Index